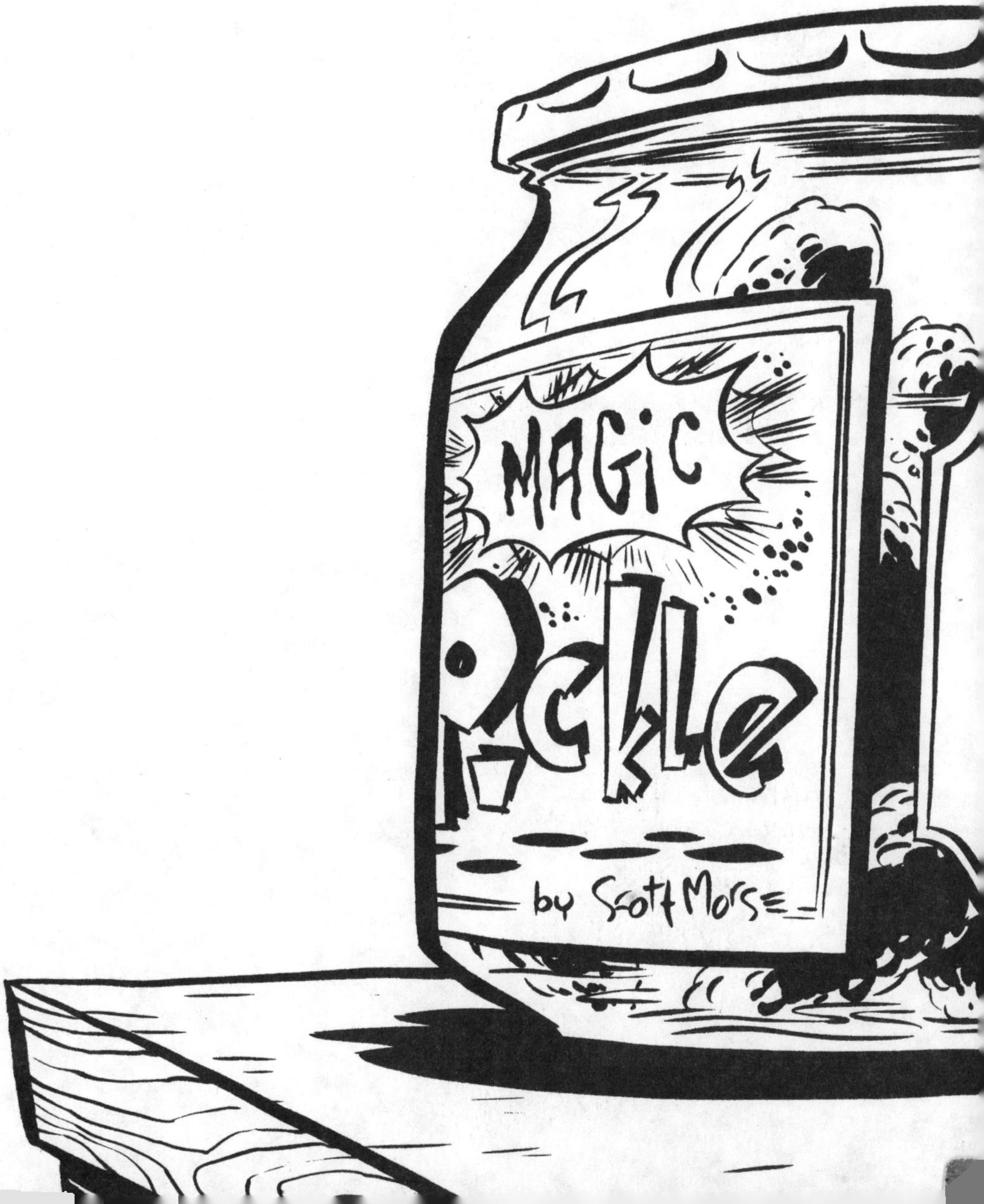
MAGIC
Pickle
by Scott Morse

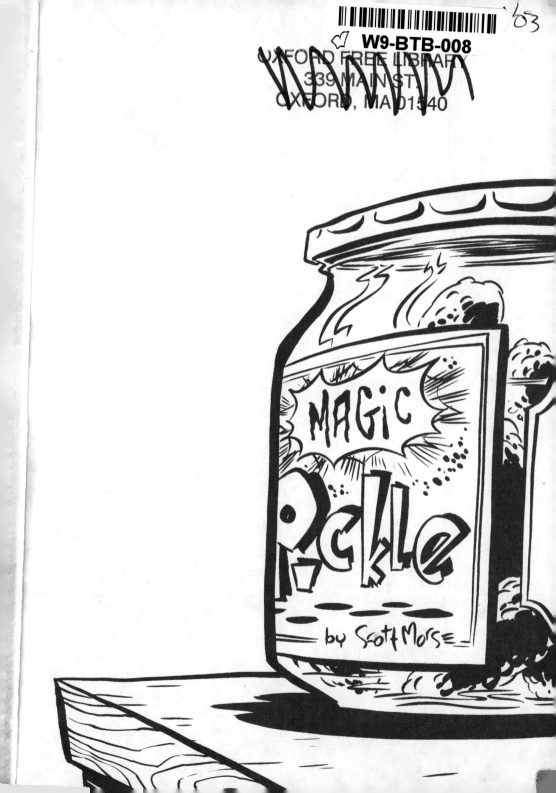

ONI PRESS, INC.
6936 SE Milwaukie Avenue,
PMB 30
Portland, OR 97202
USA
www.onipress.com

Published by Oni Press, Inc.
Joe Nozemack, publisher
Jamie S. Rich, editor in chief

Design by K. Seda & Scott Morse
Edited by James Lucas Jones

This collects issues 1-4 of
the miniseries *Magic Pickle*.

First edition: July 2002
ISBN 1929998-33-3

1 3 5 7 9 10 8 6 4 2
PRINTED IN CANADA.

Magic Pickle is ™ & © 2001, 2002 Scott Morse. Unless
otherwise specified, all other material © 2002 Oni Press,
Inc. Oni Press logo and icon are ™ & © 2002 Oni Press,
Inc. All rights reserved. Oni Press logo and icon artwork
created by Dave Gibbons. The events, institutions, and
characters presented in this book are fictional. Any
resemblance to actual persons or mutant vegetables,
living or dead, is purely coincidental. No portion of this
publication may be reproduced, by any means, without
the express written permission of the copyright holders.

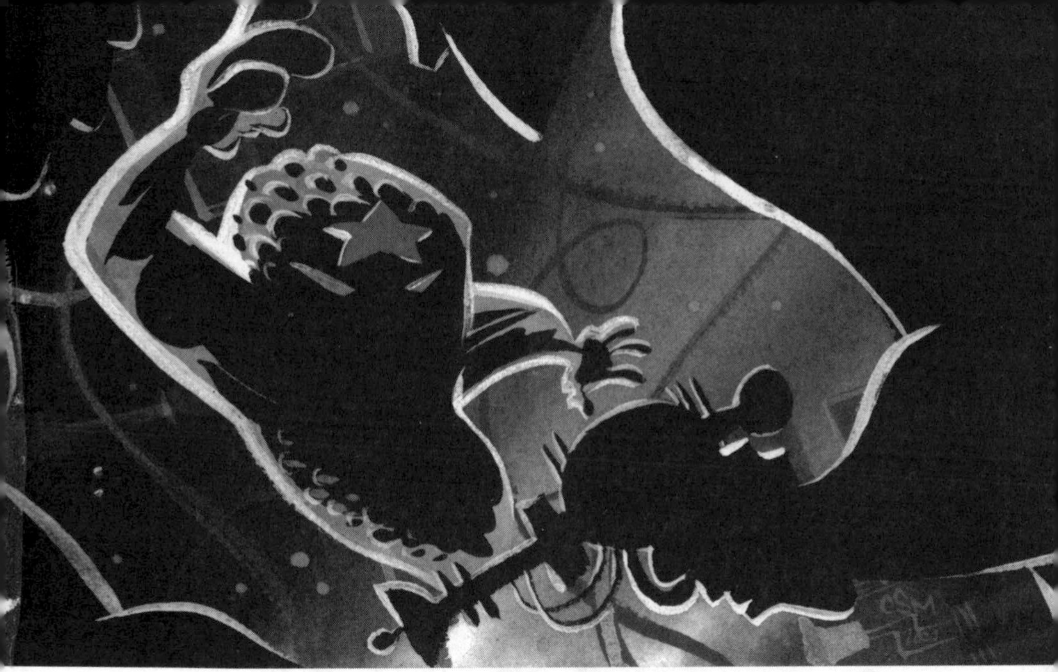

SCOTT MORSE

MAGIC PICKLE

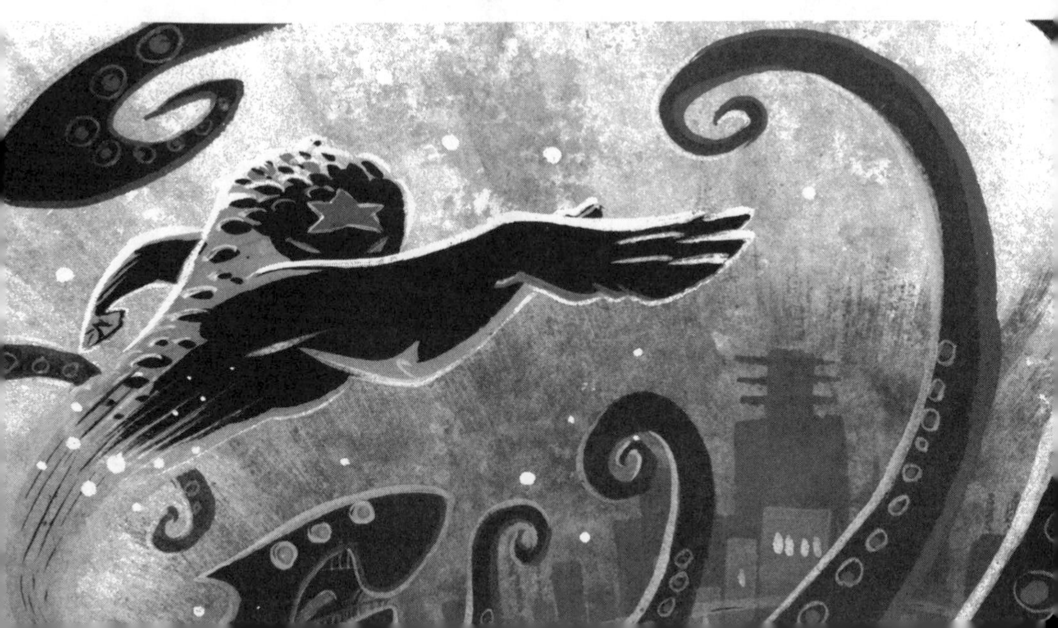

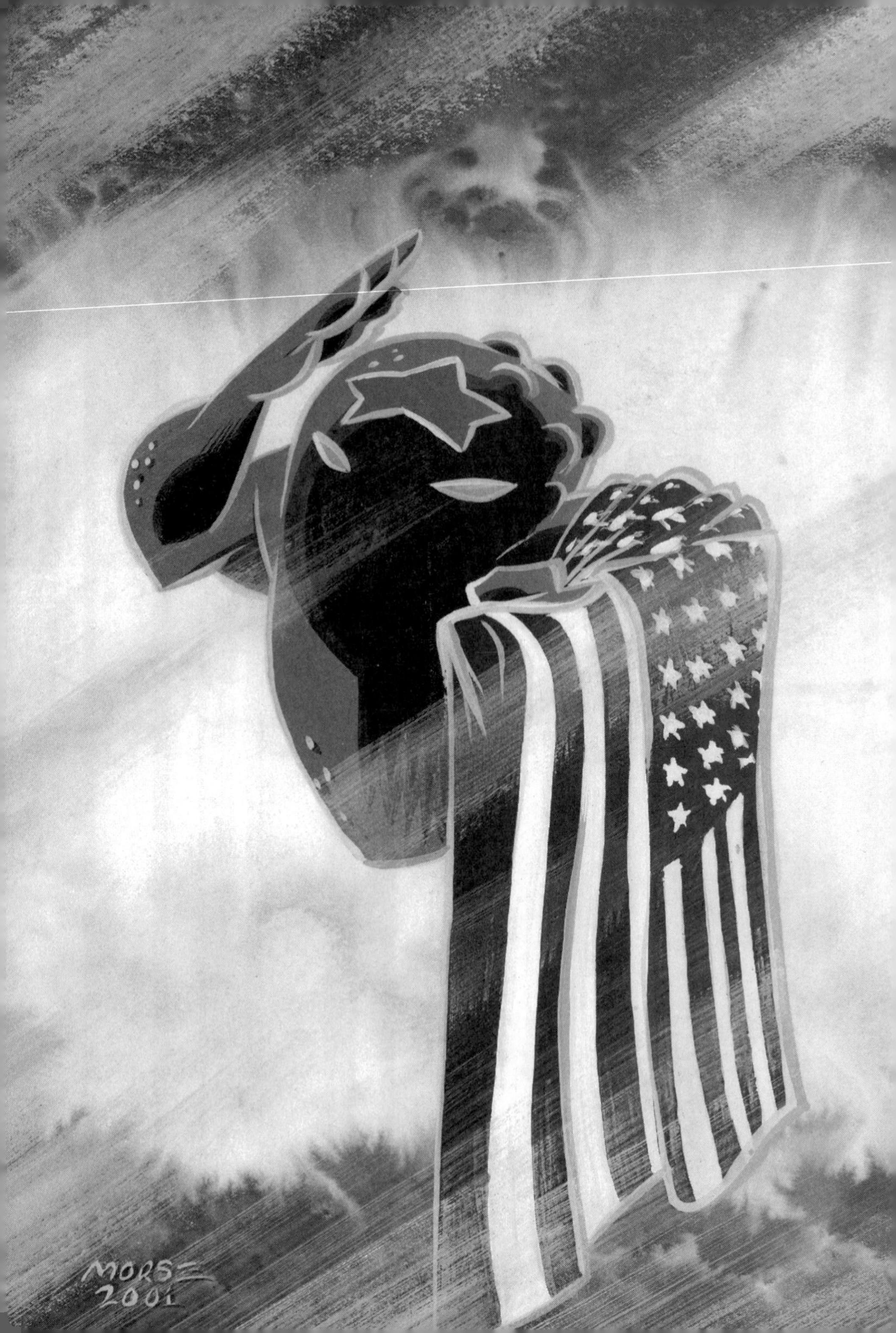
MORSE
2001

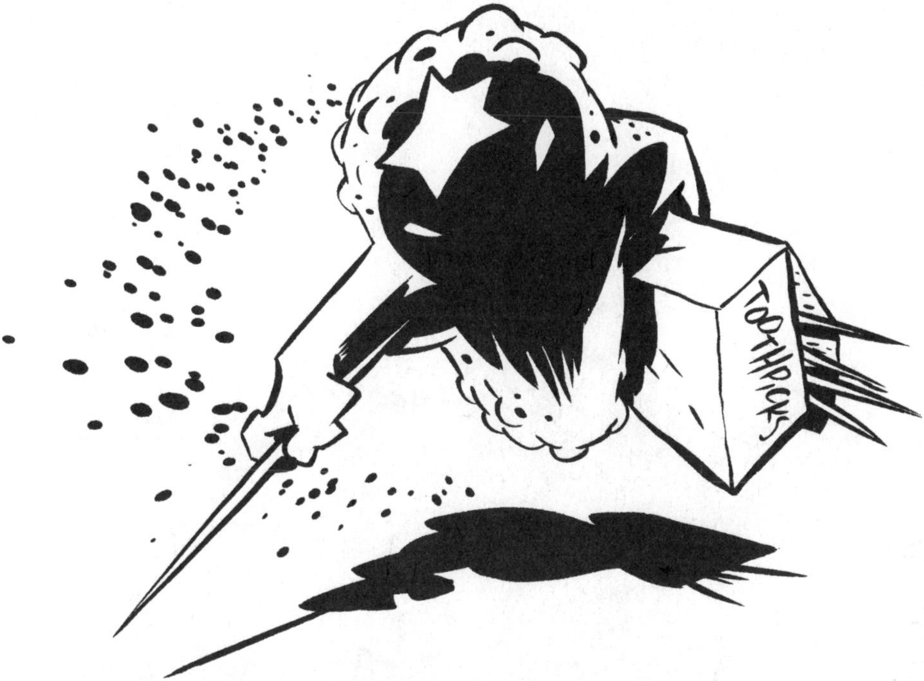
TOOTHPICKS

WHAT WILL YOU DO WHEN THEY STRIKE?

I'M AFRAID IT'S TRUE, FOLKS. EVIL IS AFOOT. WATCH WHAT YOU EAT...YOU NEVER KNOW WHAT YOUR SEEMINGLY MINDLESS TASTY MORSEL MAY HAVE IN MIND FOR ***YOU.*** I'M TALKING ABOUT PURE EVIL HERE, PEOPLE, IN THE FORM OF ***THE BROTHERHOOD OF EVIL PRODUCE--THE PHANTOM CARROT...CHILI CHILI BANG BANG...THE ROMAINE GLADIATOR.*** THEY GOT YOUR NUMBER, I GUARANTEE. DO YOU REALIZE TO WHAT EXTENT THEY'LL GO TO TAKE OVER OUR WORLD?

YOU ***DON'T***, DO YOU?

GOOD THING THE ***MAGIC PICKLE'S*** HERE TO SET THINGS STRAIGHT SO YOU'LL NEVER HAVE TO WORRY ABOUT VILLAINOUS VEGETABLES GONE BAD.

JUST THANK YOUR LUCKY STARS. AND ***HIS.***

for
KATIE MORSE
AND
ALL OF HER KIDS...

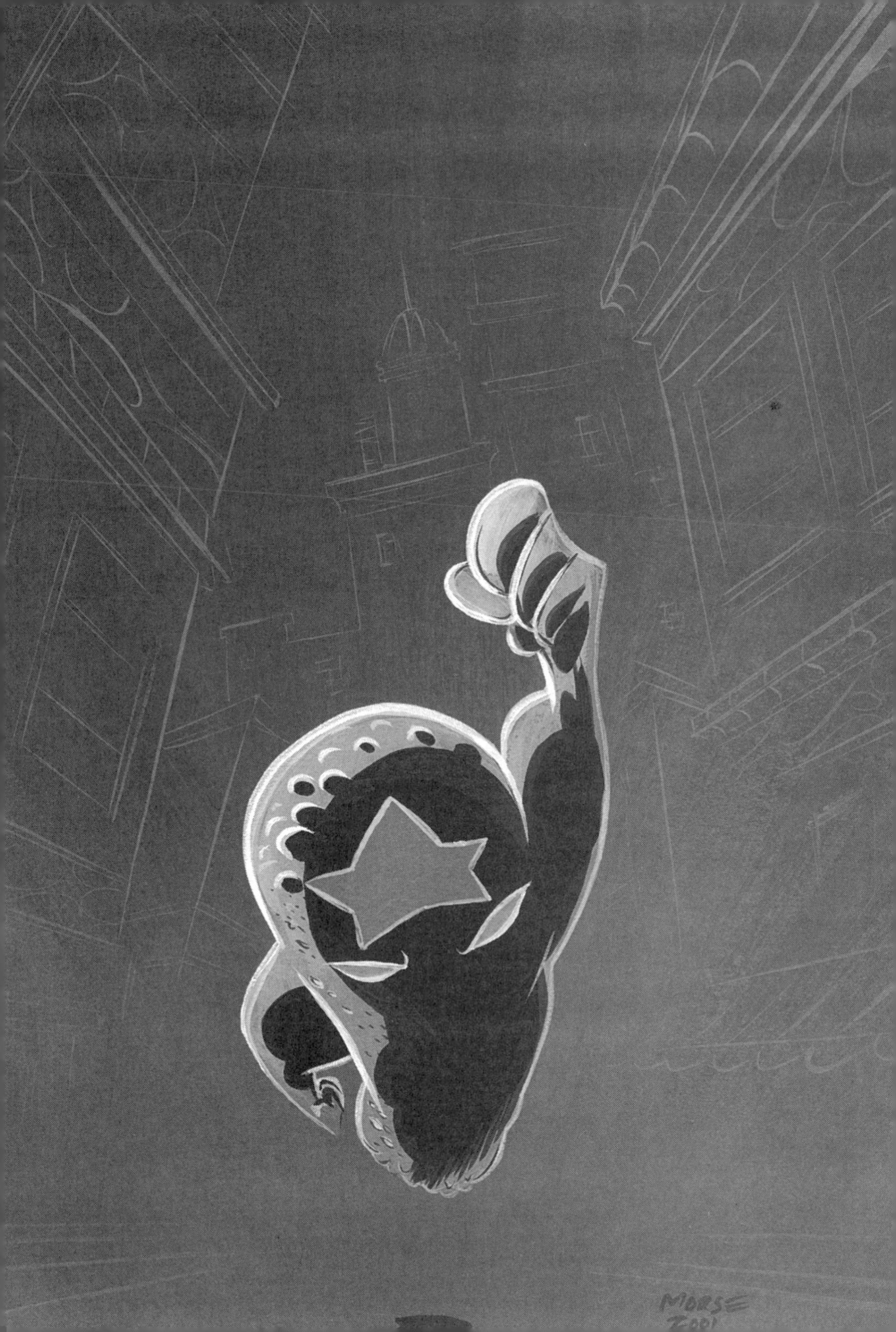
MORSE
2001

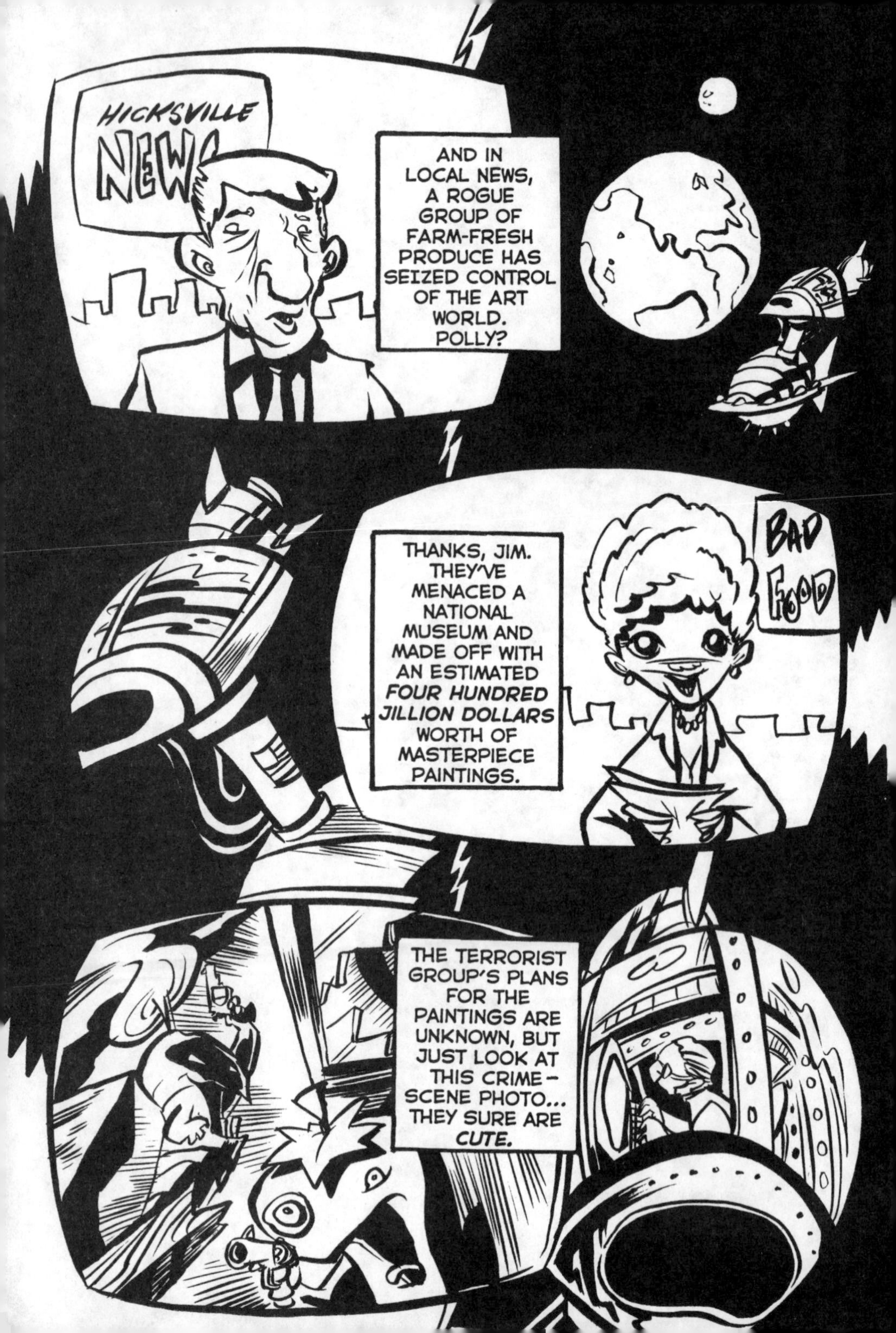
HICKSVILLE
NEWS
AND IN LOCAL NEWS, A ROGUE GROUP OF FARM-FRESH PRODUCE HAS SEIZED CONTROL OF THE ART WORLD. POLLY?
BAD FOOD
THANKS, JIM. THEY'VE MENACED A NATIONAL MUSEUM AND MADE OFF WITH AN ESTIMATED *FOUR HUNDRED JILLION DOLLARS* WORTH OF MASTERPIECE PAINTINGS.
THE TERRORIST GROUP'S PLANS FOR THE PAINTINGS ARE UNKNOWN, BUT JUST LOOK AT THIS CRIME-SCENE PHOTO... THEY SURE ARE *CUTE.*

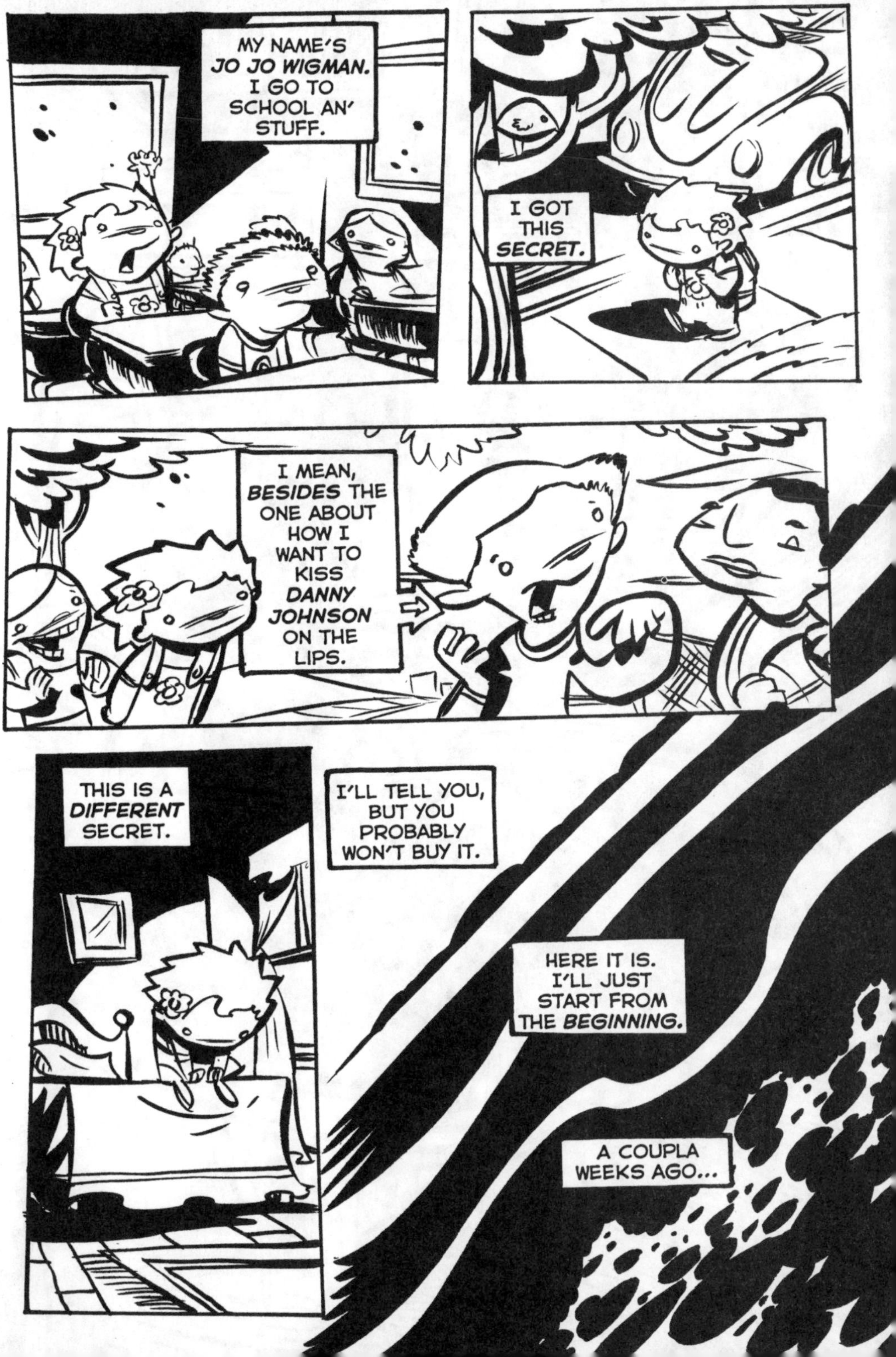
MY NAME'S *JO JO WIGMAN.* I GO TO SCHOOL AN' STUFF.
I GOT THIS *SECRET.*
I MEAN, *BESIDES* THE ONE ABOUT HOW I WANT TO KISS *DANNY JOHNSON* ON THE LIPS.
THIS IS A *DIFFERENT* SECRET.
I'LL TELL YOU, BUT YOU PROBABLY WON'T BUY IT.
HERE IT IS. I'LL JUST START FROM THE *BEGINNING.*
A COUPLA WEEKS AGO...

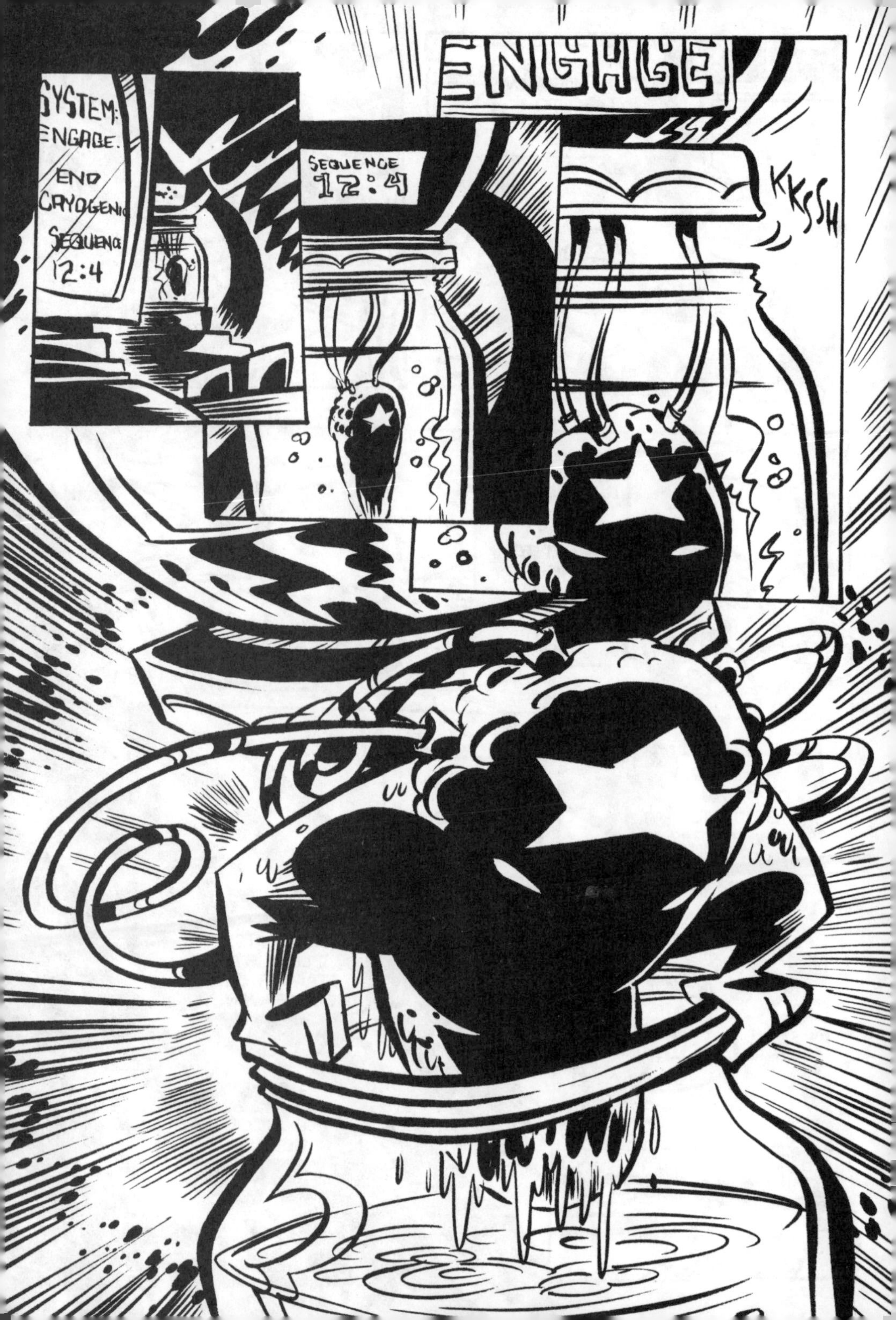
SYSTEM:
ENGAGE.
END
CRYOGENIC
SEQUENCE
12:4
SEQUENCE
12:4
ENGAGE
KKSSH

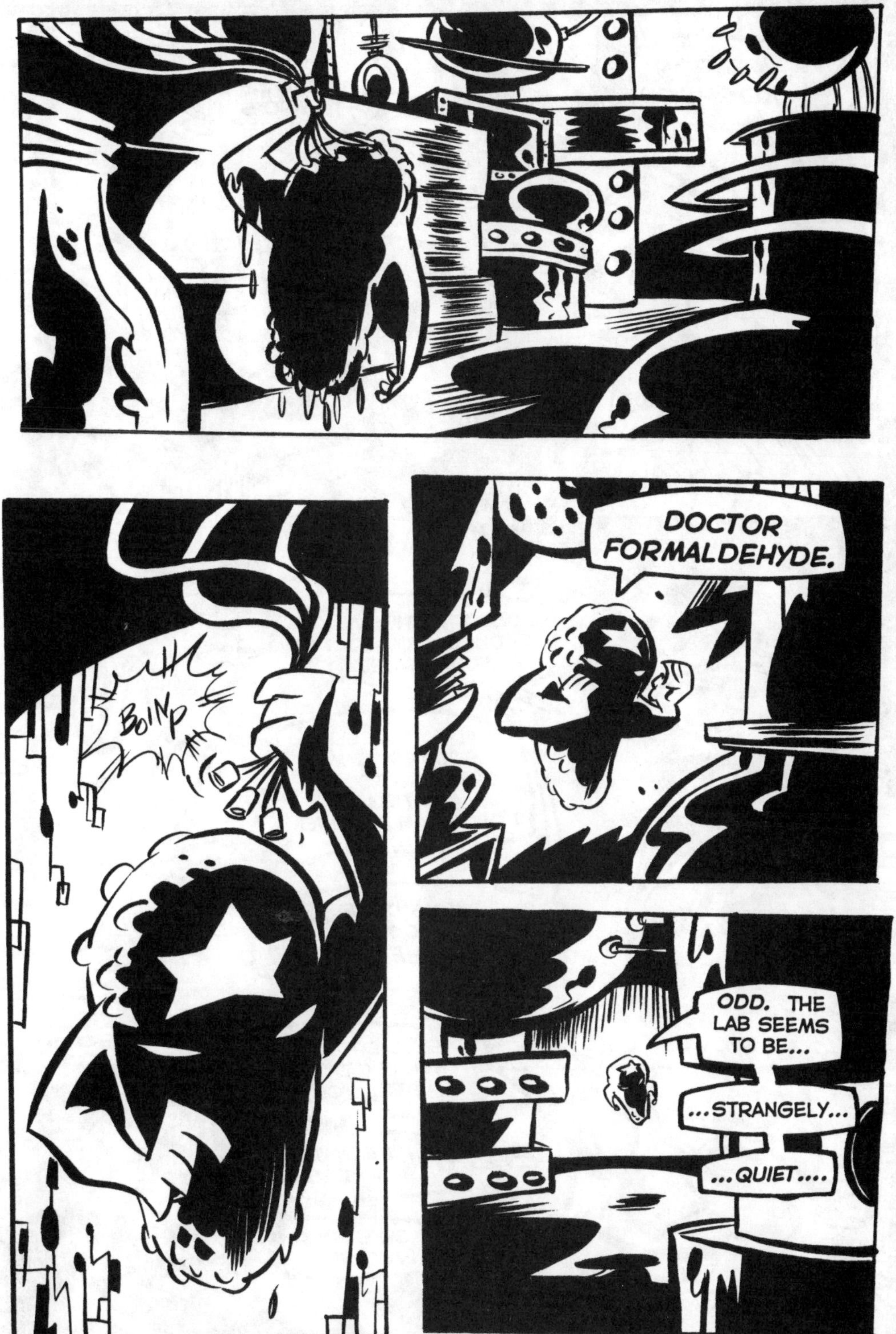
BOINP
DOCTOR FORMALDEHYDE.
ODD. THE LAB SEEMS TO BE...
...STRANGELY...
...QUIET....

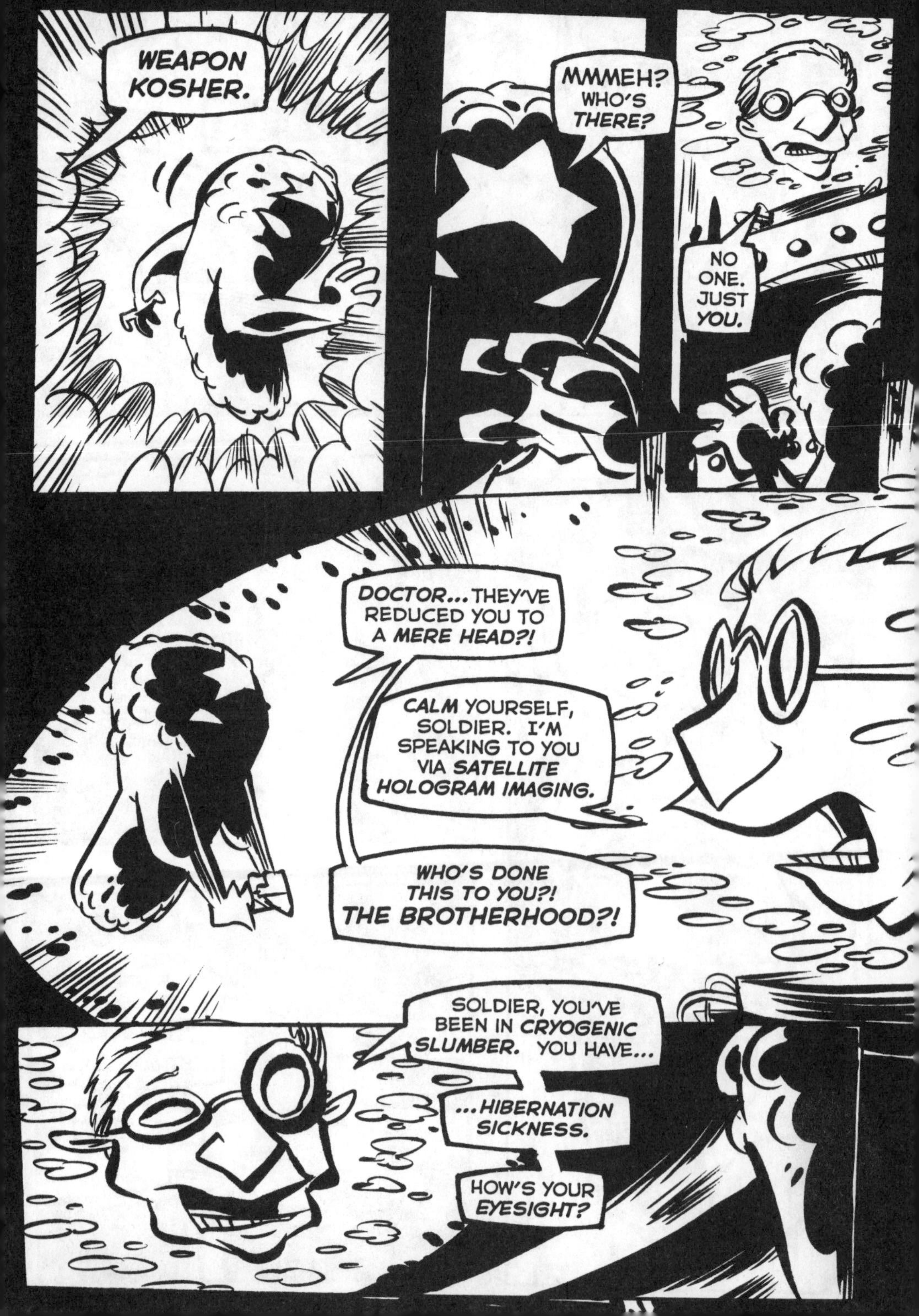
WEAPON KOSHER.
MMMEH? WHO'S THERE?
NO ONE. JUST YOU.
DOCTOR... THEY'VE REDUCED YOU TO A MERE HEAD?!
CALM YOURSELF, SOLDIER. I'M SPEAKING TO YOU VIA SATELLITE HOLOGRAM IMAGING.
WHO'S DONE THIS TO YOU?! THE BROTHERHOOD?!
SOLDIER, YOU'VE BEEN IN CRYOGENIC SLUMBER. YOU HAVE...
...HIBERNATION SICKNESS.
HOW'S YOUR EYESIGHT?

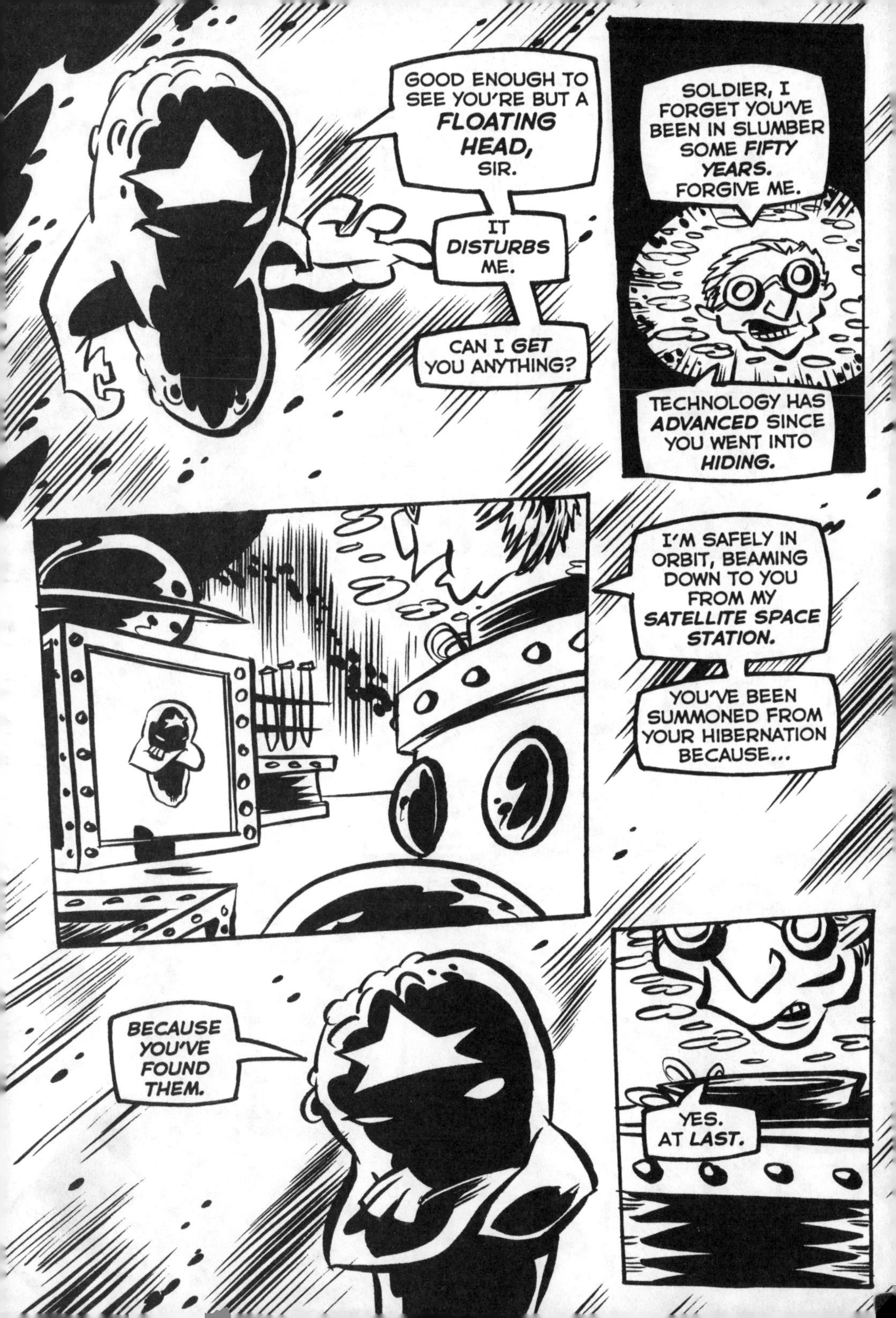
GOOD ENOUGH TO SEE YOU'RE BUT A FLOATING HEAD, SIR.
IT DISTURBS ME.
CAN I GET YOU ANYTHING?
SOLDIER, I FORGET YOU'VE BEEN IN SLUMBER SOME FIFTY YEARS. FORGIVE ME.
TECHNOLOGY HAS ADVANCED SINCE YOU WENT INTO HIDING.
I'M SAFELY IN ORBIT, BEAMING DOWN TO YOU FROM MY SATELLITE SPACE STATION.
YOU'VE BEEN SUMMONED FROM YOUR HIBERNATION BECAUSE...
BECAUSE YOU'VE FOUND THEM.
YES. AT LAST.

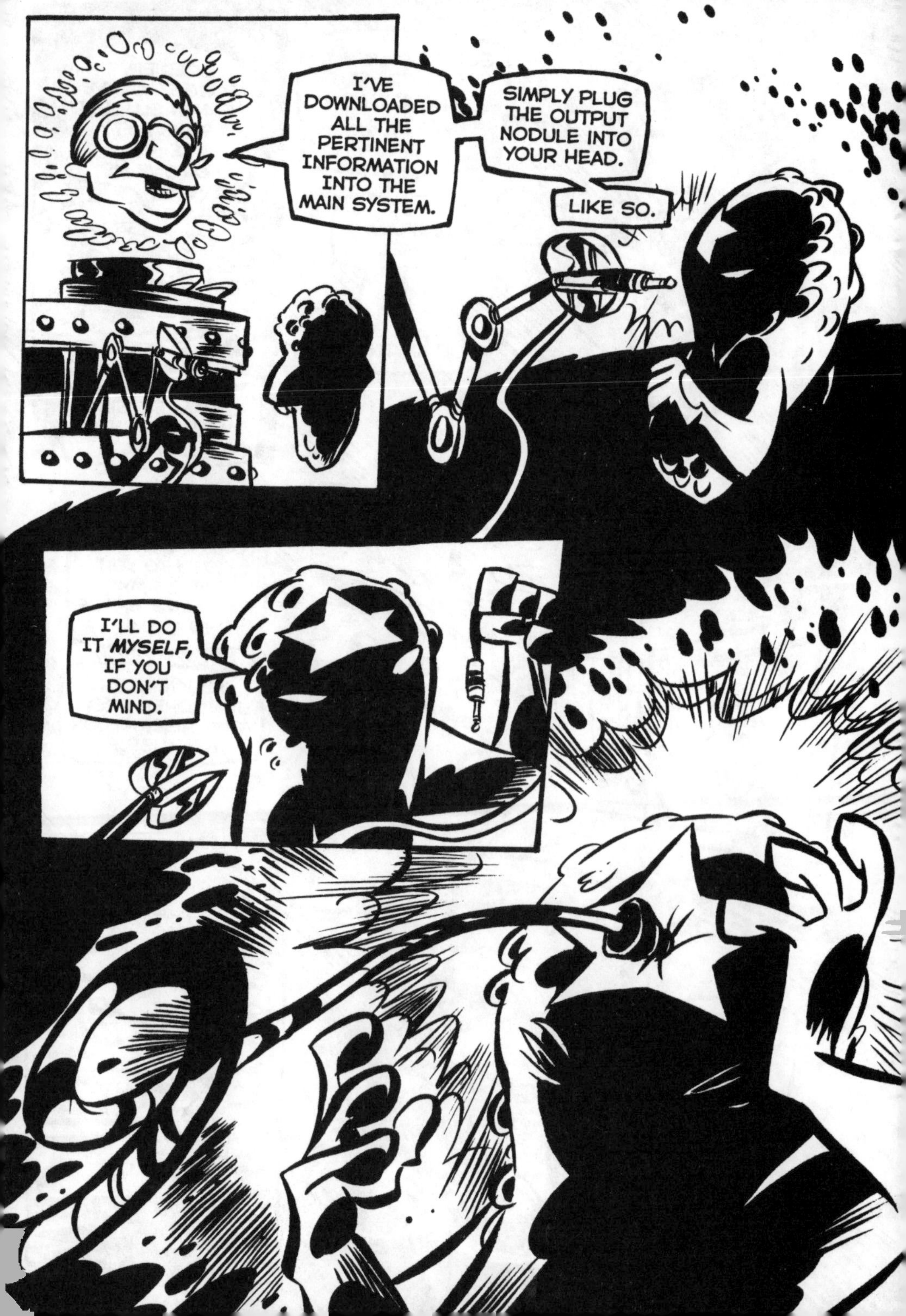
I'VE DOWNLOADED ALL THE PERTINENT INFORMATION INTO THE MAIN SYSTEM.
SIMPLY PLUG THE OUTPUT NODULE INTO YOUR HEAD.
LIKE SO.
I'LL DO IT *MYSELF,* IF YOU DON'T MIND.

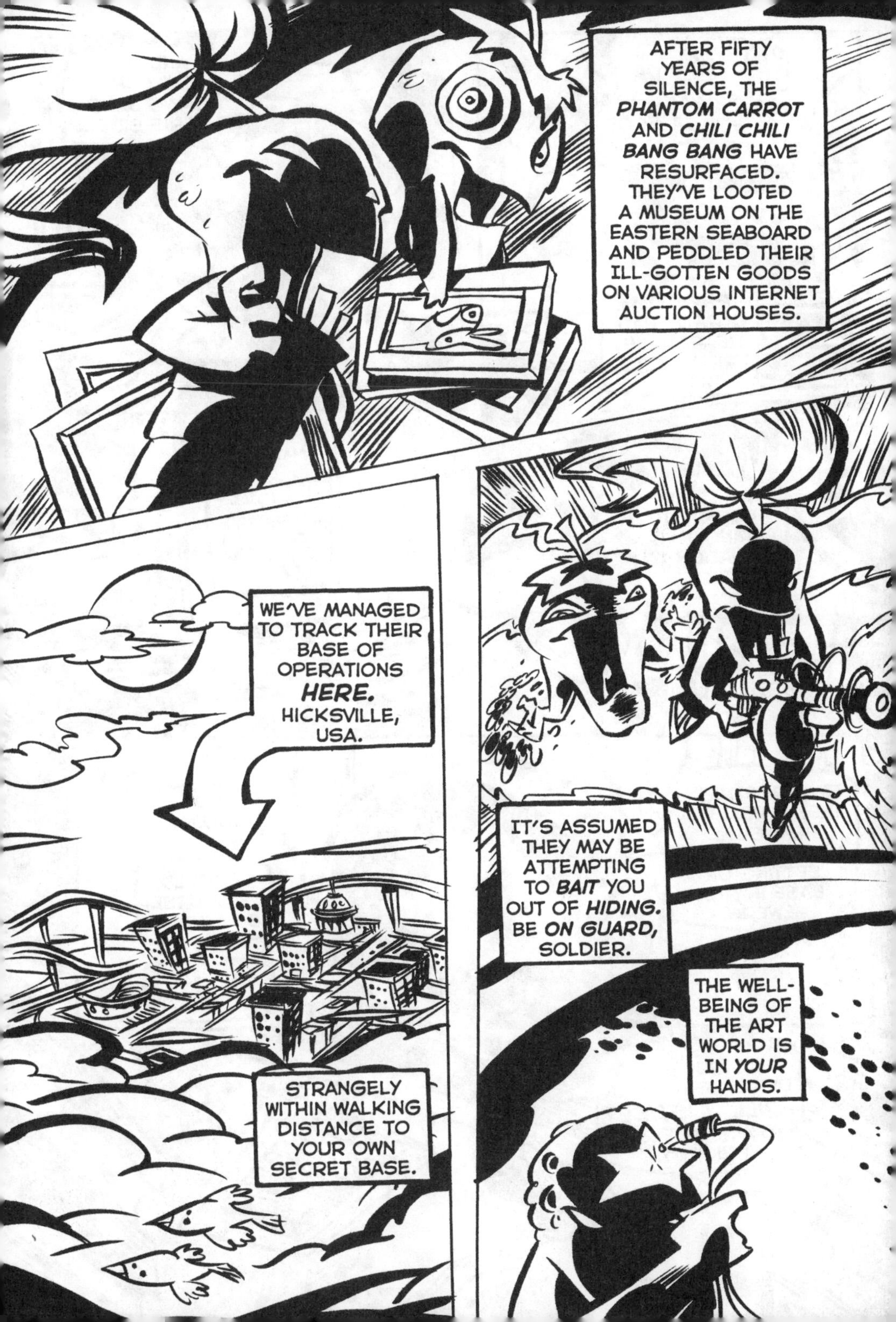
AFTER FIFTY YEARS OF SILENCE, THE *PHANTOM CARROT* AND *CHILI CHILI BANG BANG* HAVE RESURFACED. THEY'VE LOOTED A MUSEUM ON THE EASTERN SEABOARD AND PEDDLED THEIR ILL-GOTTEN GOODS ON VARIOUS INTERNET AUCTION HOUSES.
WE'VE MANAGED TO TRACK THEIR BASE OF OPERATIONS *HERE.* HICKSVILLE, USA.
STRANGELY WITHIN WALKING DISTANCE TO YOUR OWN SECRET BASE.
IT'S ASSUMED THEY MAY BE ATTEMPTING TO *BAIT* YOU OUT OF *HIDING.* BE *ON GUARD,* SOLDIER.
THE WELL-BEING OF THE ART WORLD IS IN *YOUR* HANDS.

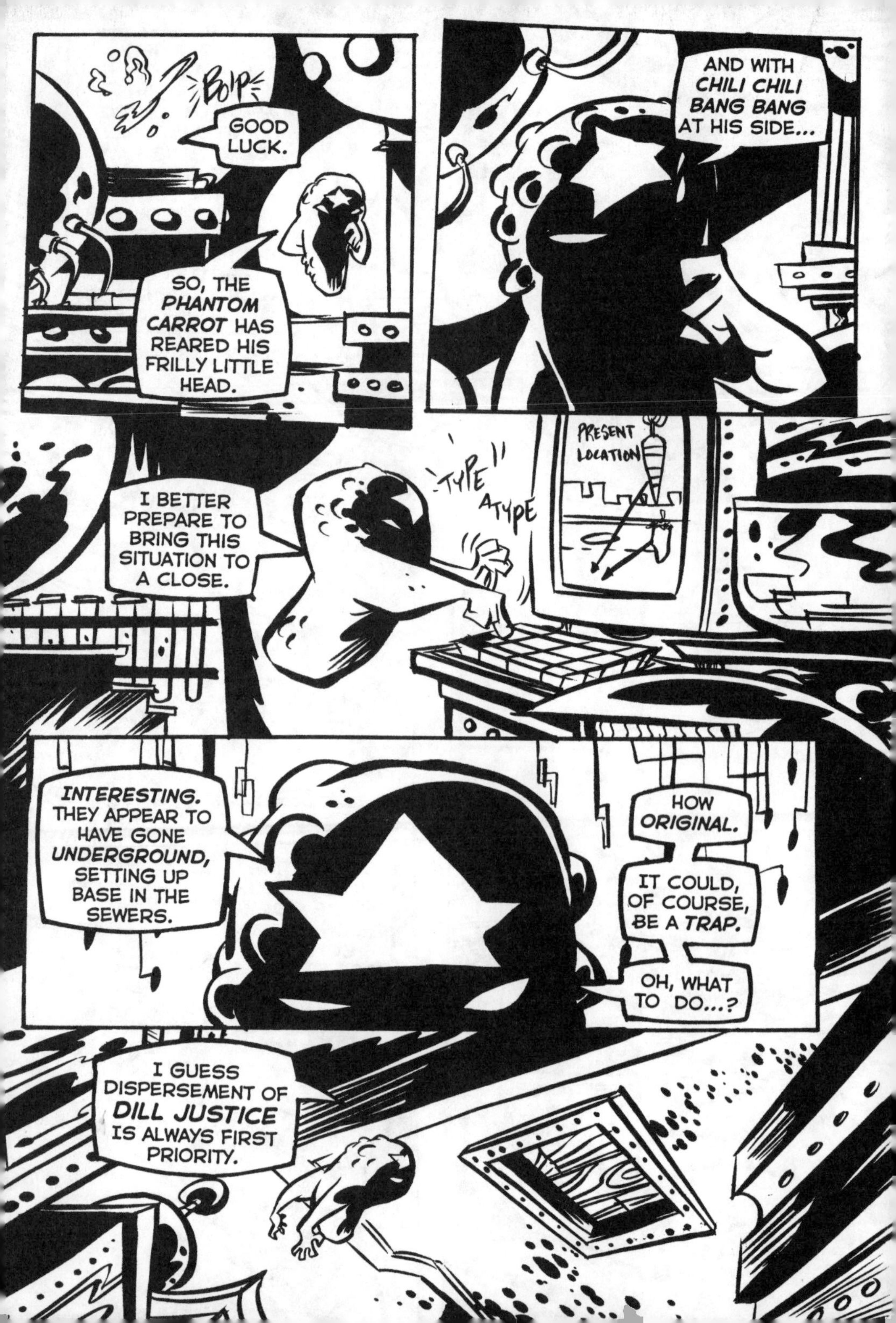
BOIP
GOOD LUCK.
SO, THE PHANTOM CARROT HAS REARED HIS FRILLY LITTLE HEAD.
AND WITH CHILI CHILI BANG BANG AT HIS SIDE...
PRESENT LOCATION
TYPE ATYPE
I BETTER PREPARE TO BRING THIS SITUATION TO A CLOSE.
INTERESTING. THEY APPEAR TO HAVE GONE UNDERGROUND, SETTING UP BASE IN THE SEWERS.
HOW ORIGINAL.
IT COULD, OF COURSE, BE A TRAP.
OH, WHAT TO DO...?
I GUESS DISPERSEMENT OF DILL JUSTICE IS ALWAYS FIRST PRIORITY.

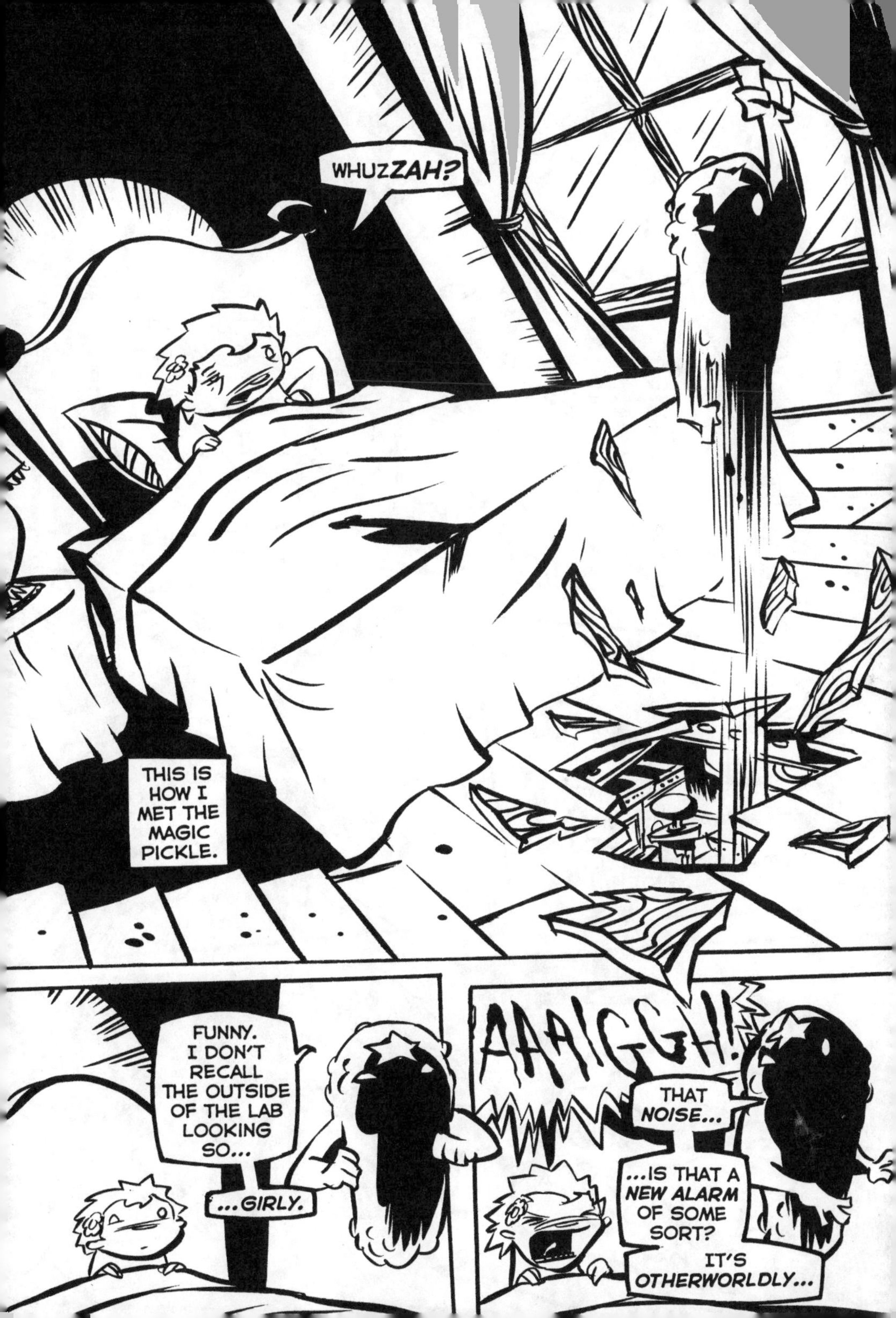
WHUZZAH?
THIS IS HOW I MET THE MAGIC PICKLE.
FUNNY. I DON'T RECALL THE OUTSIDE OF THE LAB LOOKING SO...
...GIRLY.
AAAIGGH!
THAT NOISE...
...IS THAT A NEW ALARM OF SOME SORT?
IT'S OTHERWORLDLY...

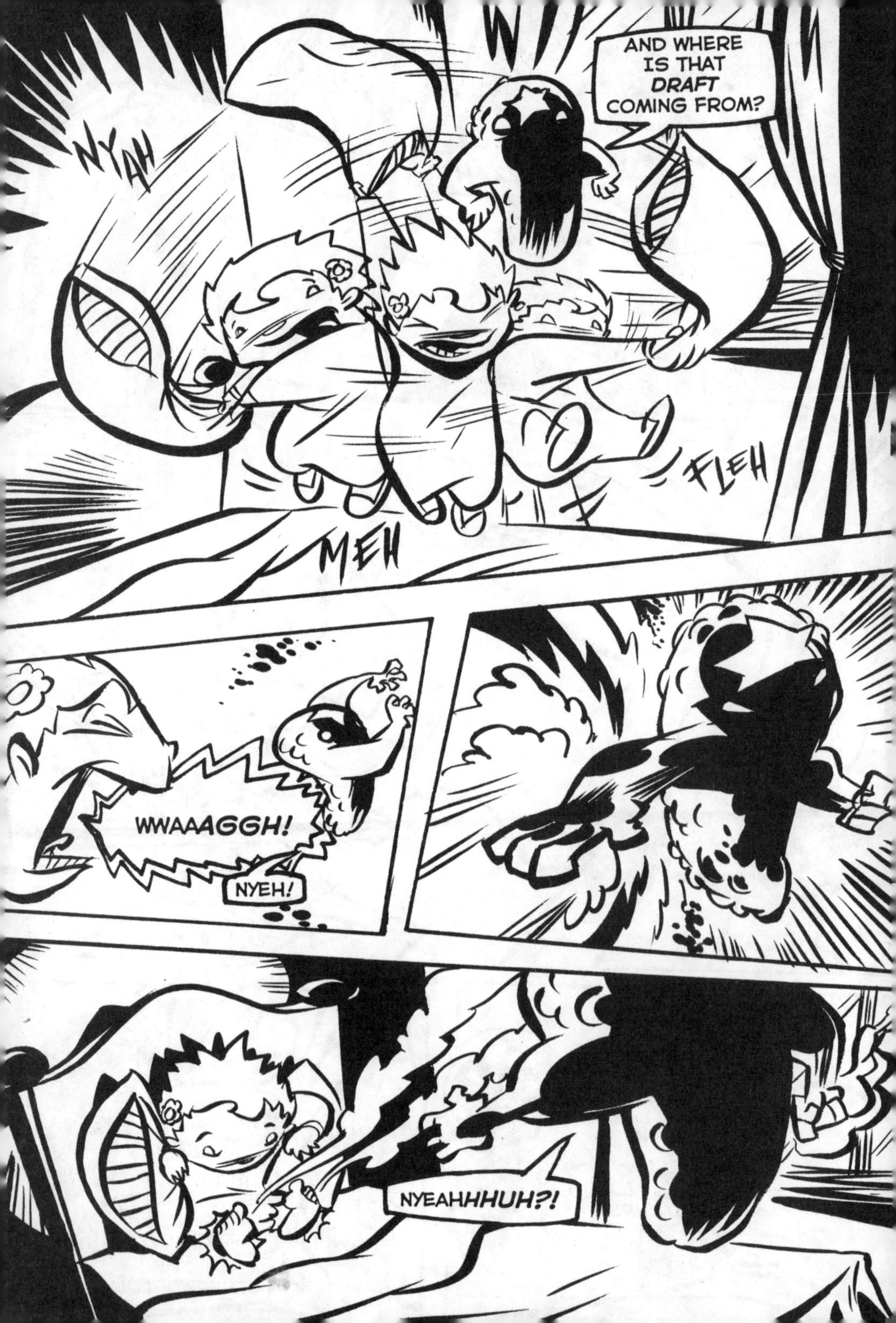

AND WHERE IS THAT *DRAFT* COMING FROM?
NYAH
FLEH
MEH
WWAAAGGH!
NYEH!
NYEAHHHUH?!

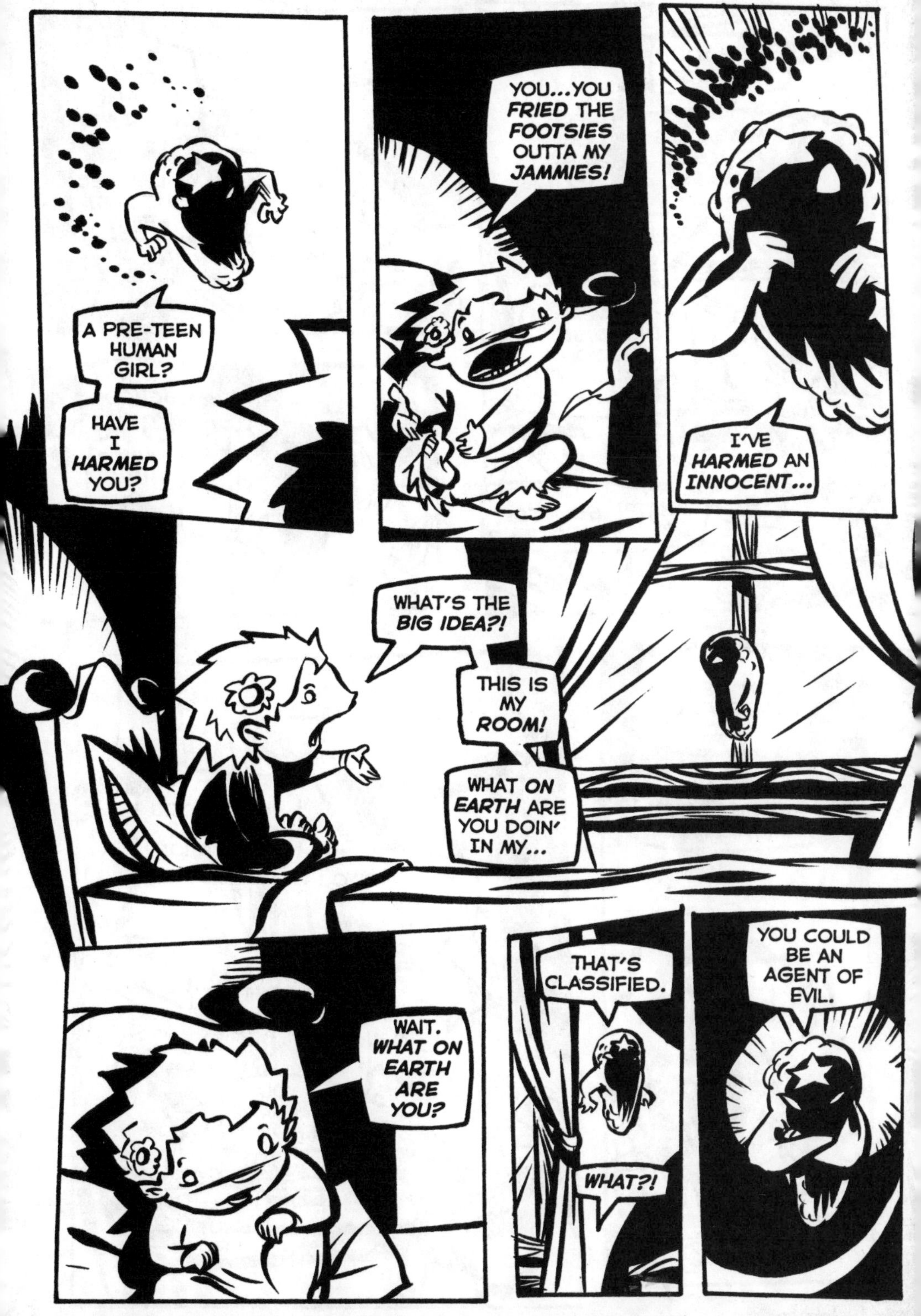
A PRE-TEEN HUMAN GIRL?
HAVE I *HARMED* YOU?
YOU...YOU *FRIED* THE *FOOTSIES* OUTTA MY *JAMMIES!*
I'VE *HARMED* AN *INNOCENT...*
WHAT'S THE *BIG IDEA?!*
THIS IS MY *ROOM!*
WHAT *ON EARTH* ARE YOU DOIN' IN MY...
WAIT. *WHAT ON EARTH ARE YOU?*
THAT'S CLASSIFIED.
WHAT?!
YOU COULD BE AN AGENT OF EVIL.

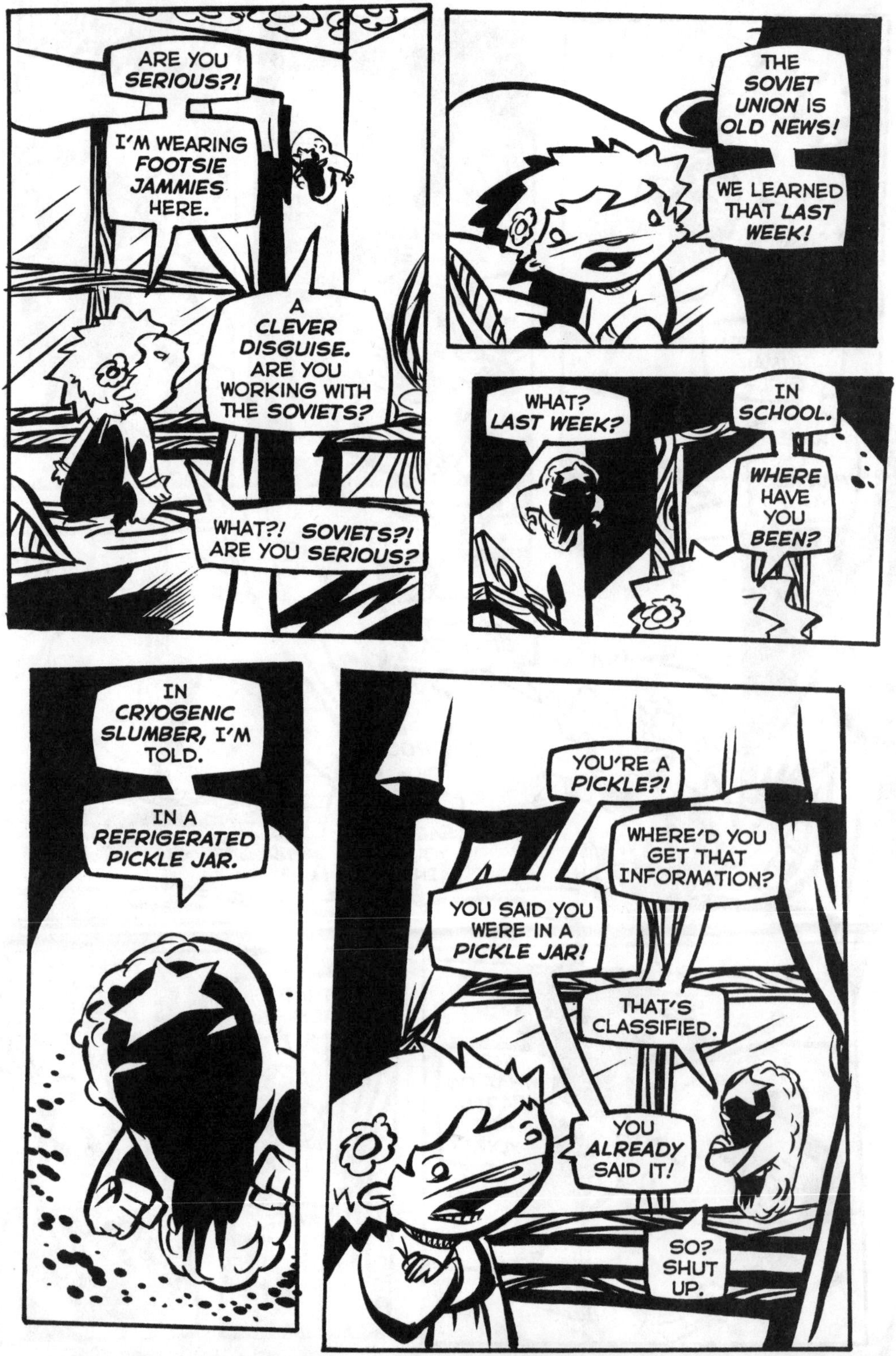
ARE YOU SERIOUS?!
I'M WEARING FOOTSIE JAMMIES HERE.
A CLEVER DISGUISE. ARE YOU WORKING WITH THE SOVIETS?
WHAT?! SOVIETS?! ARE YOU SERIOUS?
THE SOVIET UNION IS OLD NEWS!
WE LEARNED THAT LAST WEEK!
WHAT? LAST WEEK?
IN SCHOOL.
WHERE HAVE YOU BEEN?
IN CRYOGENIC SLUMBER, I'M TOLD.
IN A REFRIGERATED PICKLE JAR.
YOU'RE A PICKLE?!
WHERE'D YOU GET THAT INFORMATION?
YOU SAID YOU WERE IN A PICKLE JAR!
THAT'S CLASSIFIED.
YOU ALREADY SAID IT!
SO? SHUT UP.

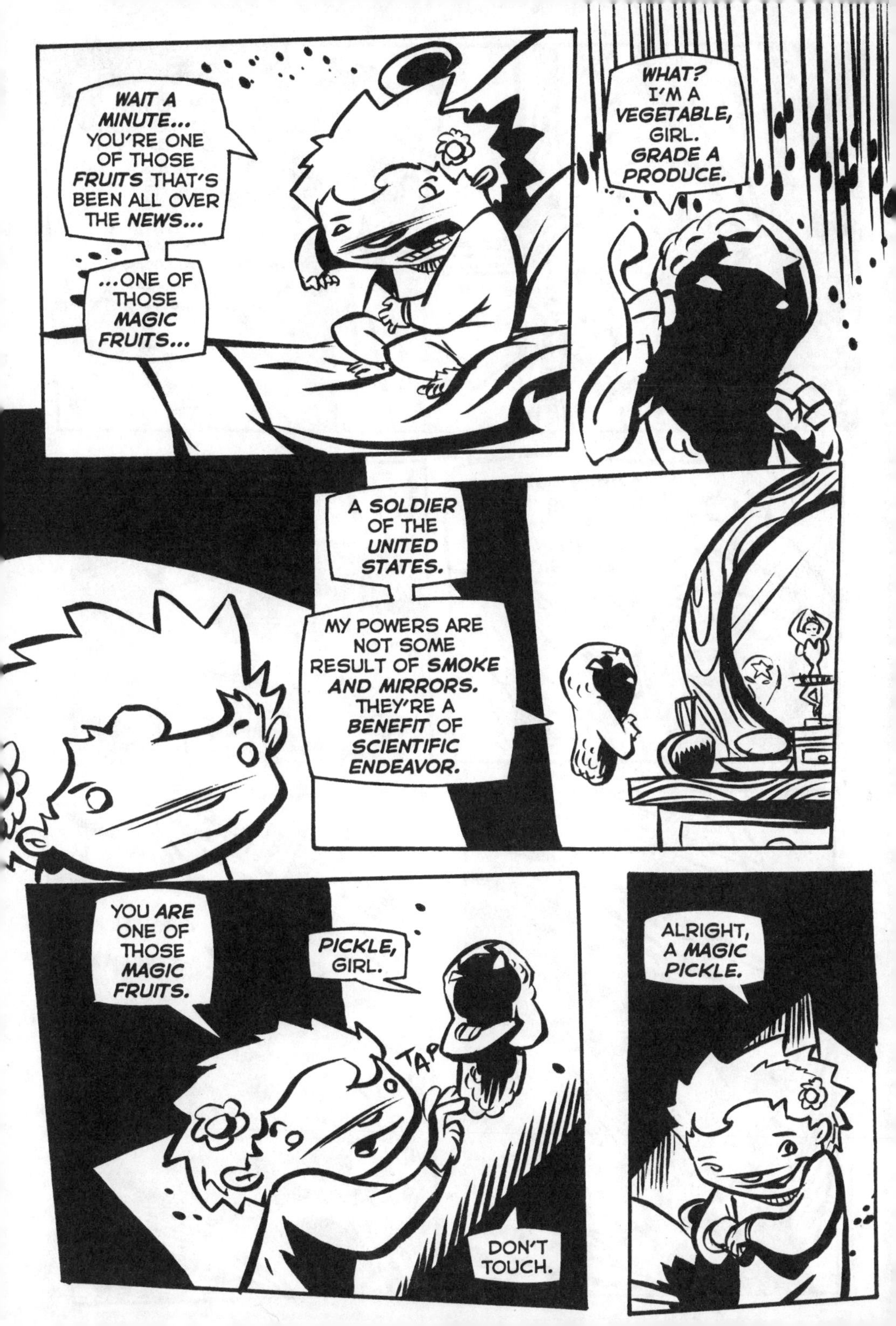
WAIT A MINUTE... YOU'RE ONE OF THOSE FRUITS THAT'S BEEN ALL OVER THE NEWS...
...ONE OF THOSE MAGIC FRUITS...
WHAT? I'M A VEGETABLE, GIRL. GRADE A PRODUCE.
A SOLDIER OF THE UNITED STATES.
MY POWERS ARE NOT SOME RESULT OF SMOKE AND MIRRORS. THEY'RE A BENEFIT OF SCIENTIFIC ENDEAVOR.
YOU ARE ONE OF THOSE MAGIC FRUITS.
PICKLE, GIRL.
TAP
DON'T TOUCH.
ALRIGHT, A MAGIC PICKLE.

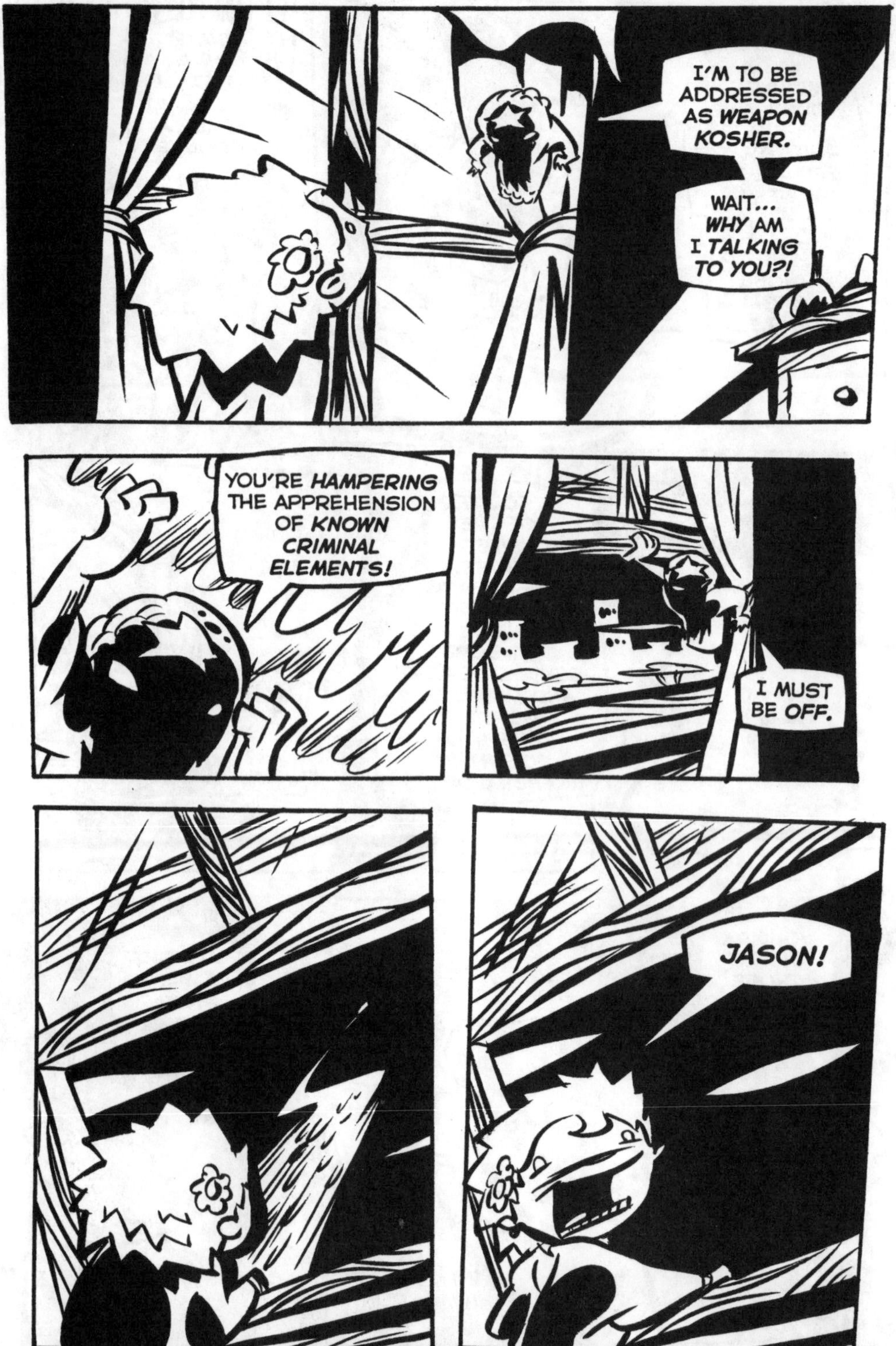
I'M TO BE ADDRESSED AS WEAPON KOSHER.
WAIT... WHY AM I TALKING TO YOU?!
YOU'RE HAMPERING THE APPREHENSION OF KNOWN CRIMINAL ELEMENTS!
I MUST BE OFF.
JASON!

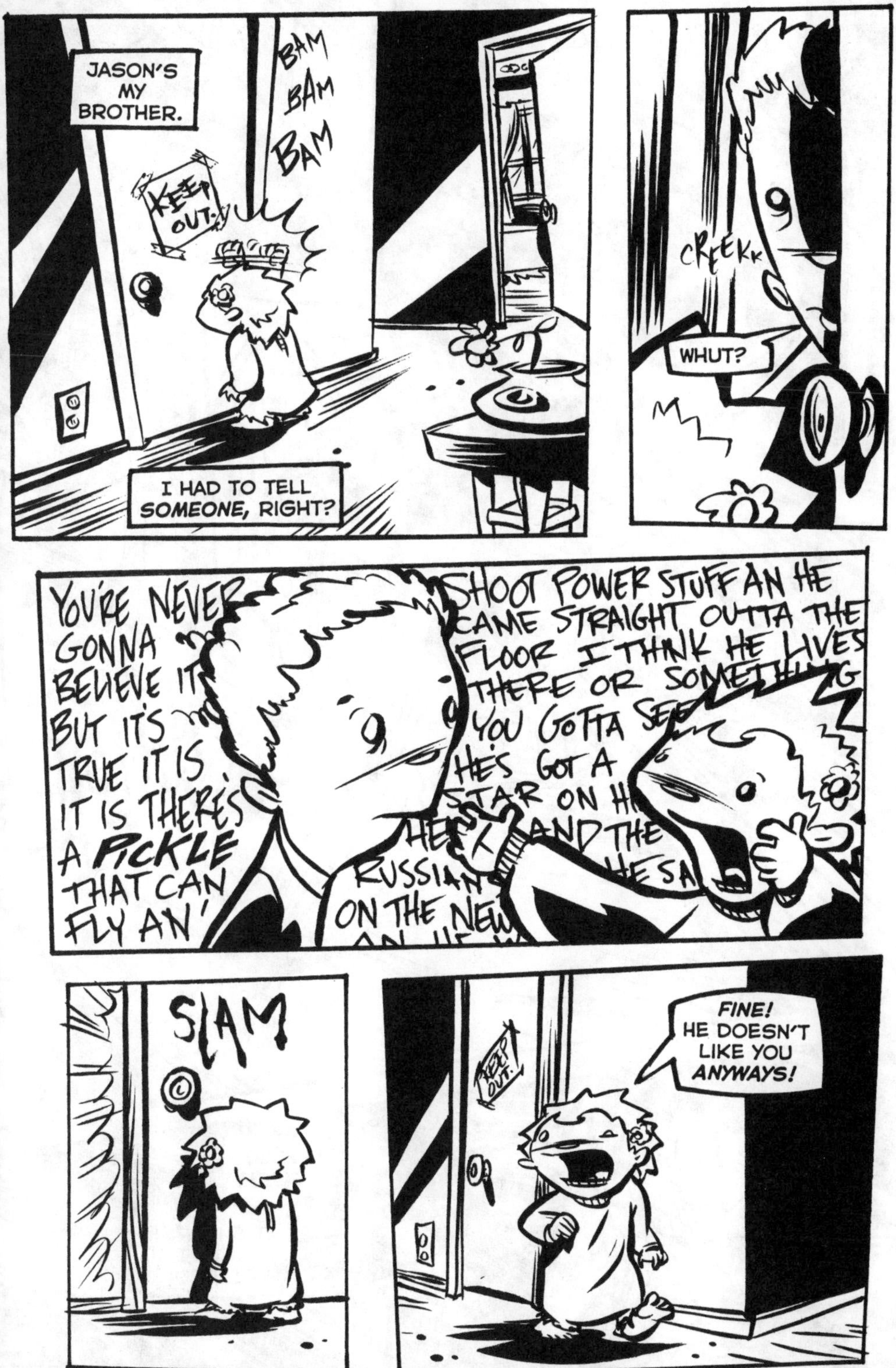
JASON'S MY BROTHER.
BAM BAM BAM
KEEP OUT.
I HAD TO TELL SOMEONE, RIGHT?
CREEKK
WHUT?
YOU'RE NEVER GONNA BELIEVE IT BUT IT'S TRUE IT IS IT IS THERE'S A PICKLE THAT CAN FLY AN'
SHOOT POWER STUFF AN HE CAME STRAIGHT OUTTA THE FLOOR I THINK HE LIVES THERE OR SOME
YOU GOTTA SE
HE'S GOT A
STAR ON H
AND THE
RUSSIAN
ON THE NEW
SLAM
KEEP OUT.
FINE! HE DOESN'T LIKE YOU ANYWAYS!

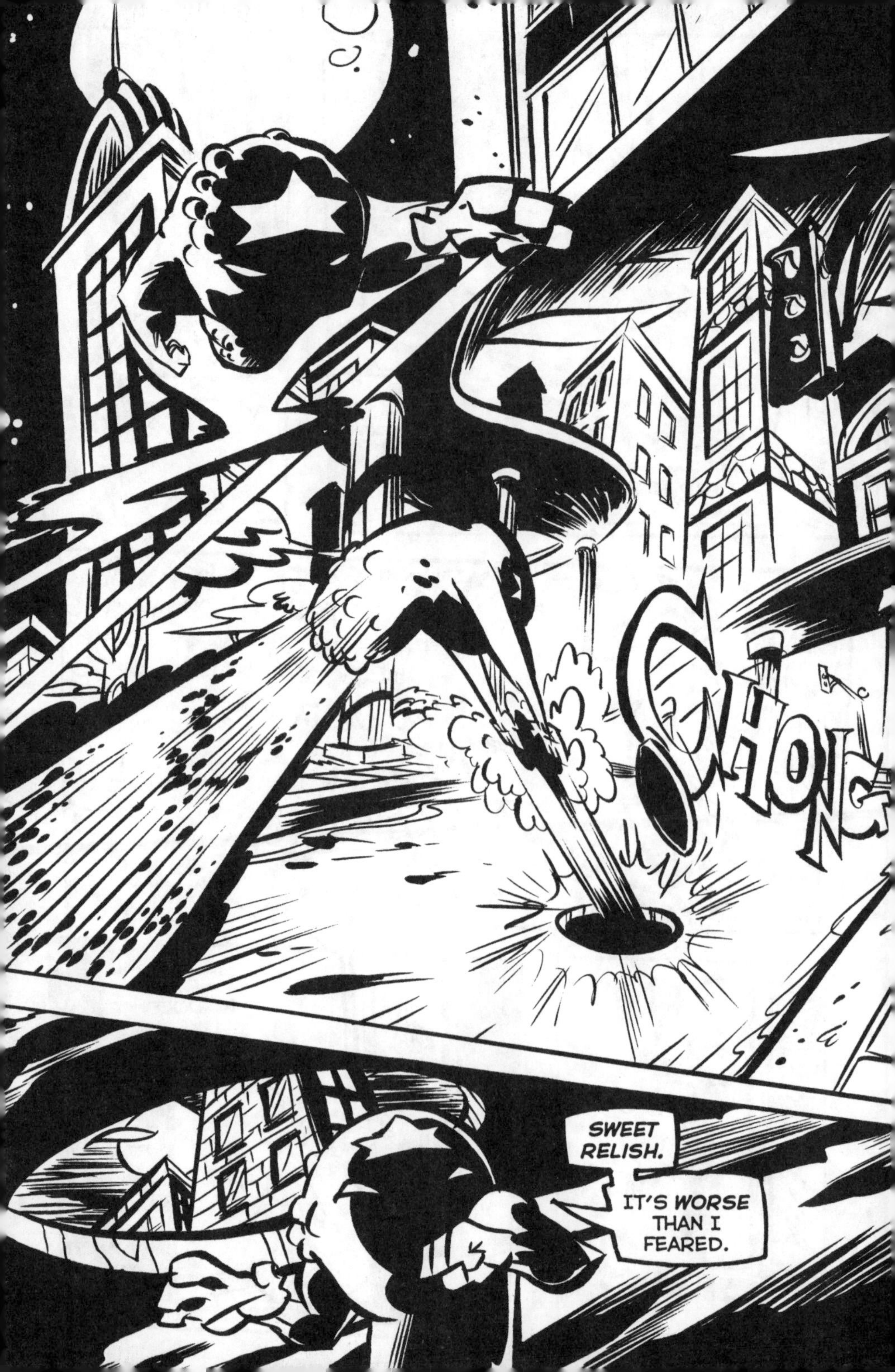
CHONG
SWEET RELISH.
IT'S *WORSE* THAN I FEARED.

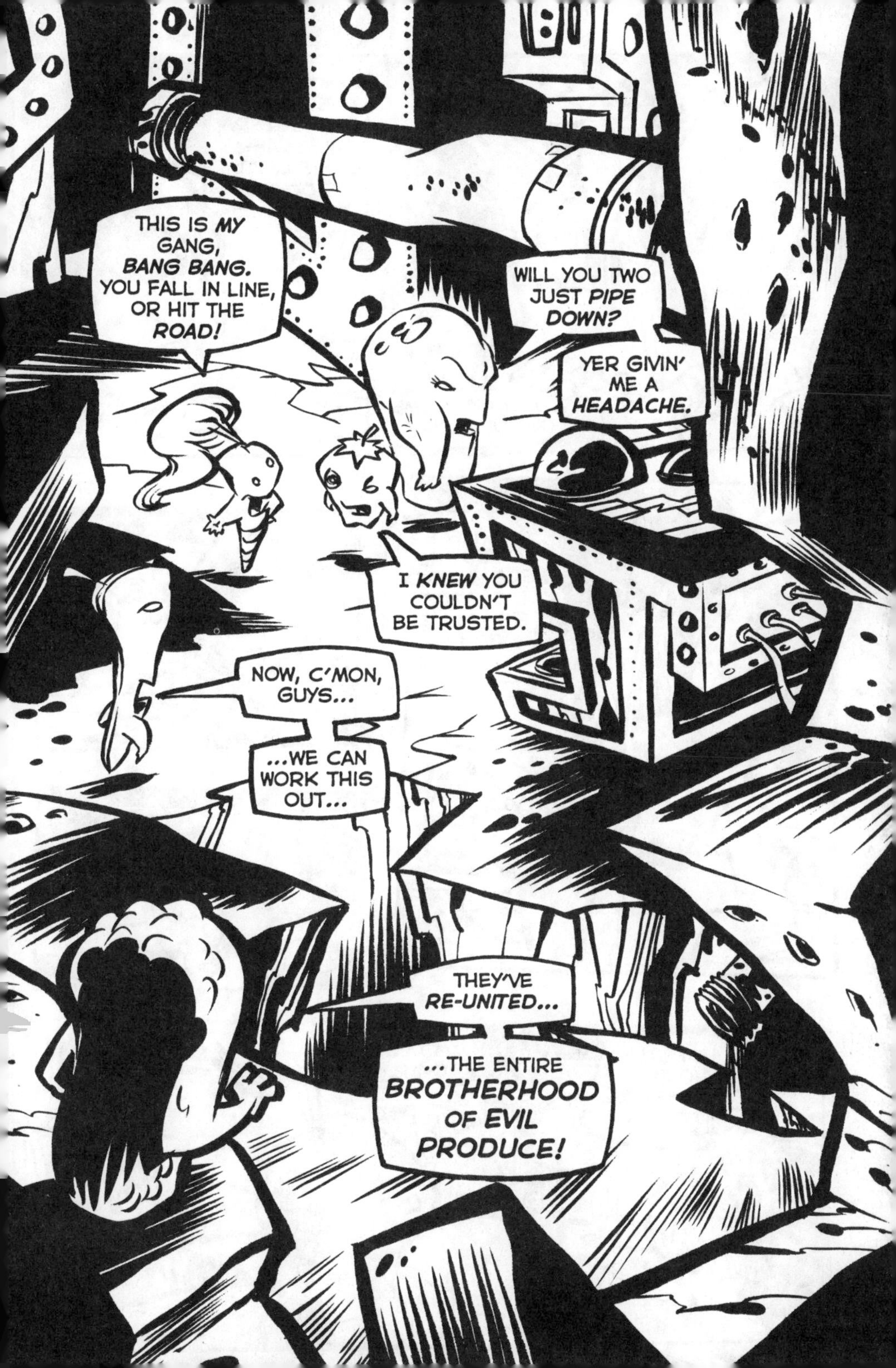
THIS IS MY GANG, BANG BANG. YOU FALL IN LINE, OR HIT THE ROAD!
WILL YOU TWO JUST PIPE DOWN?
YER GIVIN' ME A HEADACHE.
I KNEW YOU COULDN'T BE TRUSTED.
NOW, C'MON, GUYS...
...WE CAN WORK THIS OUT...
THEY'VE RE-UNITED...
...THE ENTIRE BROTHERHOOD OF EVIL PRODUCE!

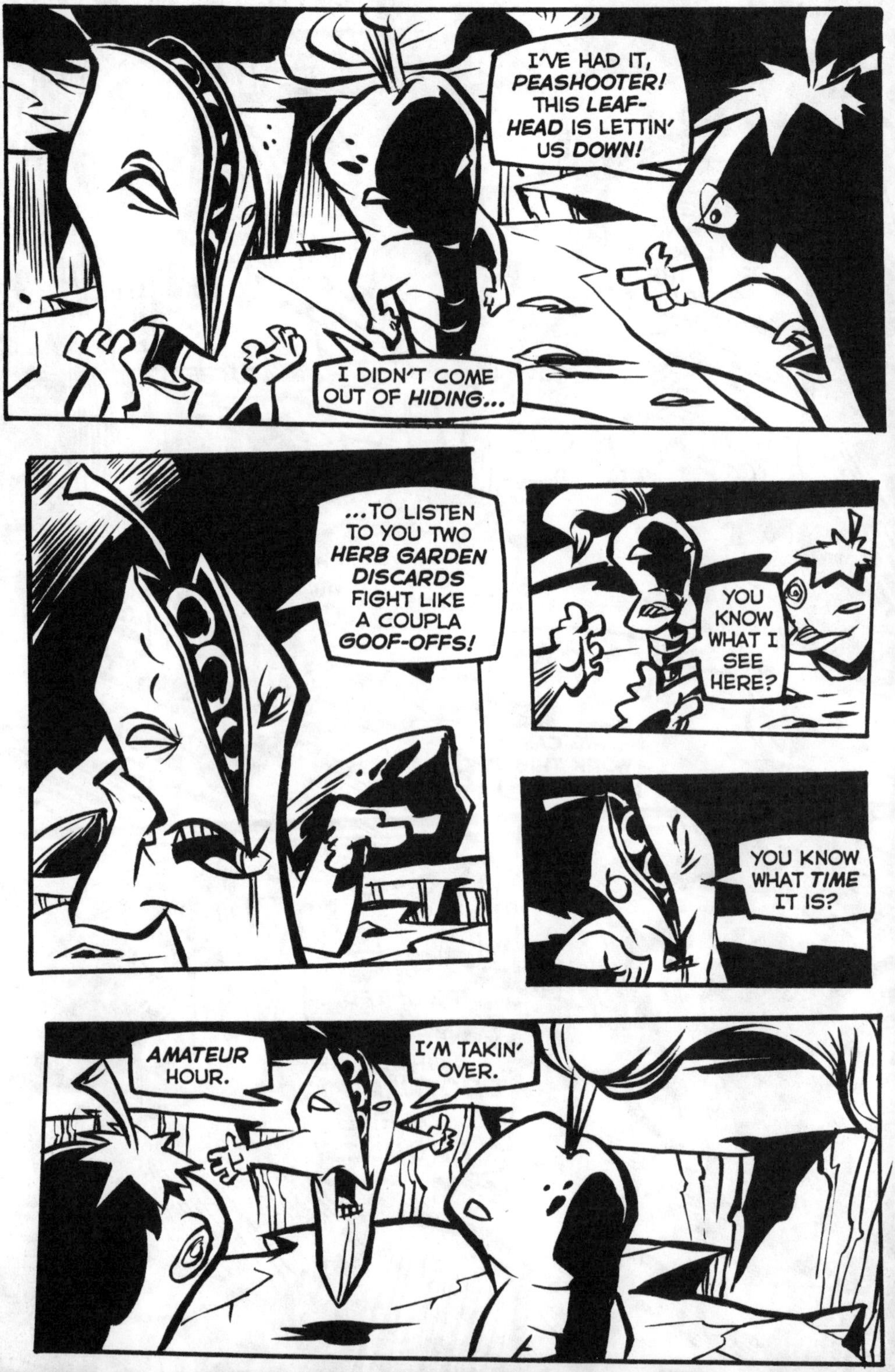

I'VE HAD IT, *PEASHOOTER!* THIS *LEAF-HEAD* IS LETTIN' US *DOWN!*
I DIDN'T COME OUT OF *HIDING...*
*...*TO LISTEN TO YOU TWO *HERB GARDEN DISCARDS* FIGHT LIKE A COUPLA *GOOF-OFFS!*
YOU KNOW WHAT I SEE HERE?
YOU KNOW WHAT *TIME* IT IS?
AMATEUR HOUR.
I'M TAKIN' OVER.

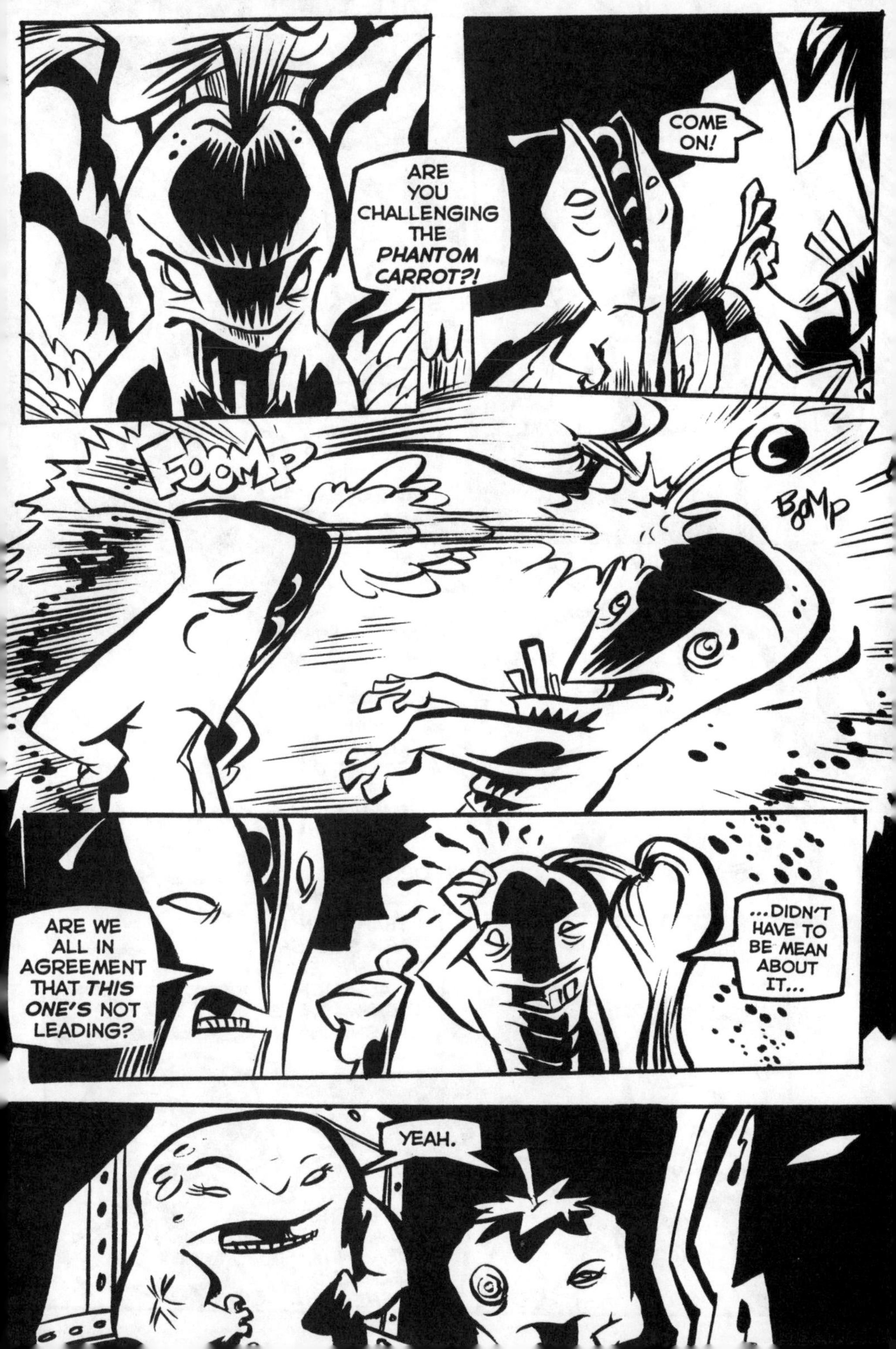
ARE YOU CHALLENGING THE PHANTOM CARROT?!
COME ON!
FOOMP
BOOMP
ARE WE ALL IN AGREEMENT THAT THIS ONE'S NOT LEADING?
...DIDN'T HAVE TO BE MEAN ABOUT IT...
YEAH.

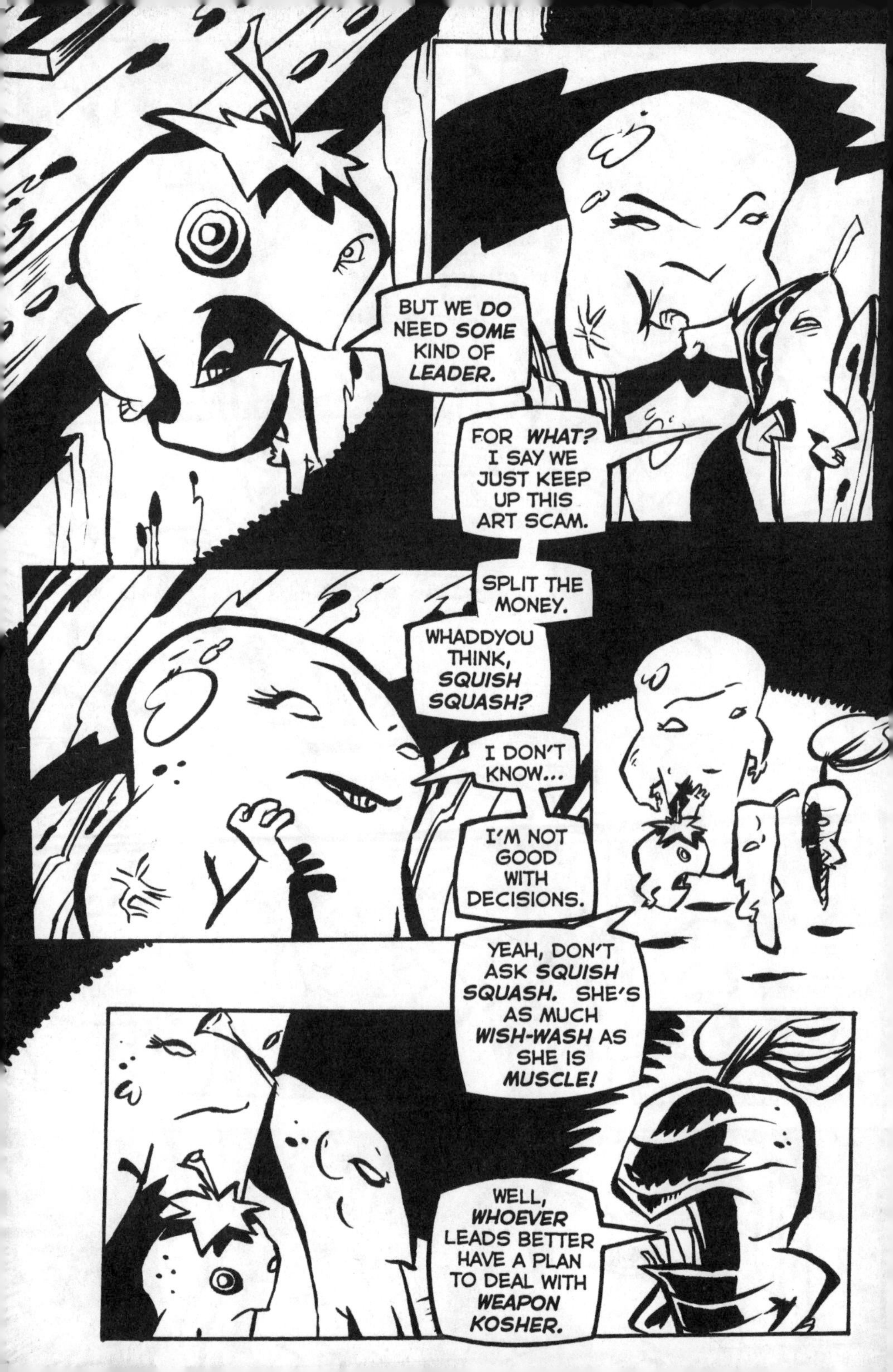

BUT WE DO NEED SOME KIND OF LEADER.
FOR WHAT? I SAY WE JUST KEEP UP THIS ART SCAM.
SPLIT THE MONEY.
WHADDYOU THINK, SQUISH SQUASH?
I DON'T KNOW...
I'M NOT GOOD WITH DECISIONS.
YEAH, DON'T ASK SQUISH SQUASH. SHE'S AS MUCH WISH-WASH AS SHE IS MUSCLE!
WELL, WHOEVER LEADS BETTER HAVE A PLAN TO DEAL WITH WEAPON KOSHER.

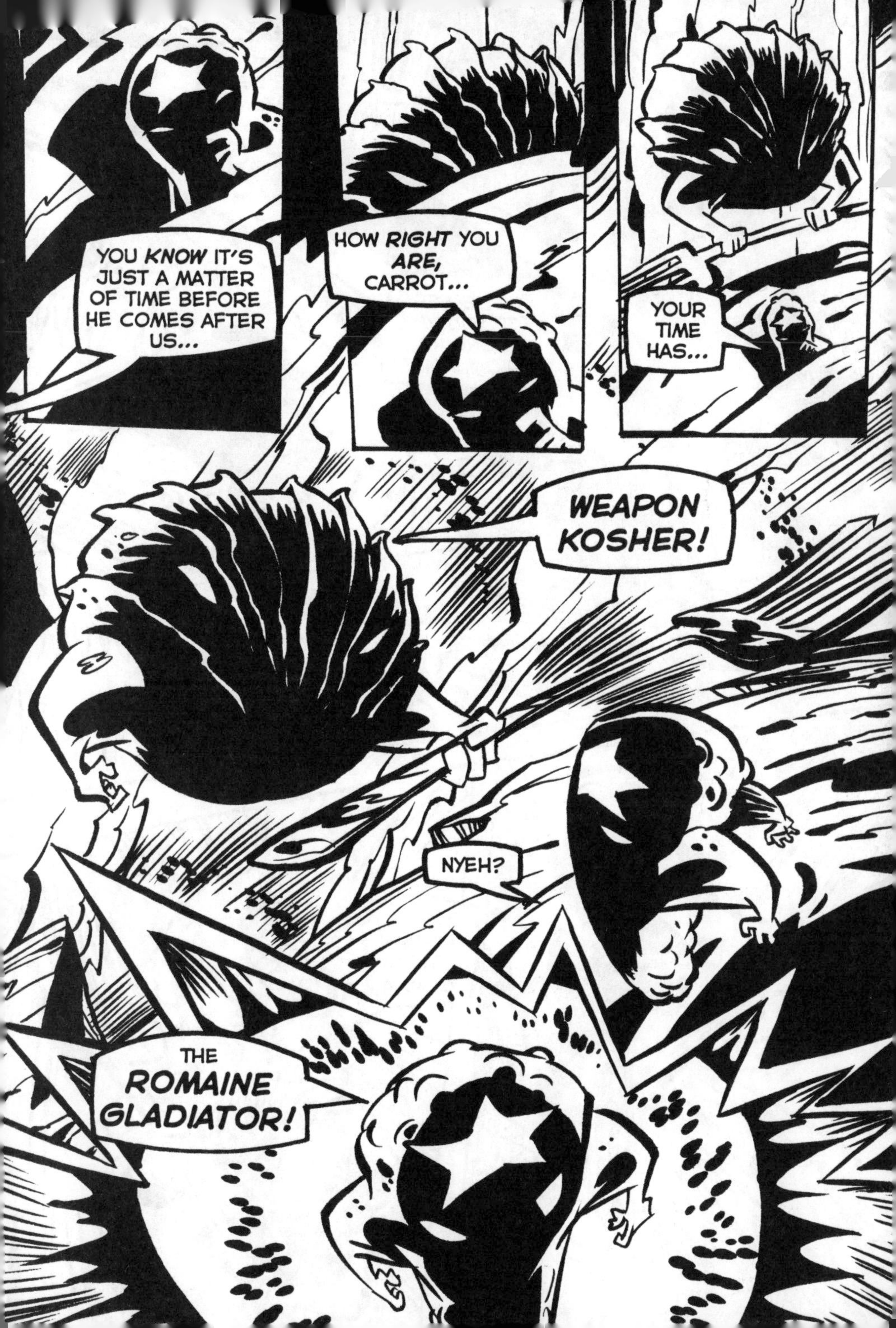
YOU KNOW IT'S JUST A MATTER OF TIME BEFORE HE COMES AFTER US...
HOW RIGHT YOU ARE, CARROT...
YOUR TIME HAS...
WEAPON KOSHER!
NYEH?
THE ROMAINE GLADIATOR!

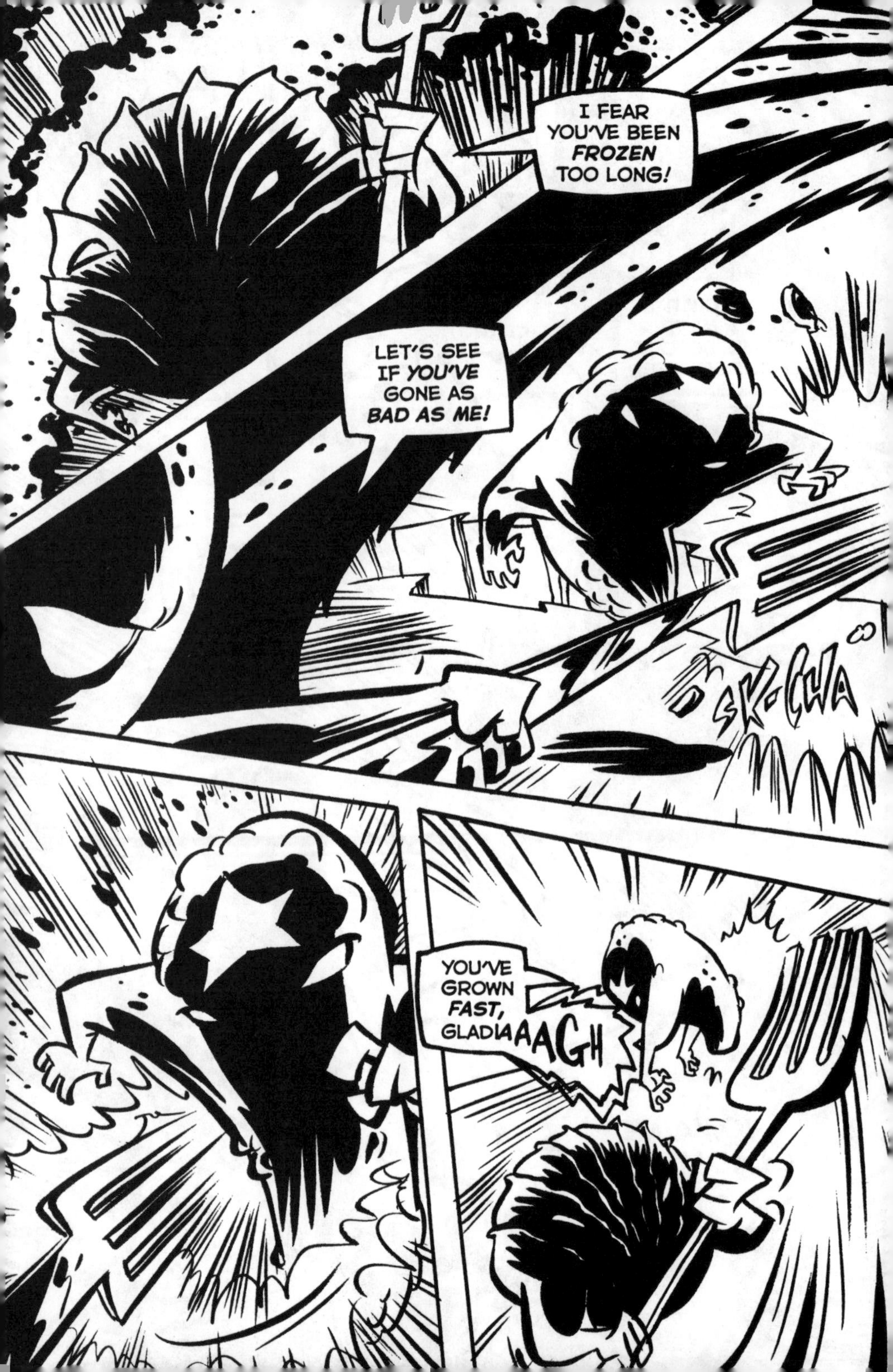
I FEAR YOU'VE BEEN *FROZEN* TOO LONG!
LET'S SEE IF *YOU'VE* GONE AS *BAD AS ME!*
SK-CHA
YOU'VE GROWN *FAST,* GLADIAAAGH

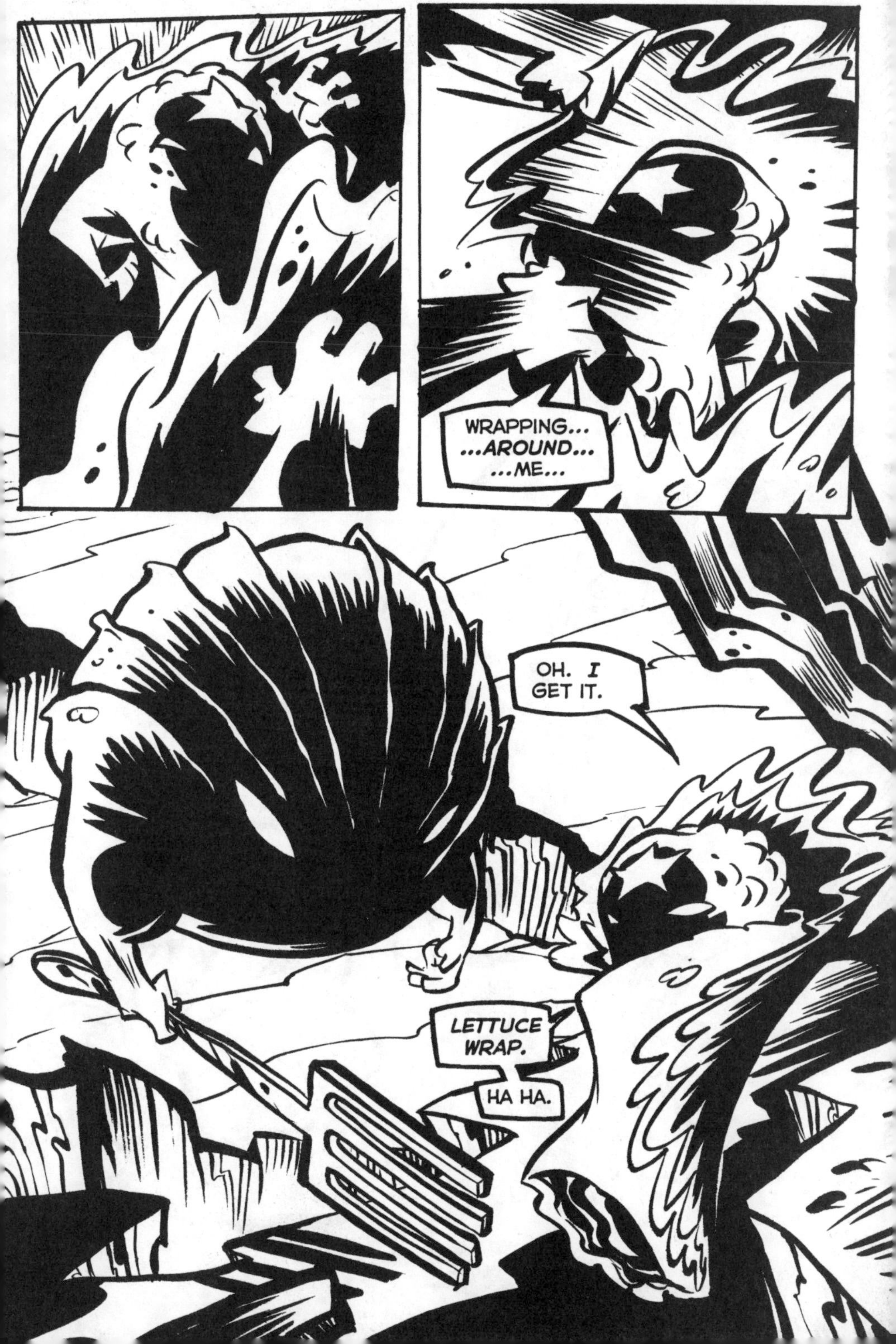
WRAPPING...
...AROUND...
...ME...
OH. I GET IT.
LETTUCE WRAP.
HA HA.

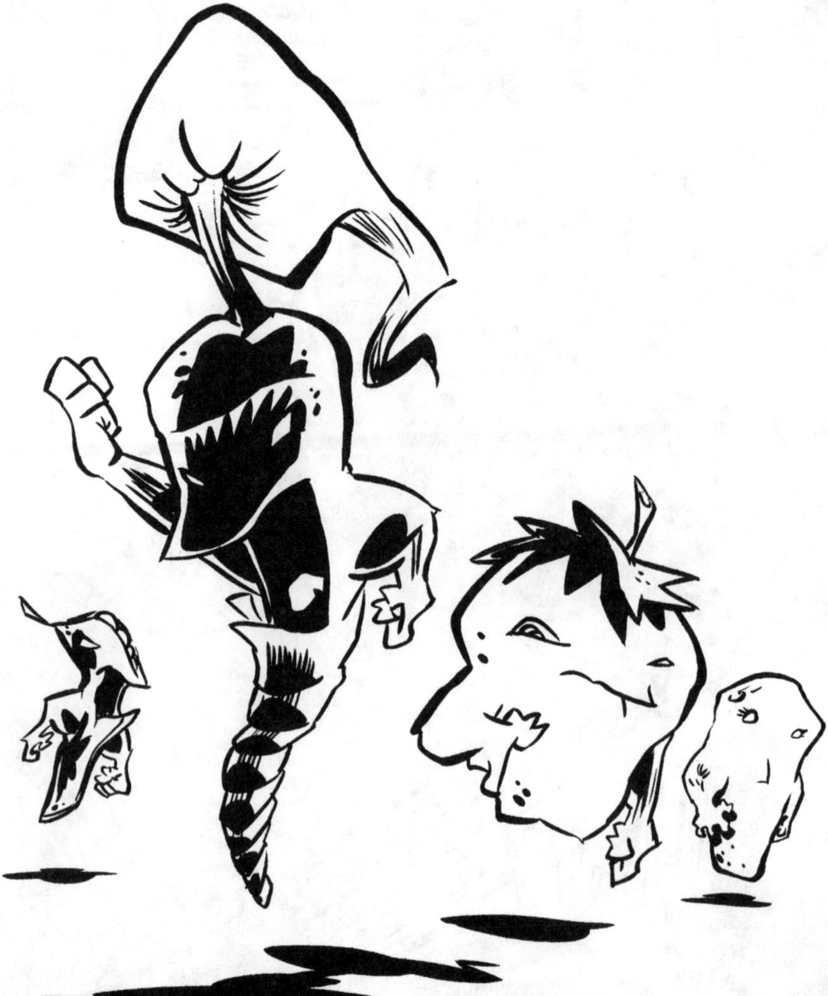

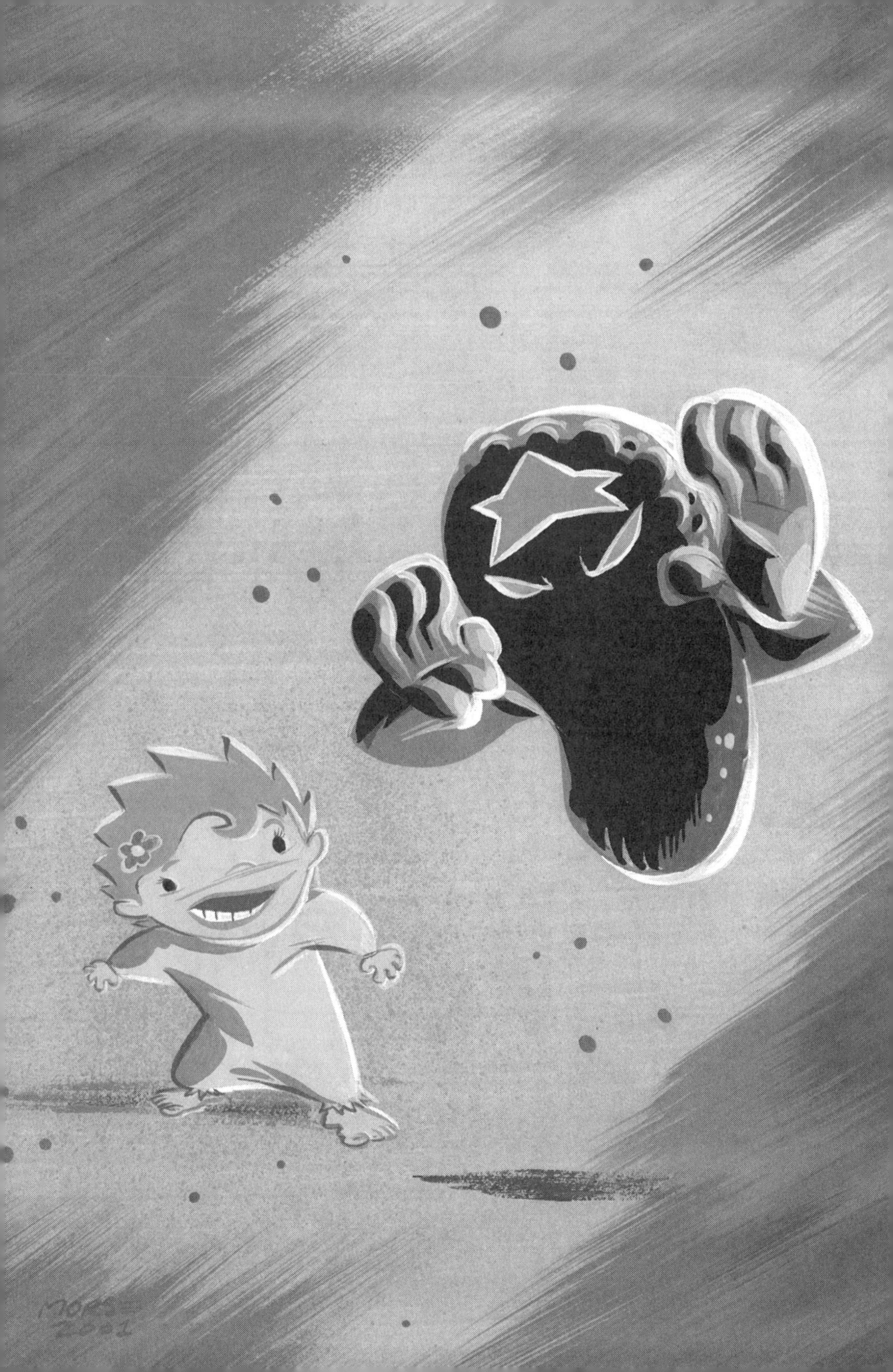
MORSE
2001

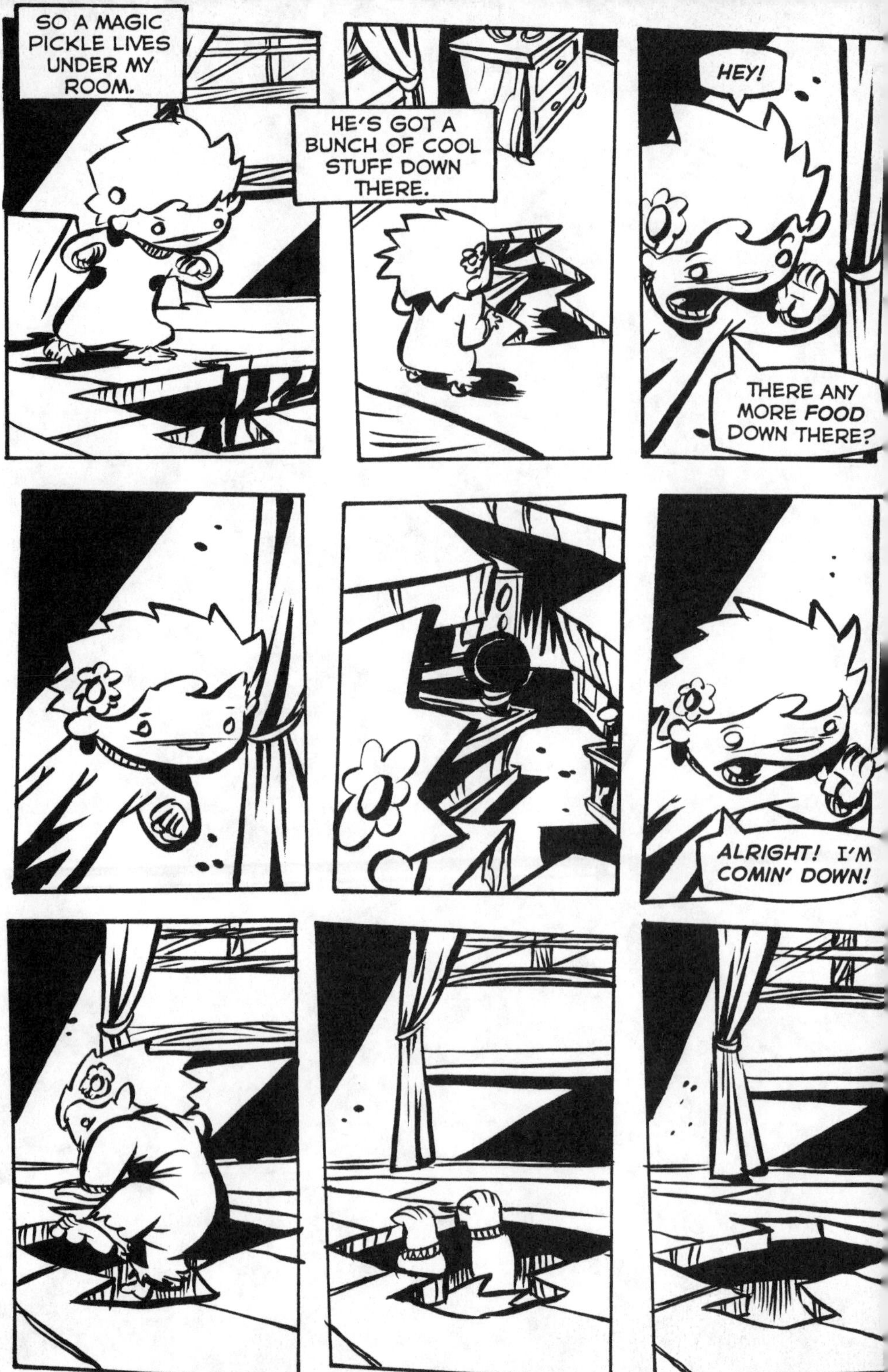
SO A MAGIC PICKLE LIVES UNDER MY ROOM.
HE'S GOT A BUNCH OF COOL STUFF DOWN THERE.
HEY!
THERE ANY MORE FOOD DOWN THERE?
ALRIGHT! I'M COMIN' DOWN!

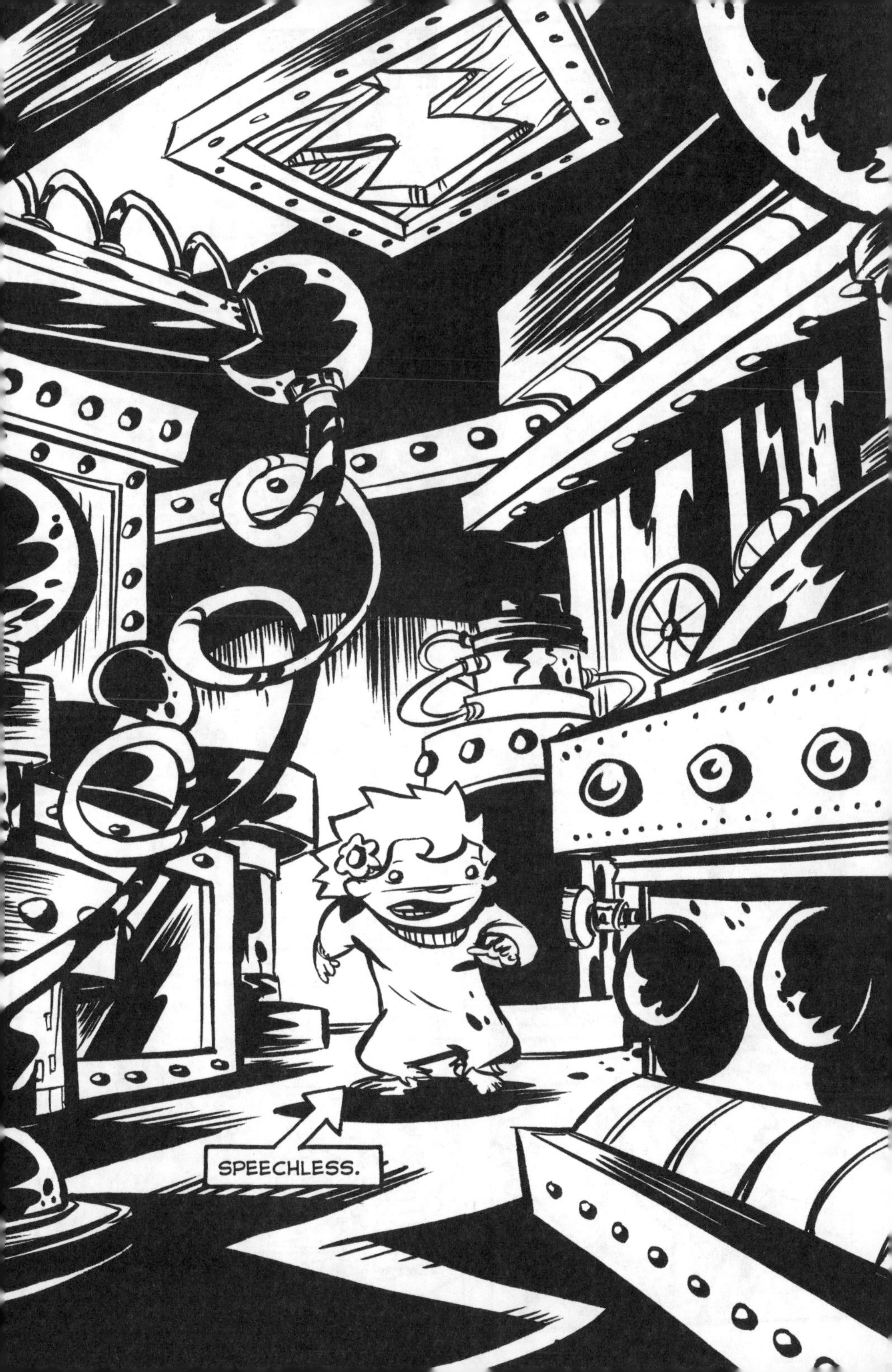
SPEECHLESS.

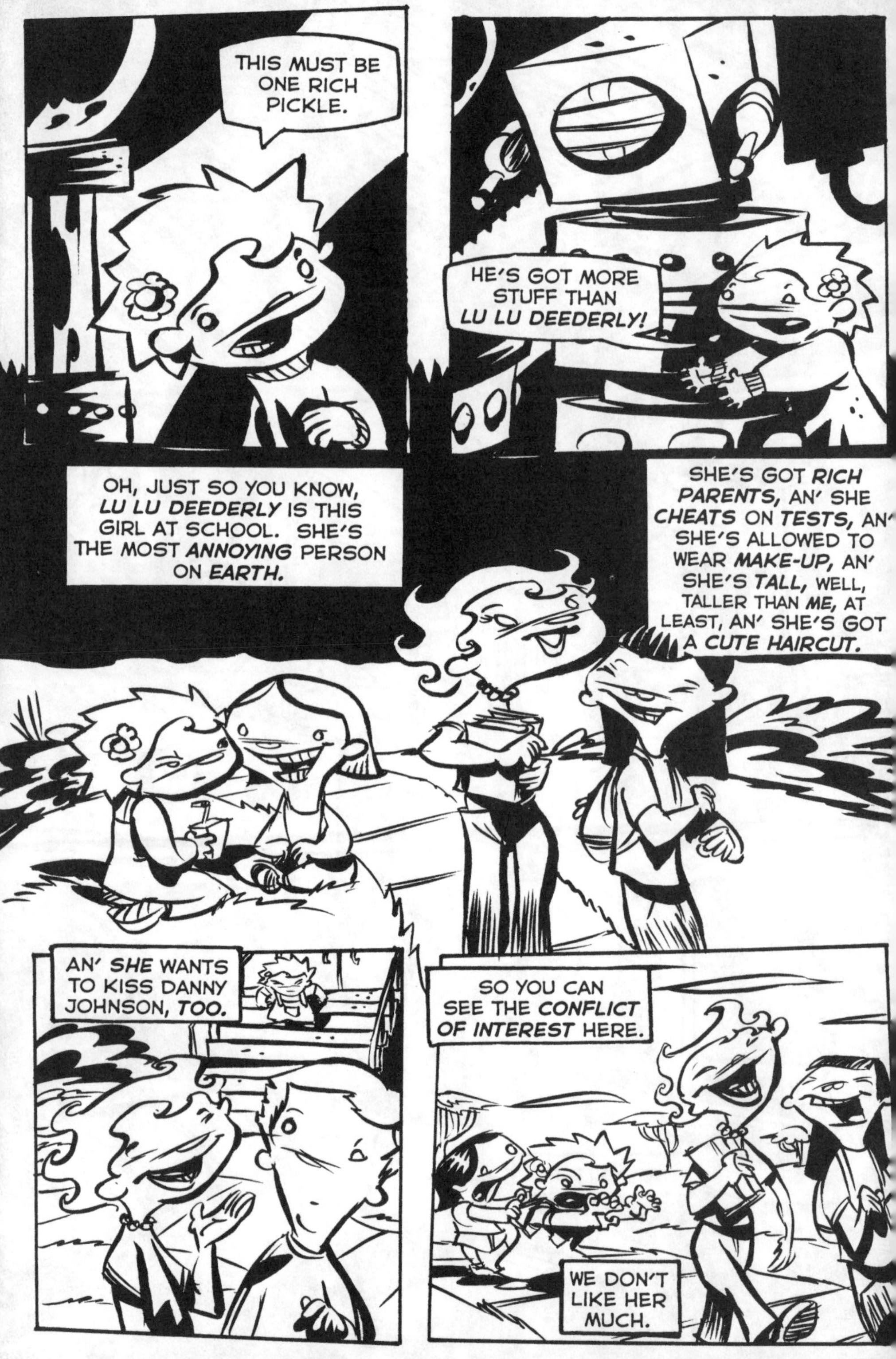

THIS MUST BE ONE RICH PICKLE.
HE'S GOT MORE STUFF THAN *LU LU DEEDERLY!*
OH, JUST SO YOU KNOW, *LU LU DEEDERLY* IS THIS GIRL AT SCHOOL. SHE'S THE MOST *ANNOYING* PERSON ON *EARTH.*
SHE'S GOT *RICH PARENTS,* AN' SHE *CHEATS* ON *TESTS,* AN' SHE'S ALLOWED TO WEAR *MAKE-UP,* AN' SHE'S *TALL,* WELL, TALLER THAN *ME,* AT LEAST, AN' SHE'S GOT A *CUTE HAIRCUT.*
AN' *SHE* WANTS TO KISS DANNY JOHNSON, *TOO.*
SO YOU CAN SEE THE *CONFLICT OF INTEREST* HERE.
WE DON'T LIKE HER MUCH.

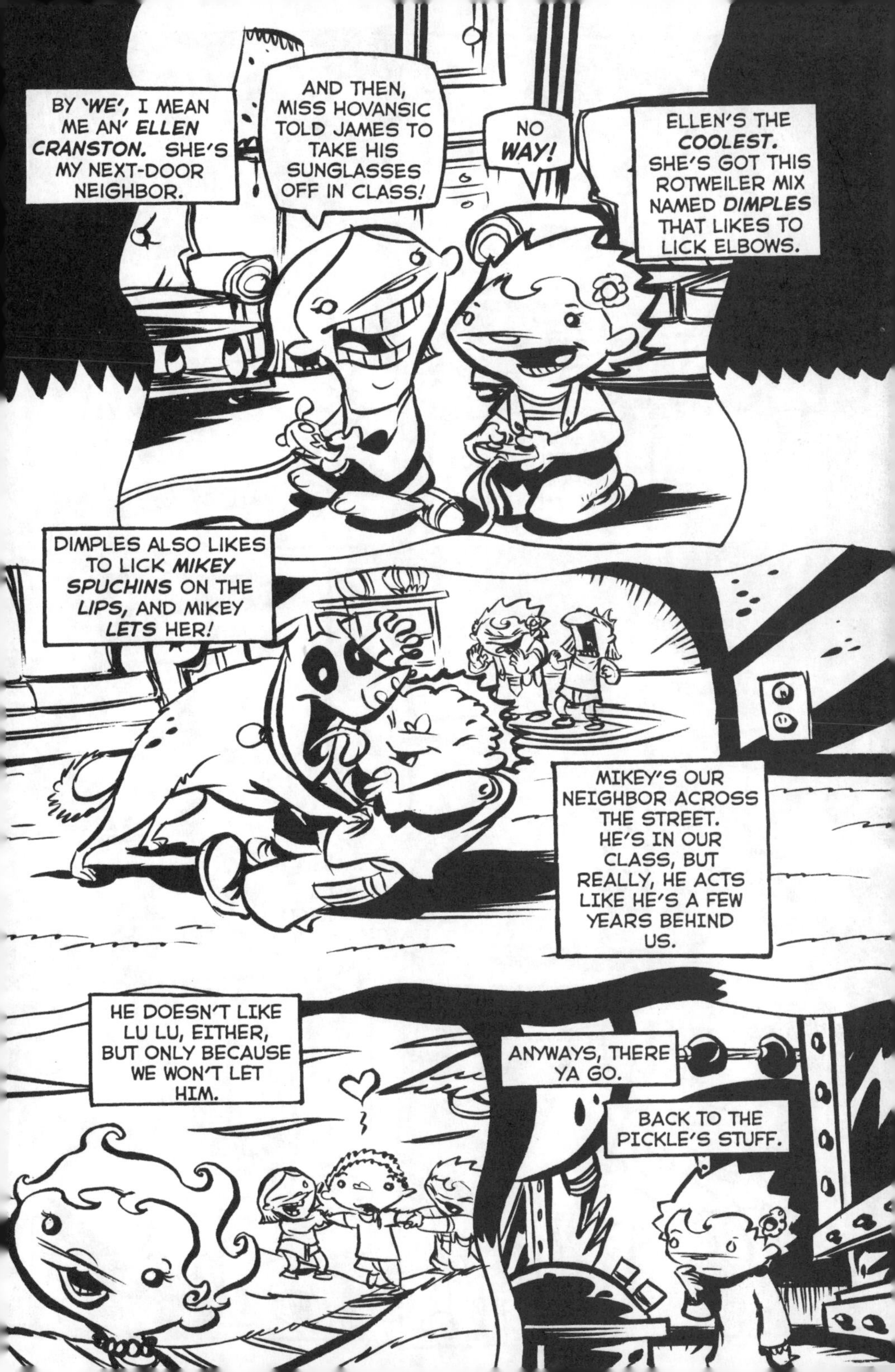
BY 'WE', I MEAN ME AN' ELLEN CRANSTON. SHE'S MY NEXT-DOOR NEIGHBOR.
AND THEN, MISS HOVANSIC TOLD JAMES TO TAKE HIS SUNGLASSES OFF IN CLASS!
NO WAY!
ELLEN'S THE COOLEST. SHE'S GOT THIS ROTWEILER MIX NAMED DIMPLES THAT LIKES TO LICK ELBOWS.
DIMPLES ALSO LIKES TO LICK MIKEY SPUCHINS ON THE LIPS, AND MIKEY LETS HER!
MIKEY'S OUR NEIGHBOR ACROSS THE STREET. HE'S IN OUR CLASS, BUT REALLY, HE ACTS LIKE HE'S A FEW YEARS BEHIND US.
HE DOESN'T LIKE LU LU, EITHER, BUT ONLY BECAUSE WE WON'T LET HIM.
ANYWAYS, THERE YA GO.
BACK TO THE PICKLE'S STUFF.

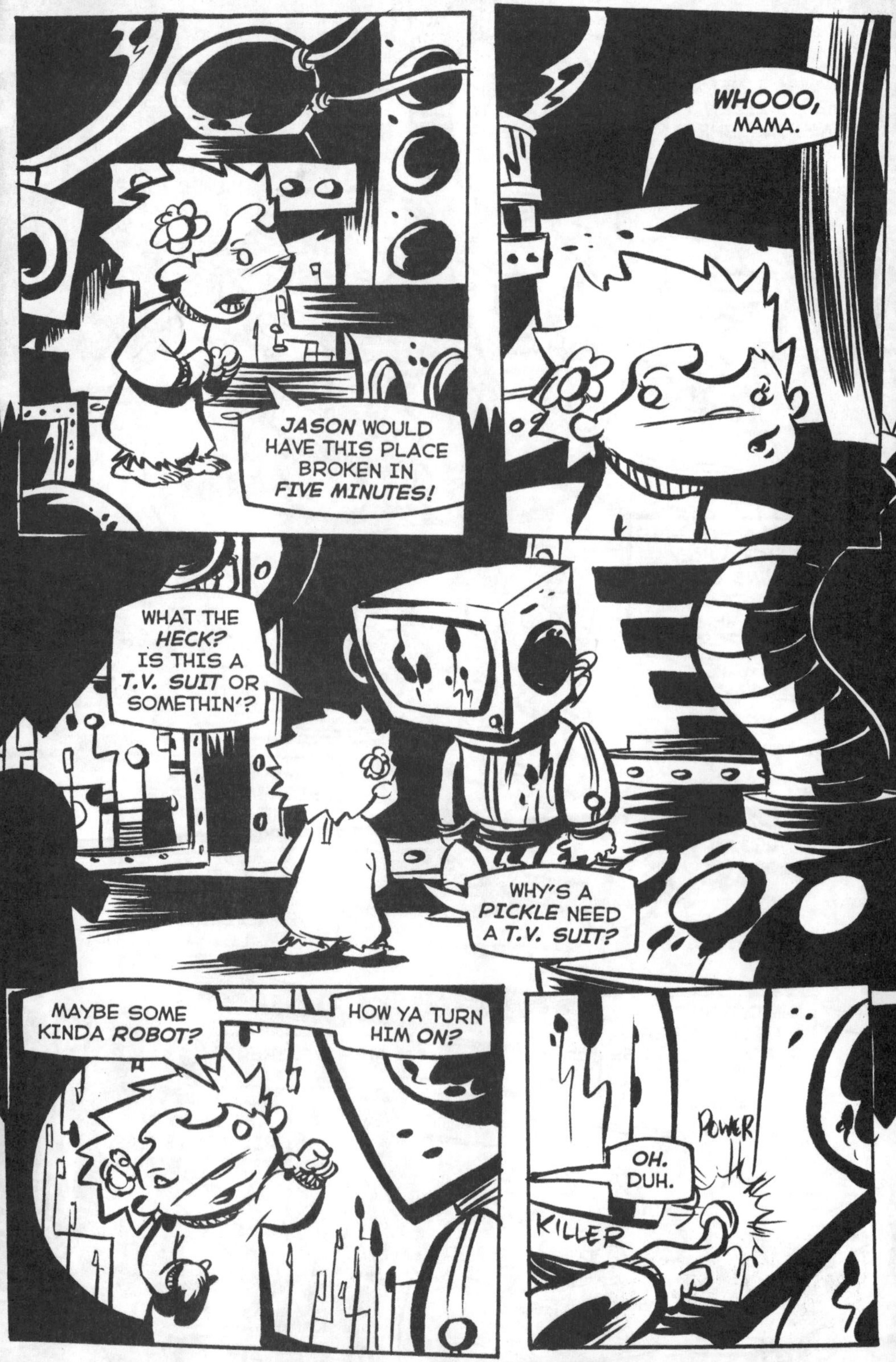
JASON WOULD HAVE THIS PLACE BROKEN IN FIVE MINUTES!
WHOOO, MAMA.
WHAT THE HECK? IS THIS A T.V. SUIT OR SOMETHIN'?
WHY'S A PICKLE NEED A T.V. SUIT?
MAYBE SOME KINDA ROBOT?
HOW YA TURN HIM ON?
POWER
KILLER
OH. DUH.

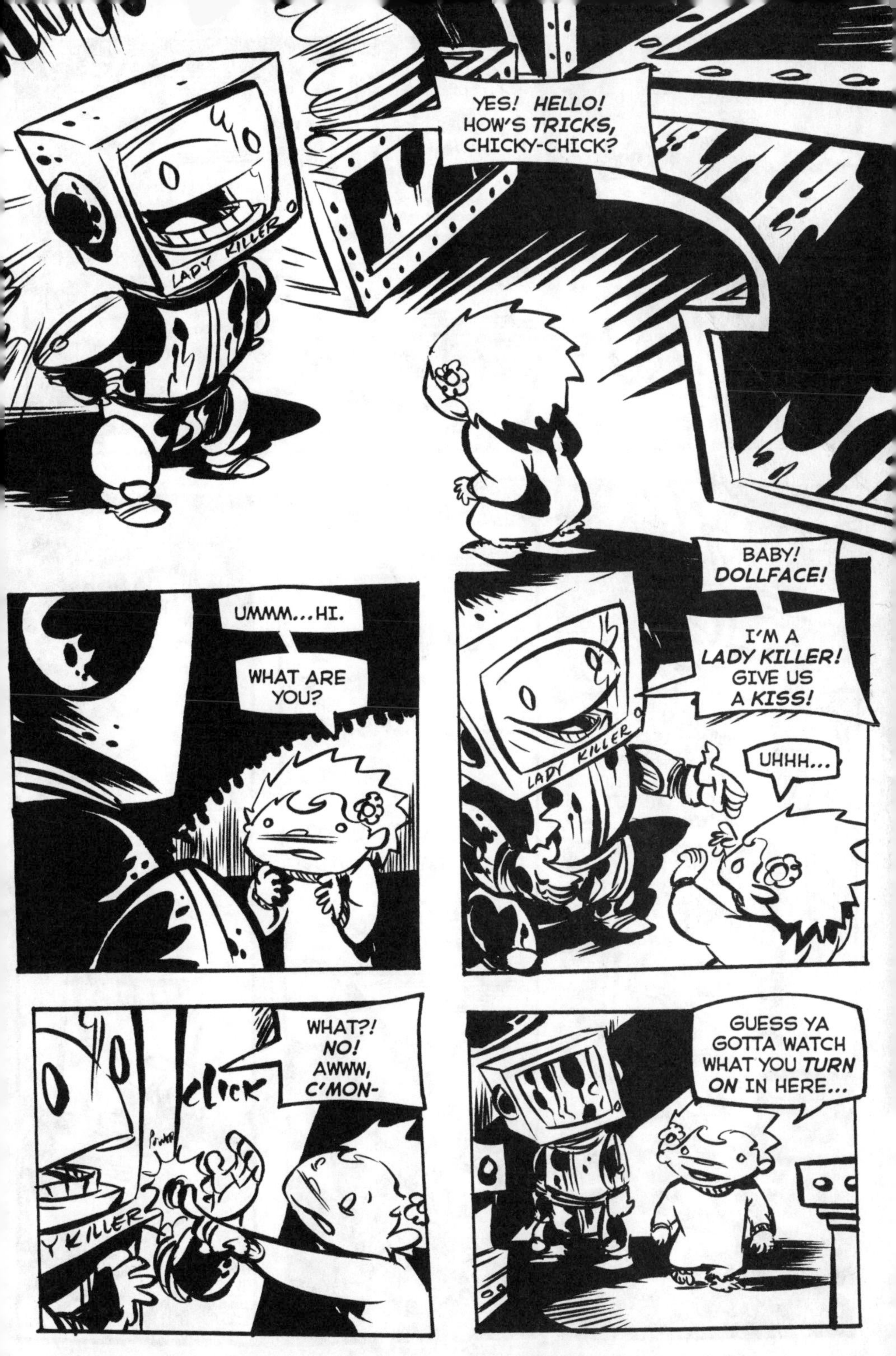

YES! HELLO! HOW'S TRICKS, CHICKY-CHICK?
LADY KILLER
UMMM...HI.
WHAT ARE YOU?
BABY! DOLLFACE!
I'M A LADY KILLER! GIVE US A KISS!
LADY KILLER
UHHH...
WHAT?! NO! AWWW, C'MON-
click
Y KILLER
GUESS YA GOTTA WATCH WHAT YOU TURN ON IN HERE...

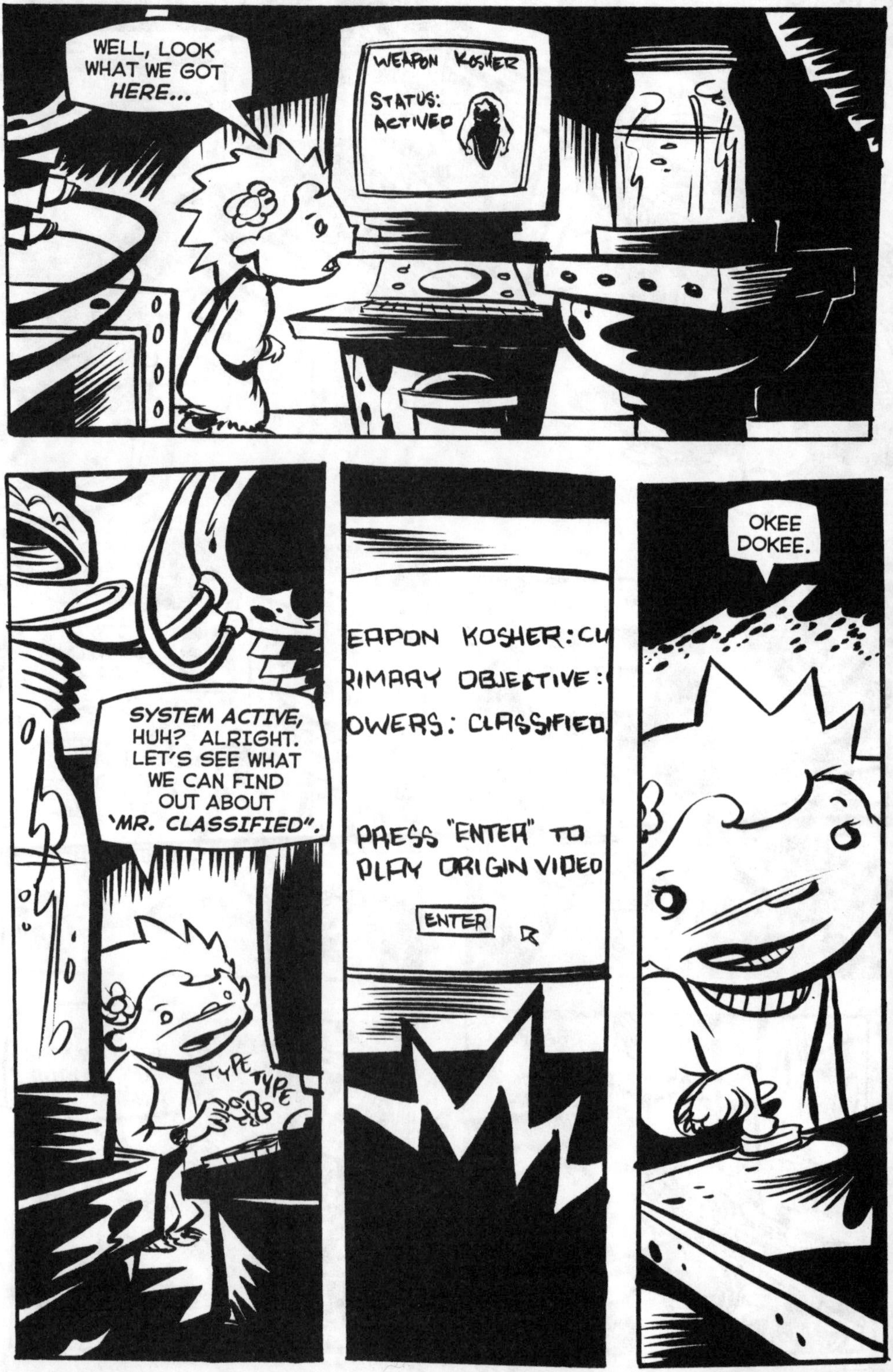

WELL, LOOK WHAT WE GOT HERE...
WEAPON KOSHER
STATUS: ACTIVED
SYSTEM ACTIVE, HUH? ALRIGHT. LET'S SEE WHAT WE CAN FIND OUT ABOUT 'MR. CLASSIFIED".
TYPE TYPE
EAPON KOSHER:CL
RIMARY OBJECTIVE:
OWERS: CLASSIFIED
PRESS "ENTER" TO PLAY ORIGIN VIDEO
ENTER
OKEE DOKEE.

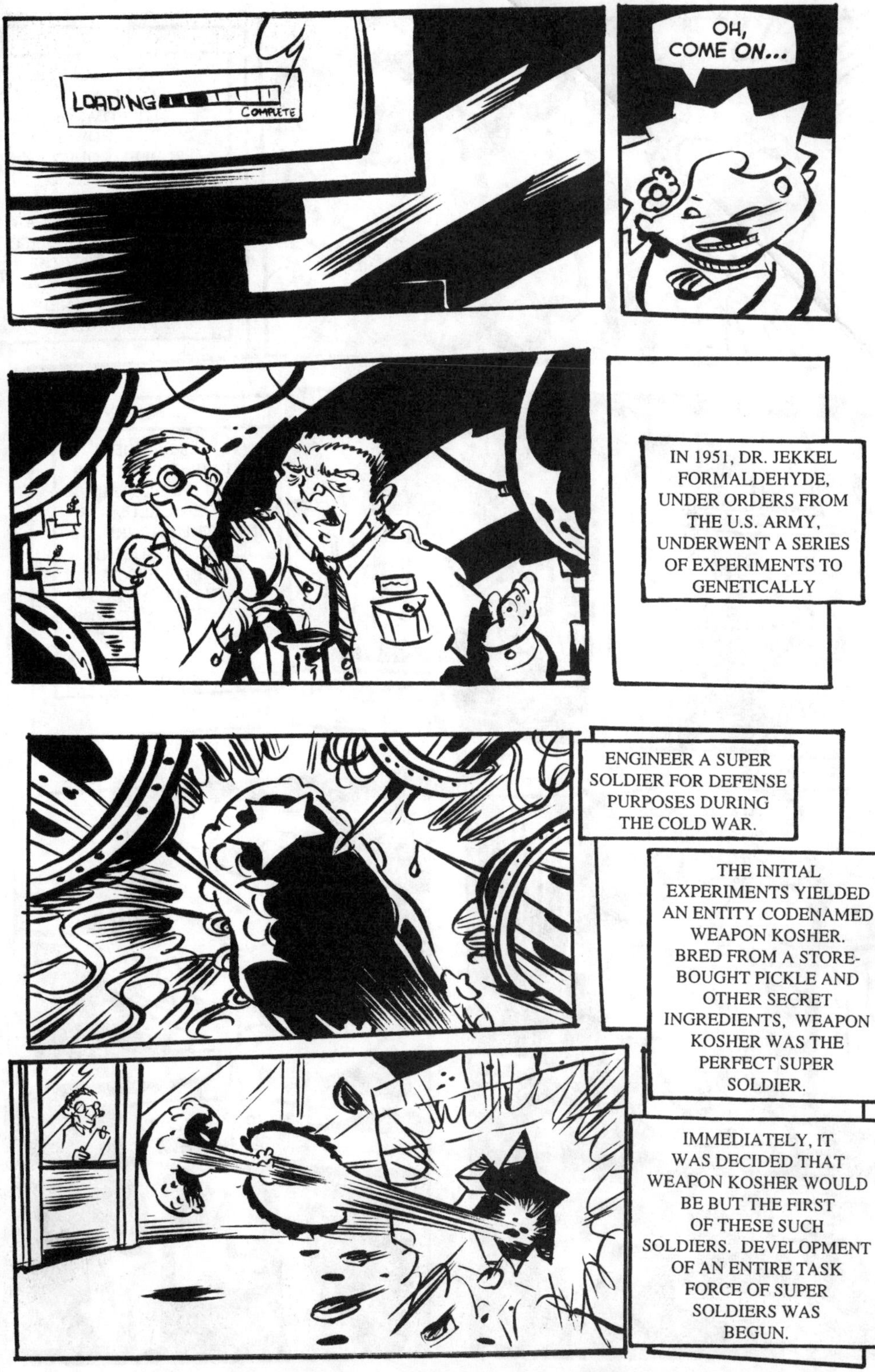
LOADING
COMPLETE
OH, COME ON...
IN 1951, DR. JEKKEL FORMALDEHYDE, UNDER ORDERS FROM THE U.S. ARMY, UNDERWENT A SERIES OF EXPERIMENTS TO GENETICALLY
ENGINEER A SUPER SOLDIER FOR DEFENSE PURPOSES DURING THE COLD WAR.
THE INITIAL EXPERIMENTS YIELDED AN ENTITY CODENAMED WEAPON KOSHER. BRED FROM A STORE-BOUGHT PICKLE AND OTHER SECRET INGREDIENTS, WEAPON KOSHER WAS THE PERFECT SUPER SOLDIER.
IMMEDIATELY, IT WAS DECIDED THAT WEAPON KOSHER WOULD BE BUT THE FIRST OF THESE SUCH SOLDIERS. DEVELOPMENT OF AN ENTIRE TASK FORCE OF SUPER SOLDIERS WAS BEGUN.

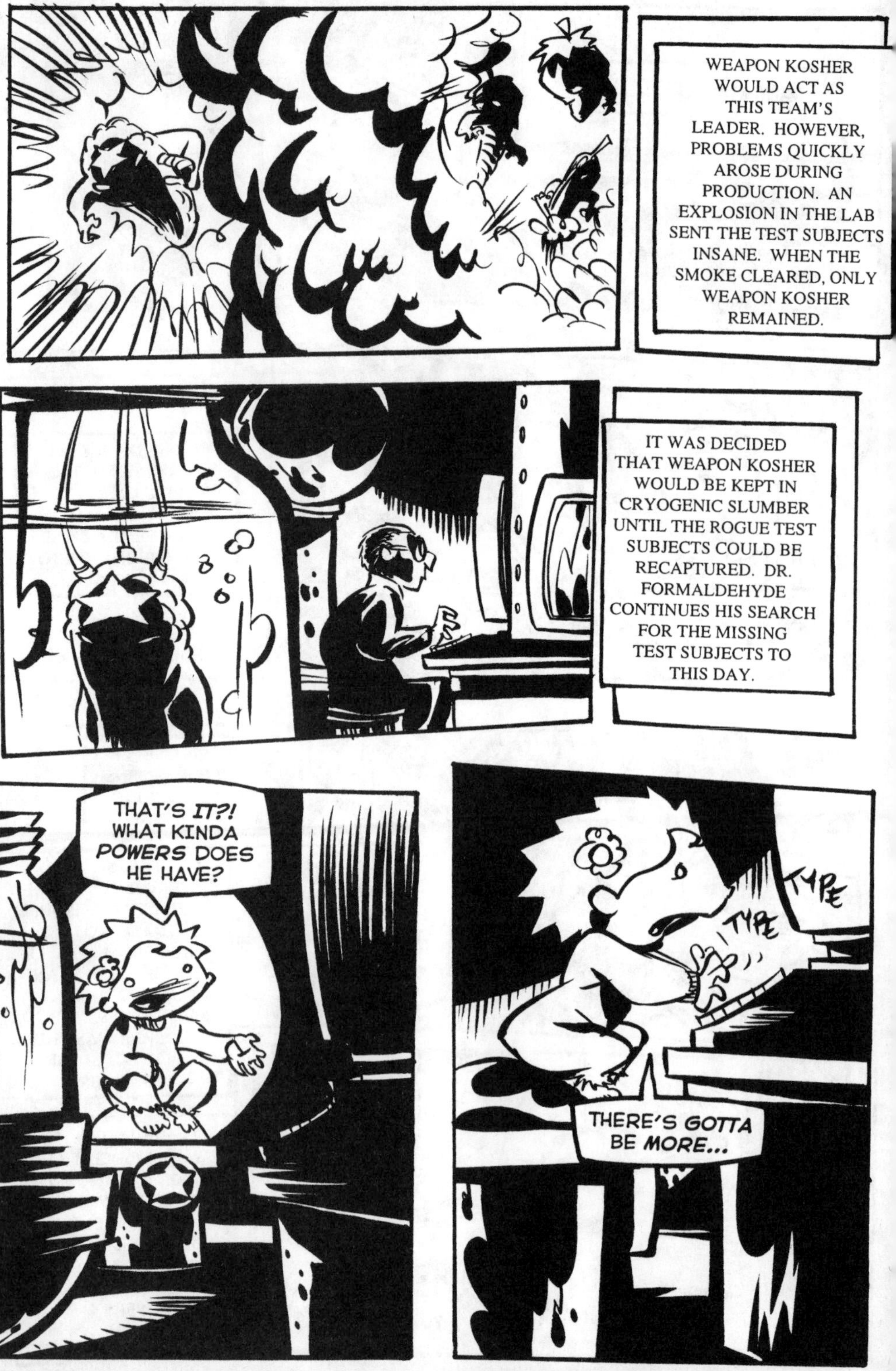
WEAPON KOSHER WOULD ACT AS THIS TEAM'S LEADER. HOWEVER, PROBLEMS QUICKLY AROSE DURING PRODUCTION. AN EXPLOSION IN THE LAB SENT THE TEST SUBJECTS INSANE. WHEN THE SMOKE CLEARED, ONLY WEAPON KOSHER REMAINED.
IT WAS DECIDED THAT WEAPON KOSHER WOULD BE KEPT IN CRYOGENIC SLUMBER UNTIL THE ROGUE TEST SUBJECTS COULD BE RECAPTURED. DR. FORMALDEHYDE CONTINUES HIS SEARCH FOR THE MISSING TEST SUBJECTS TO THIS DAY.
THAT'S *IT?!* WHAT KINDA *POWERS* DOES HE HAVE?
TYPE
TYPE
THERE'S *GOTTA* BE *MORE...*

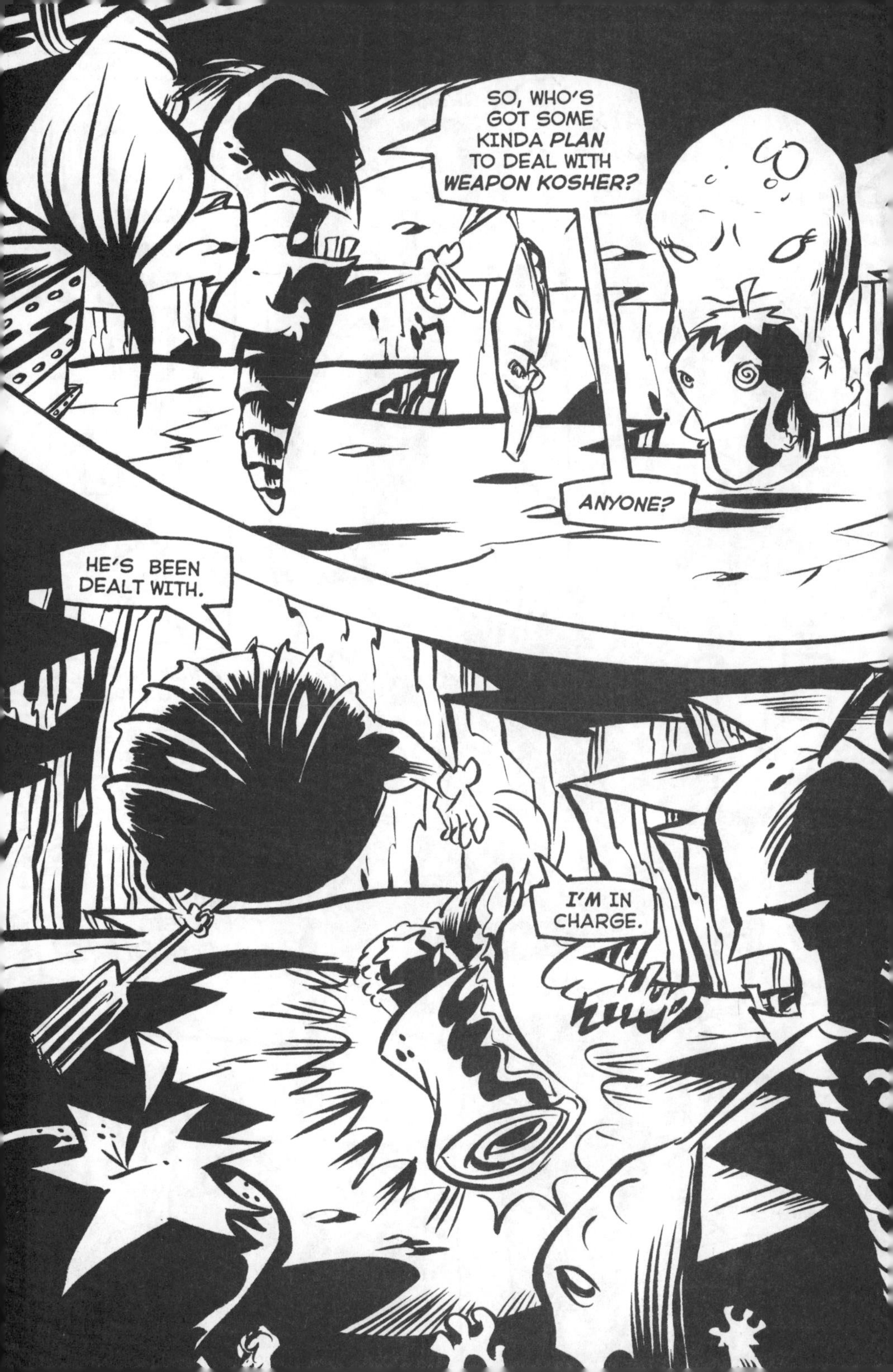
SO, WHO'S GOT SOME KINDA *PLAN* TO DEAL WITH *WEAPON KOSHER?*
ANYONE?
HE'S BEEN DEALT WITH.
I'M IN CHARGE.

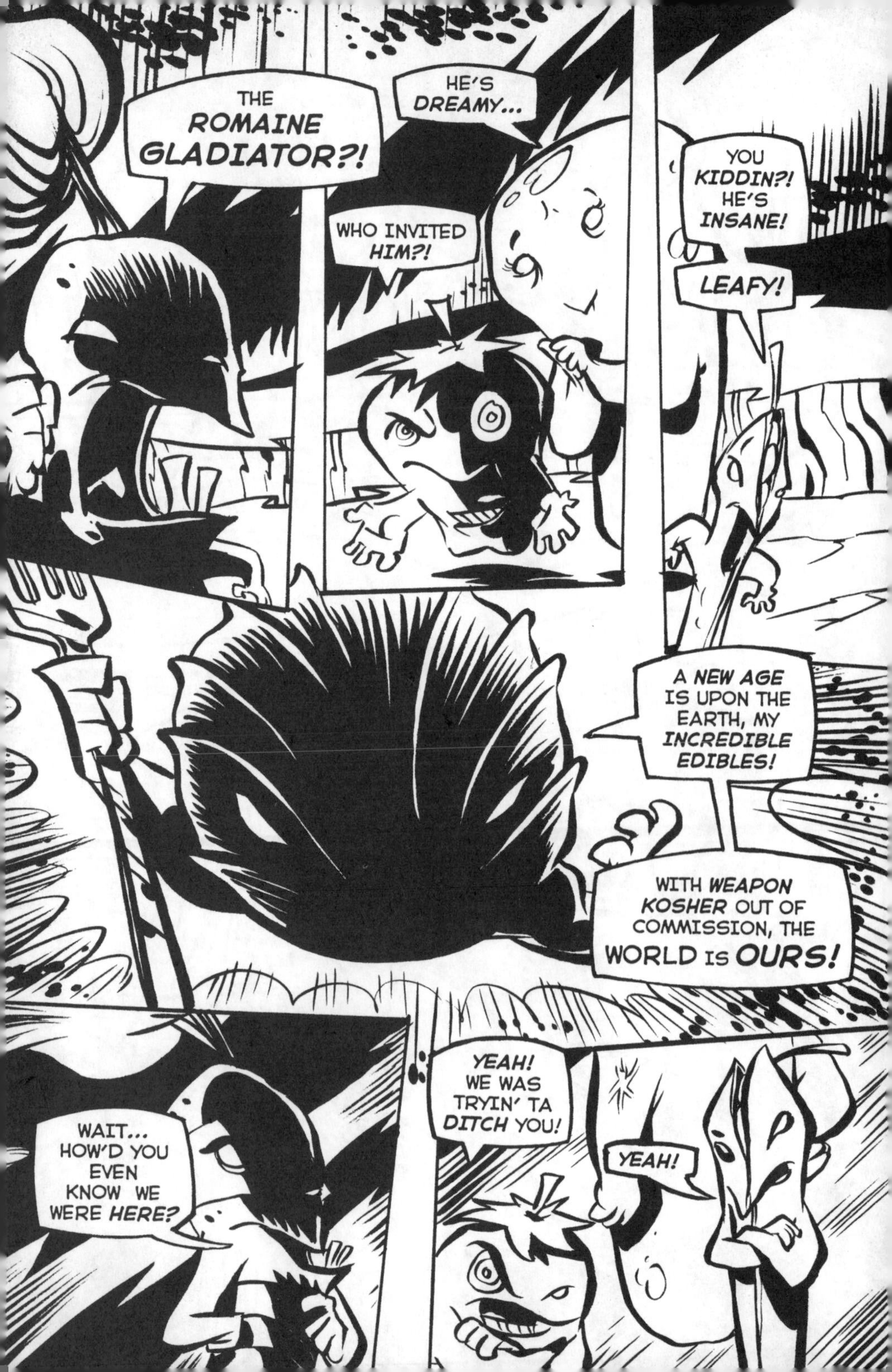
THE ROMAINE GLADIATOR?!
HE'S DREAMY...
WHO INVITED HIM?!
YOU KIDDIN?! HE'S INSANE!
LEAFY!
A NEW AGE IS UPON THE EARTH, MY INCREDIBLE EDIBLES!
WITH WEAPON KOSHER OUT OF COMMISSION, THE WORLD IS OURS!
WAIT... HOW'D YOU EVEN KNOW WE WERE HERE?
YEAH! WE WAS TRYIN' TA DITCH YOU!
YEAH!

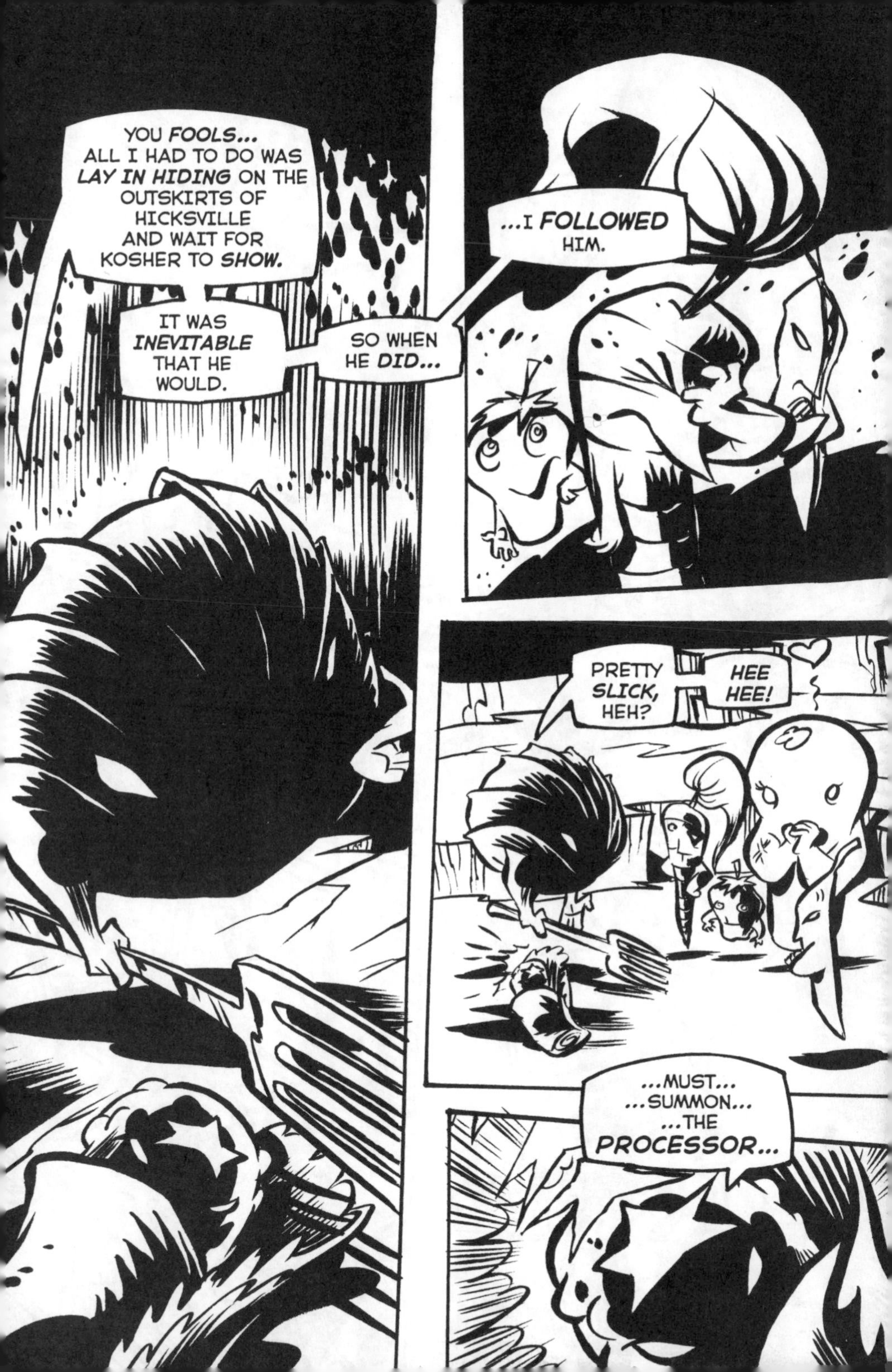
YOU FOOLS... ALL I HAD TO DO WAS LAY IN HIDING ON THE OUTSKIRTS OF HICKSVILLE AND WAIT FOR KOSHER TO SHOW.
IT WAS INEVITABLE THAT HE WOULD.
SO WHEN HE DID...
...I FOLLOWED HIM.
PRETTY SLICK, HEH?
HEE HEE!
...MUST... ...SUMMON... ...THE PROCESSOR...

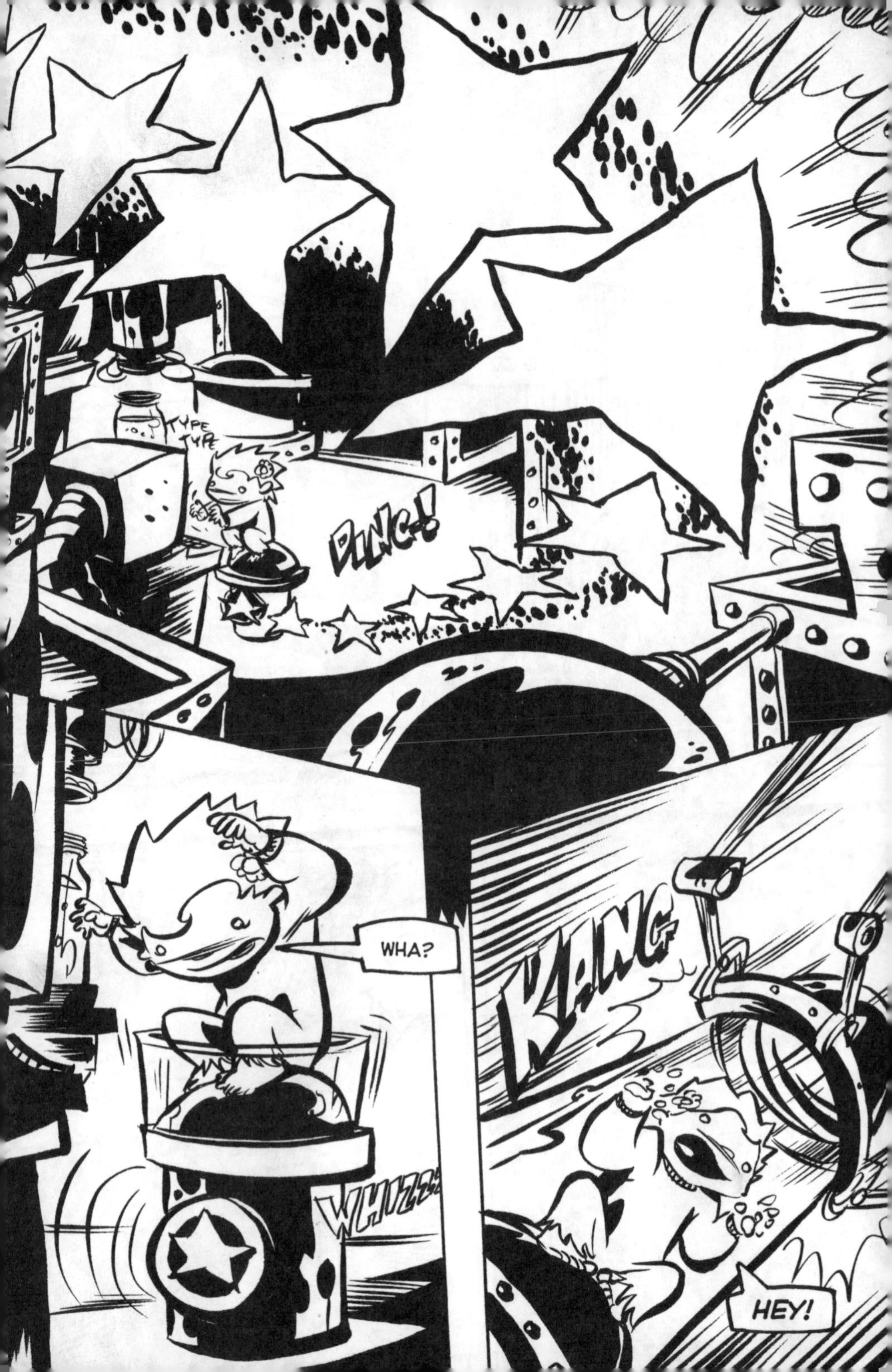
TYPE
TYPE
DING!
WHA?
KLANG
WHIZZ
HEY!

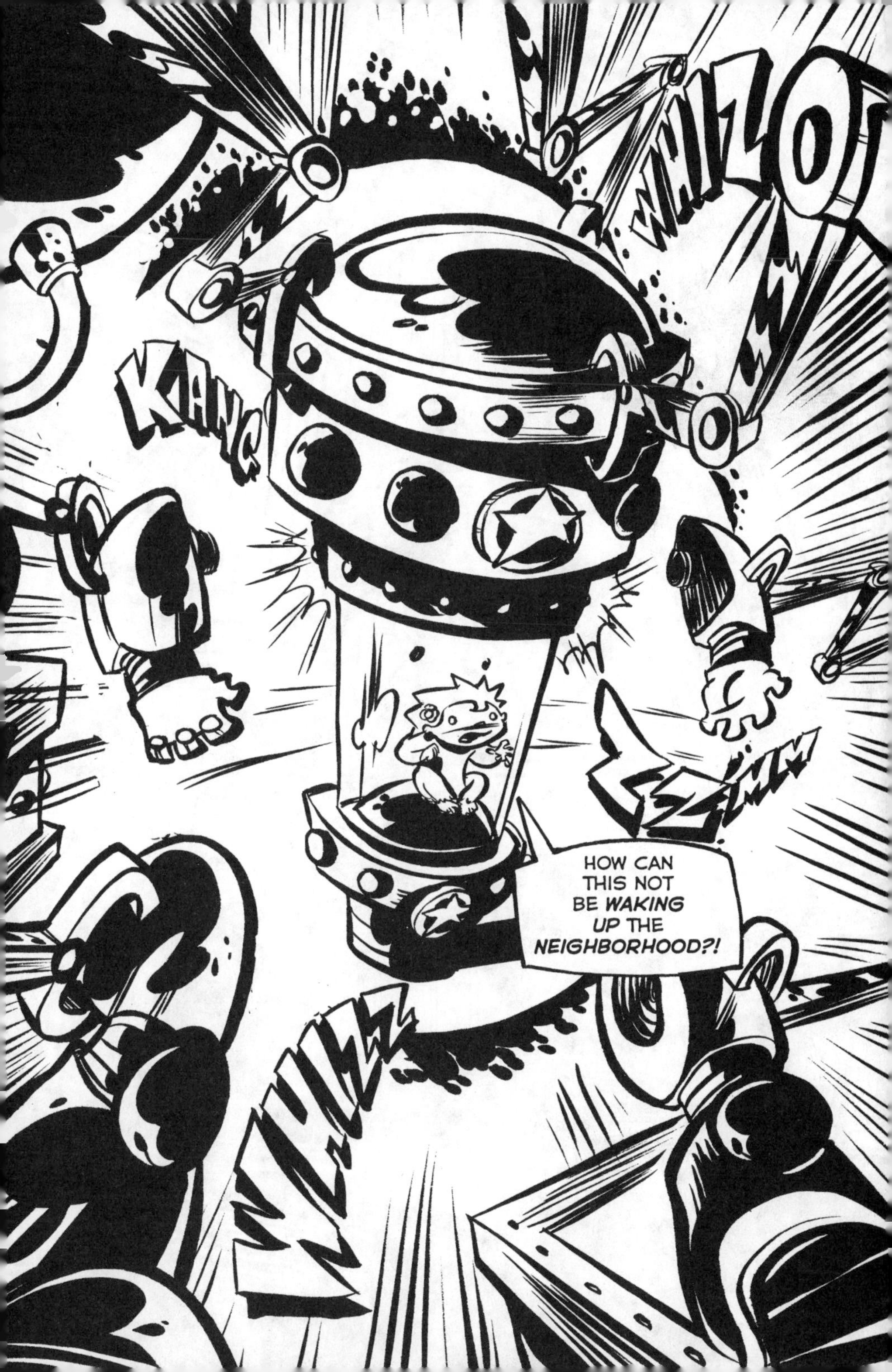
KLANG
HOW CAN THIS NOT BE *WAKING UP* THE *NEIGHBORHOOD?!*

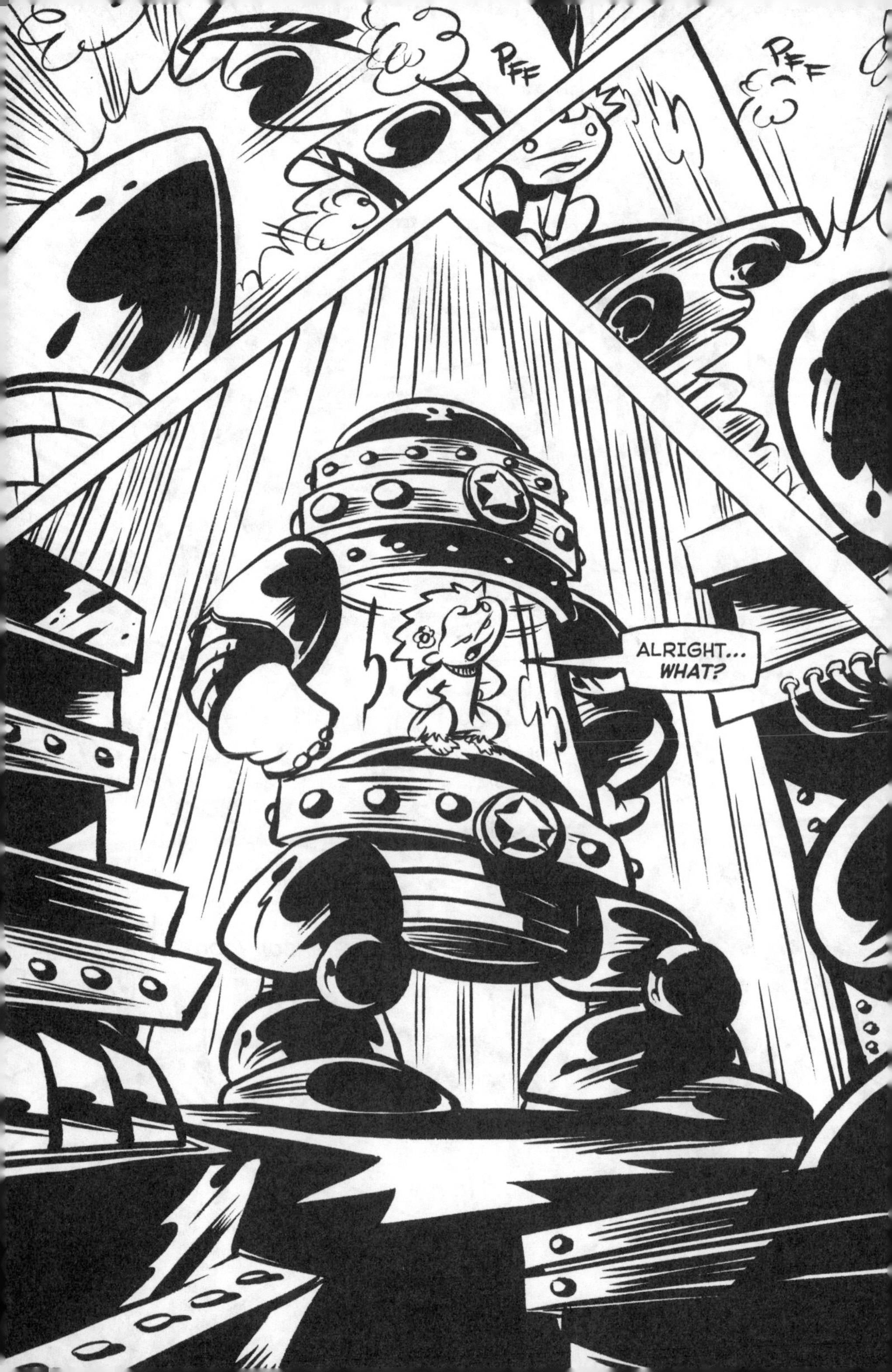
PFF
PFF
ALRIGHT... WHAT?

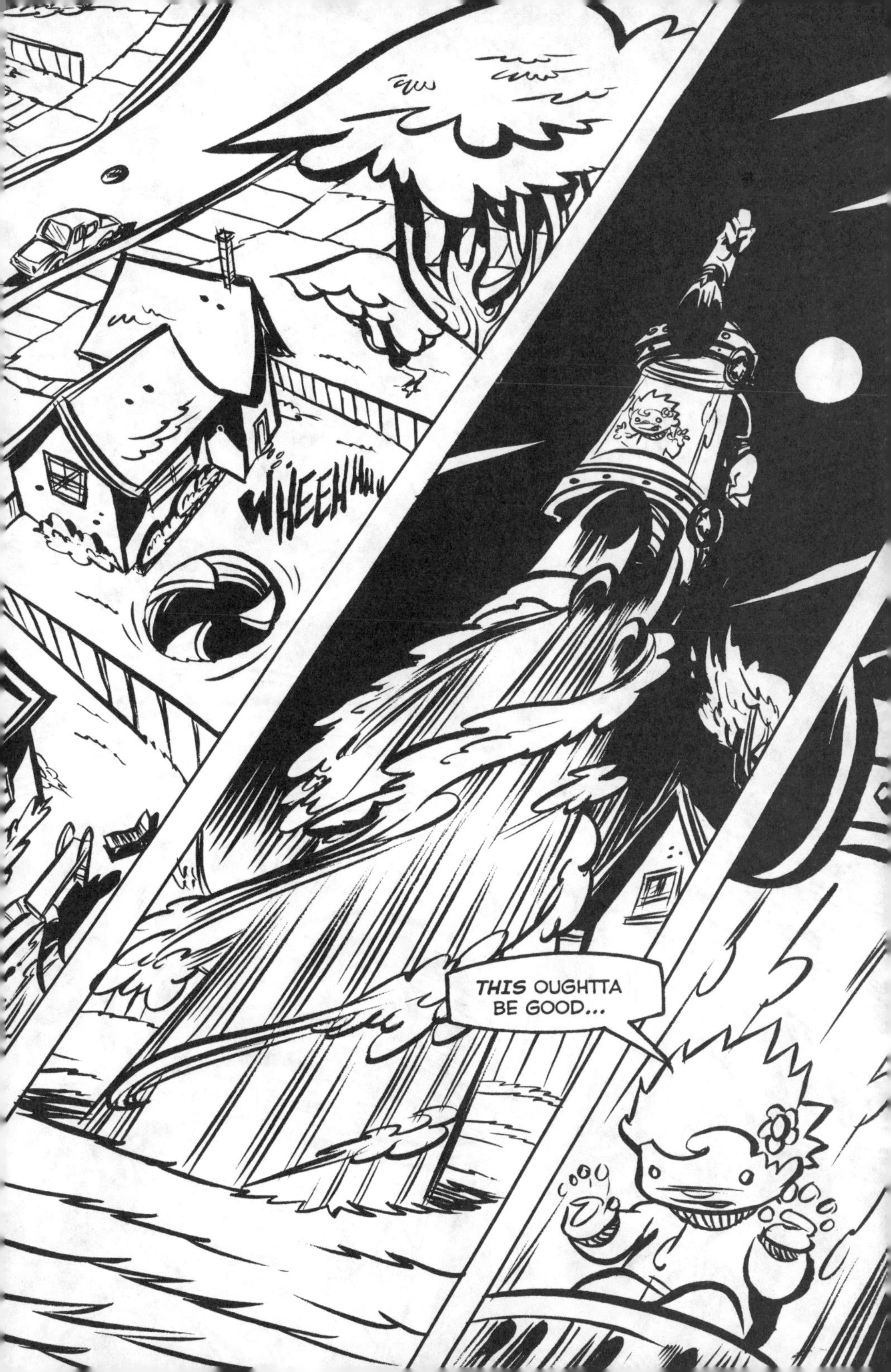
WHEEHHHH
THIS OUGHTTA BE GOOD...

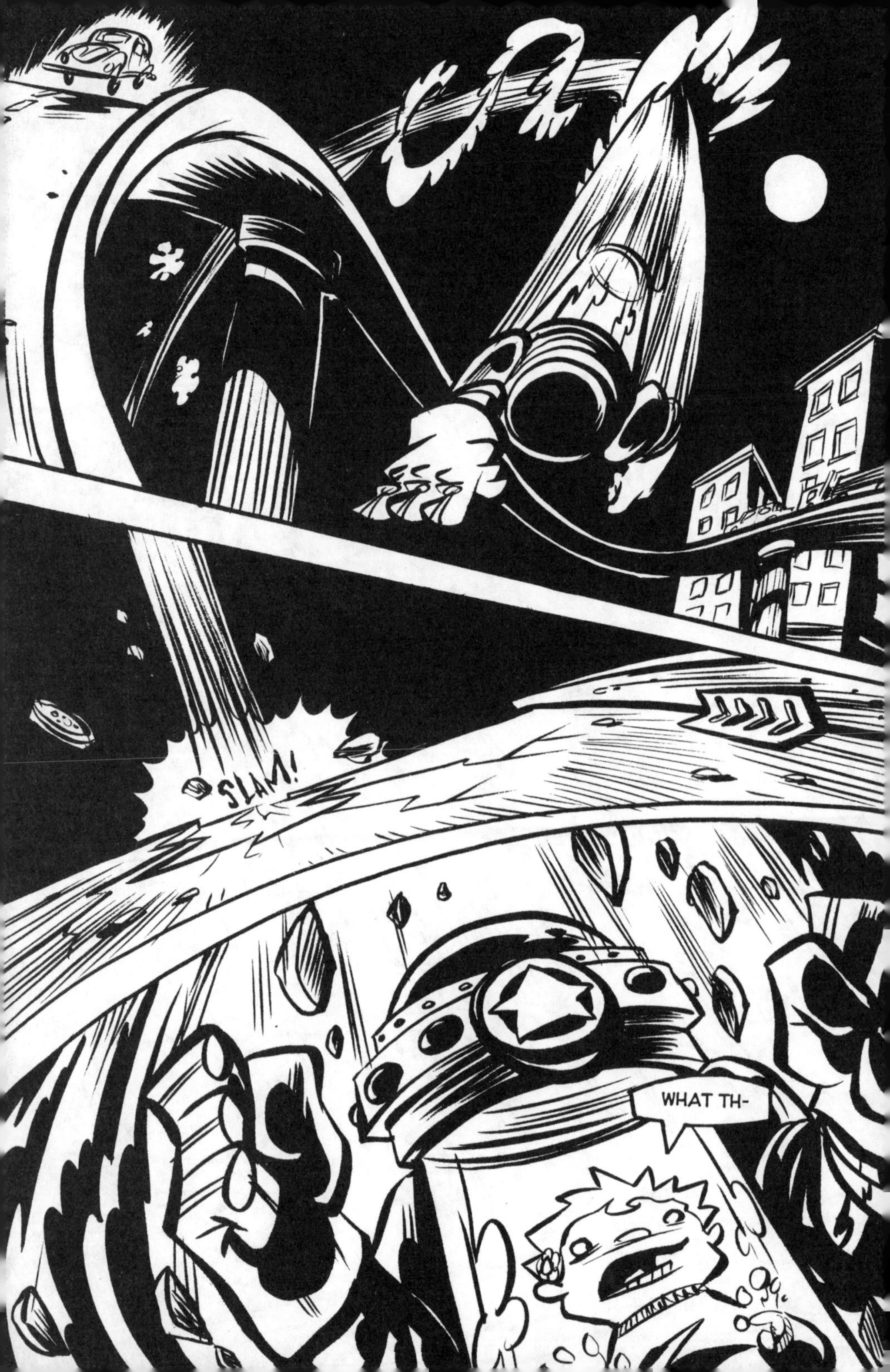
SLAM!
WHAT TH-

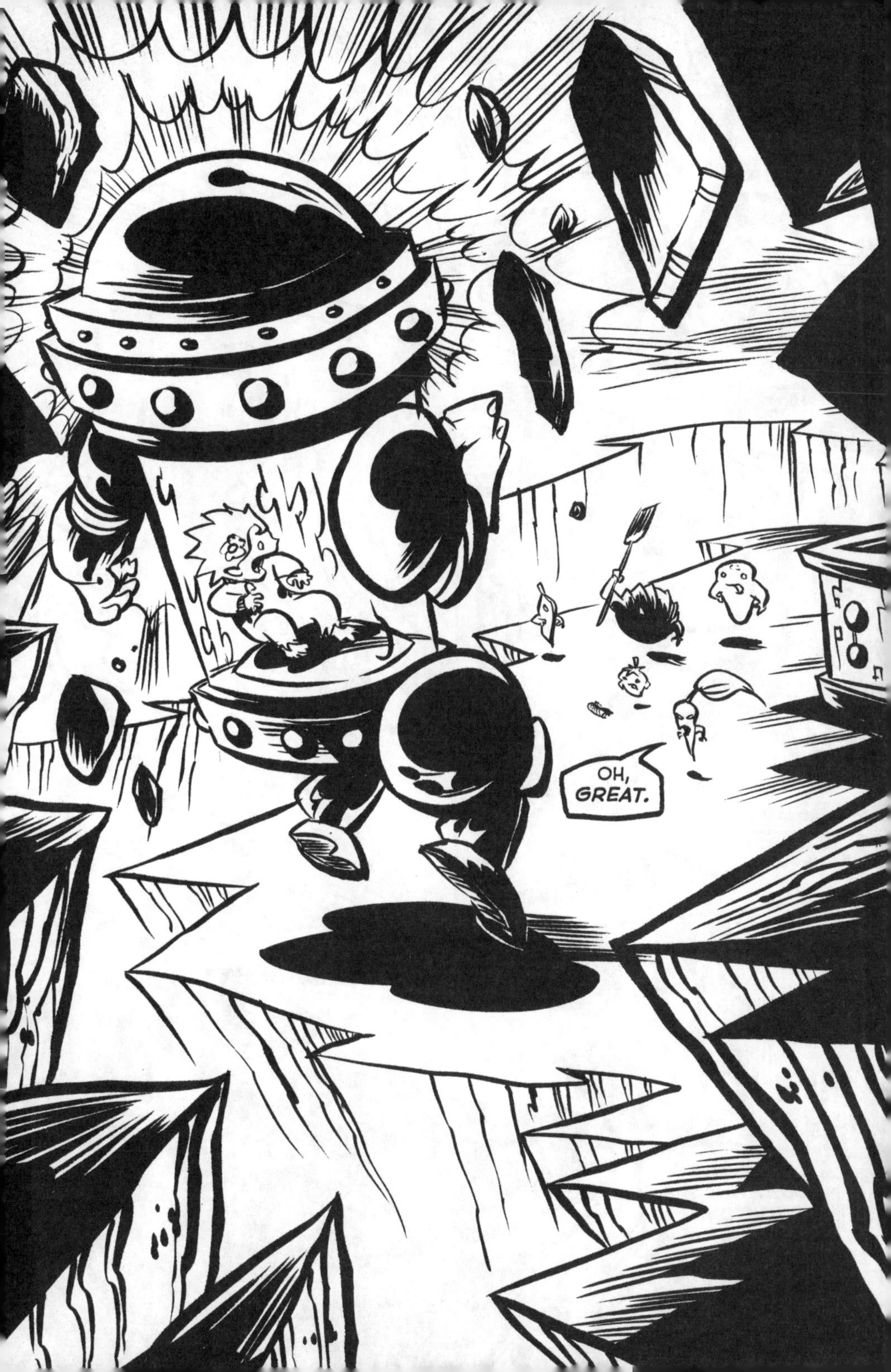
OH, GREAT.

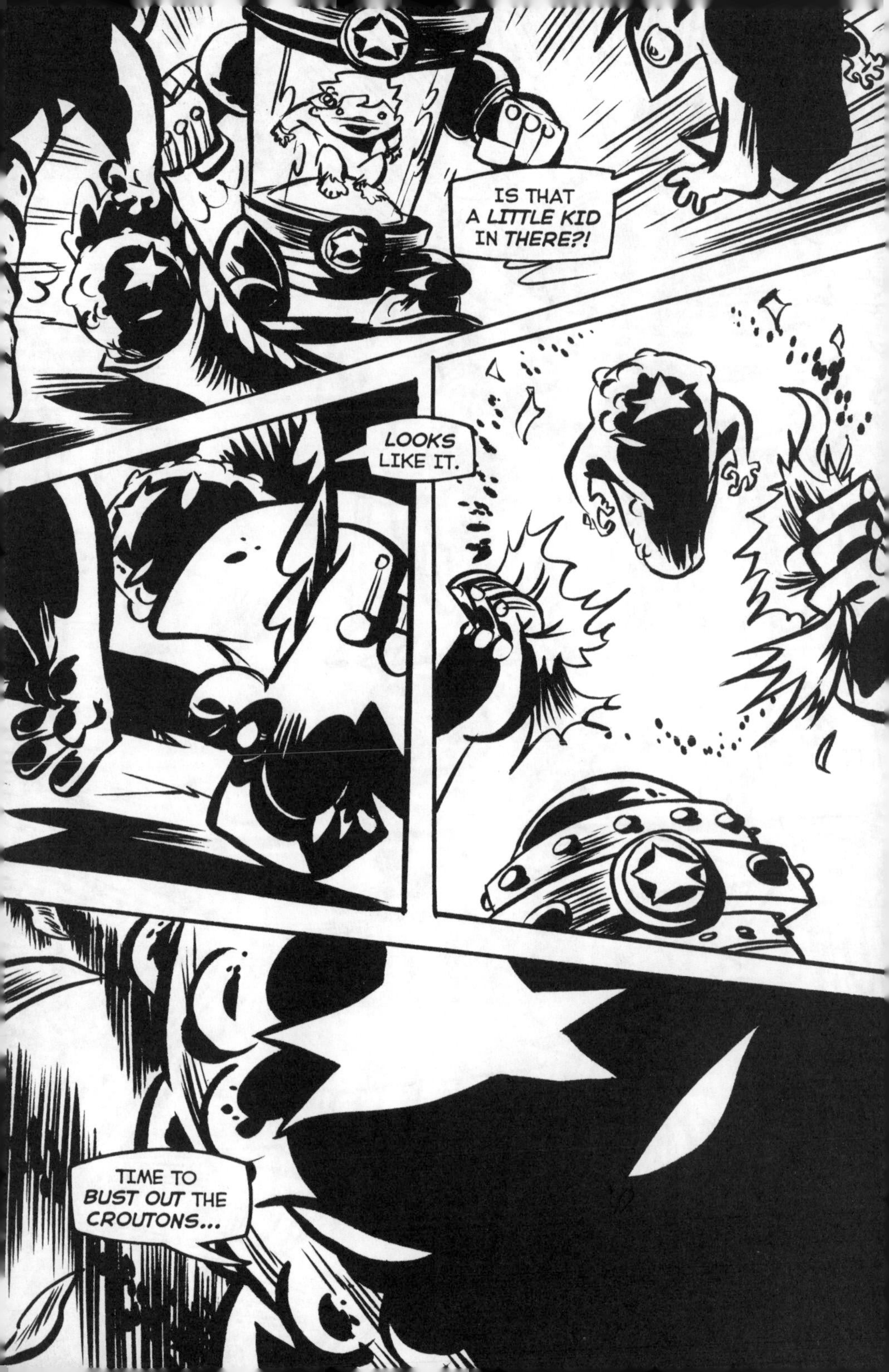
IS THAT A *LITTLE KID* IN *THERE?!*
LOOKS LIKE IT.
TIME TO *BUST OUT* THE *CROUTONS...*

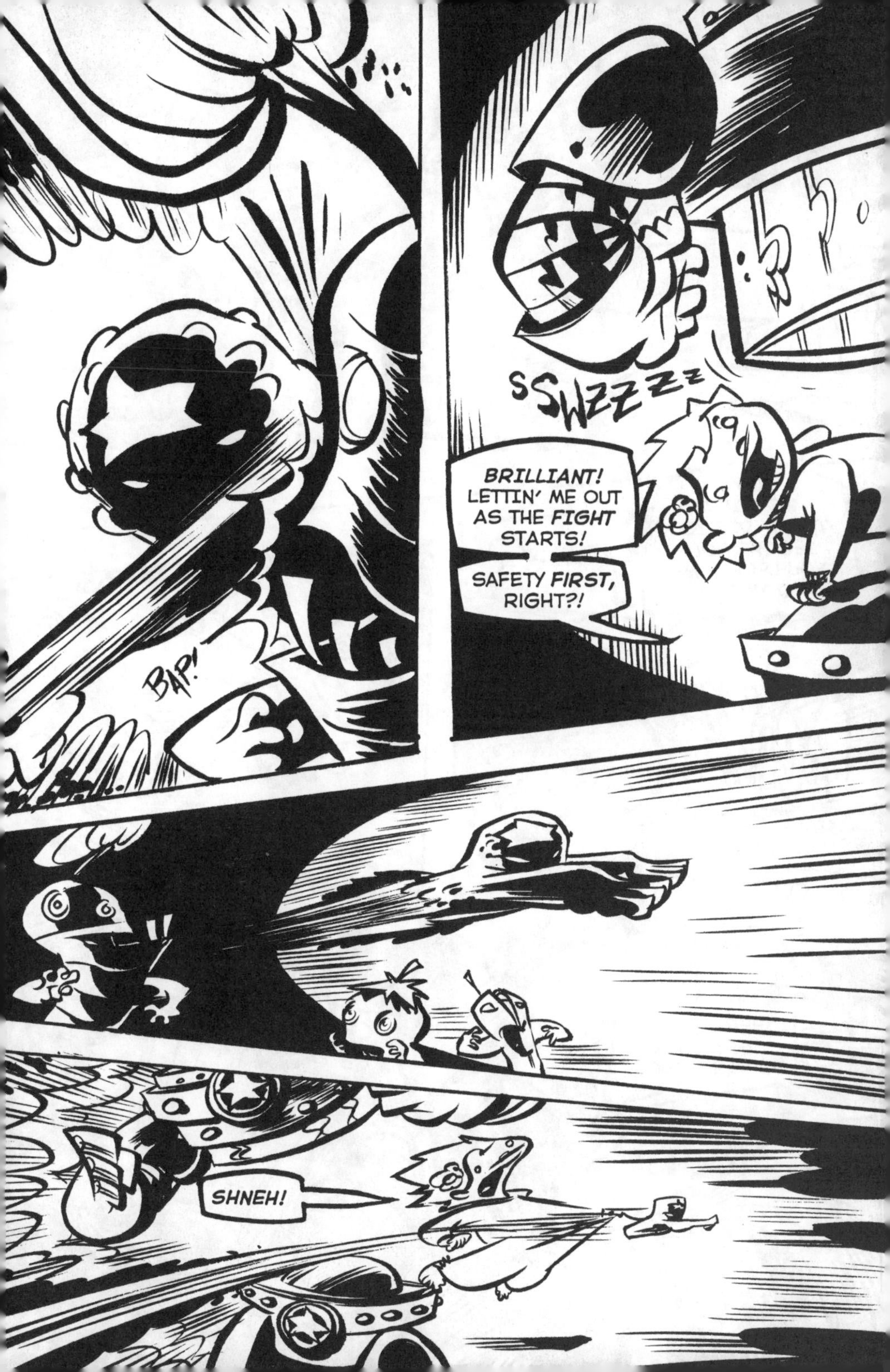

BAP!
SSWZZZZZ
BRILLIANT! LETTIN' ME OUT AS THE FIGHT STARTS!
SAFETY FIRST, RIGHT?!
SHNEH!

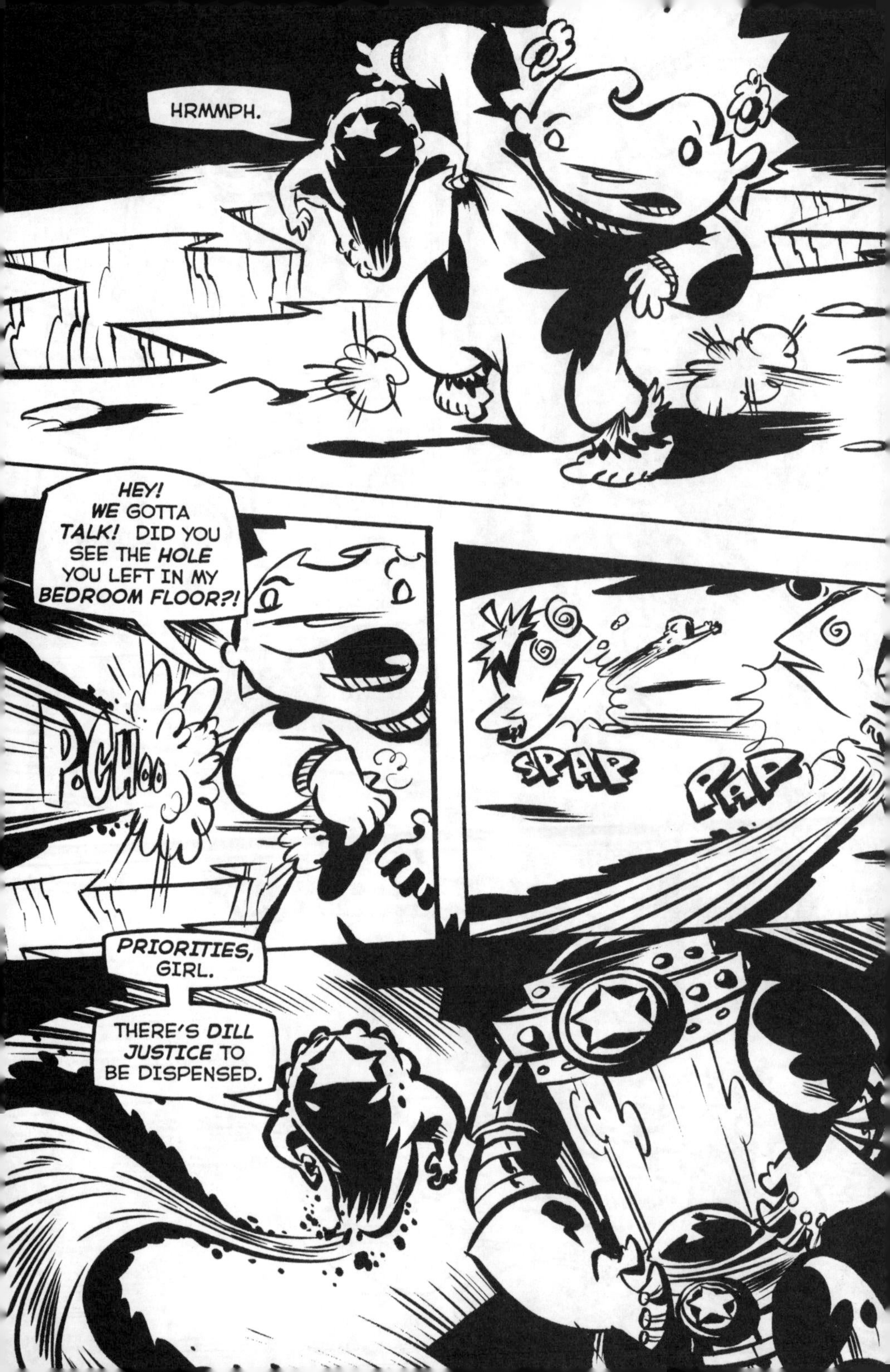
HRMMPH.
HEY! WE GOTTA TALK! DID YOU SEE THE HOLE YOU LEFT IN MY BEDROOM FLOOR?!
P.CHOO
SPAP
PAP
PRIORITIES, GIRL.
THERE'S DILL JUSTICE TO BE DISPENSED.

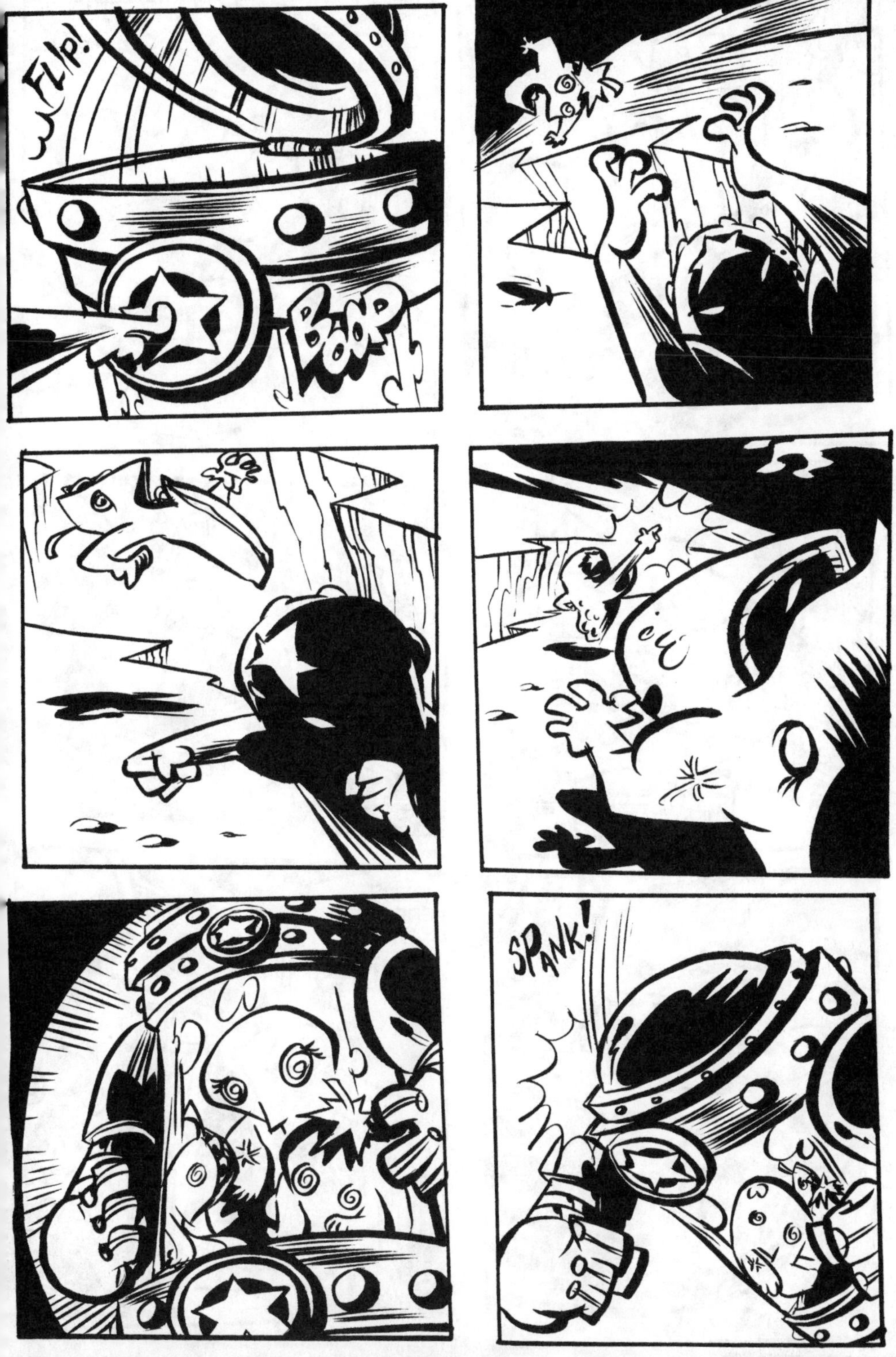
FLIP!
BOOP
SPANK!

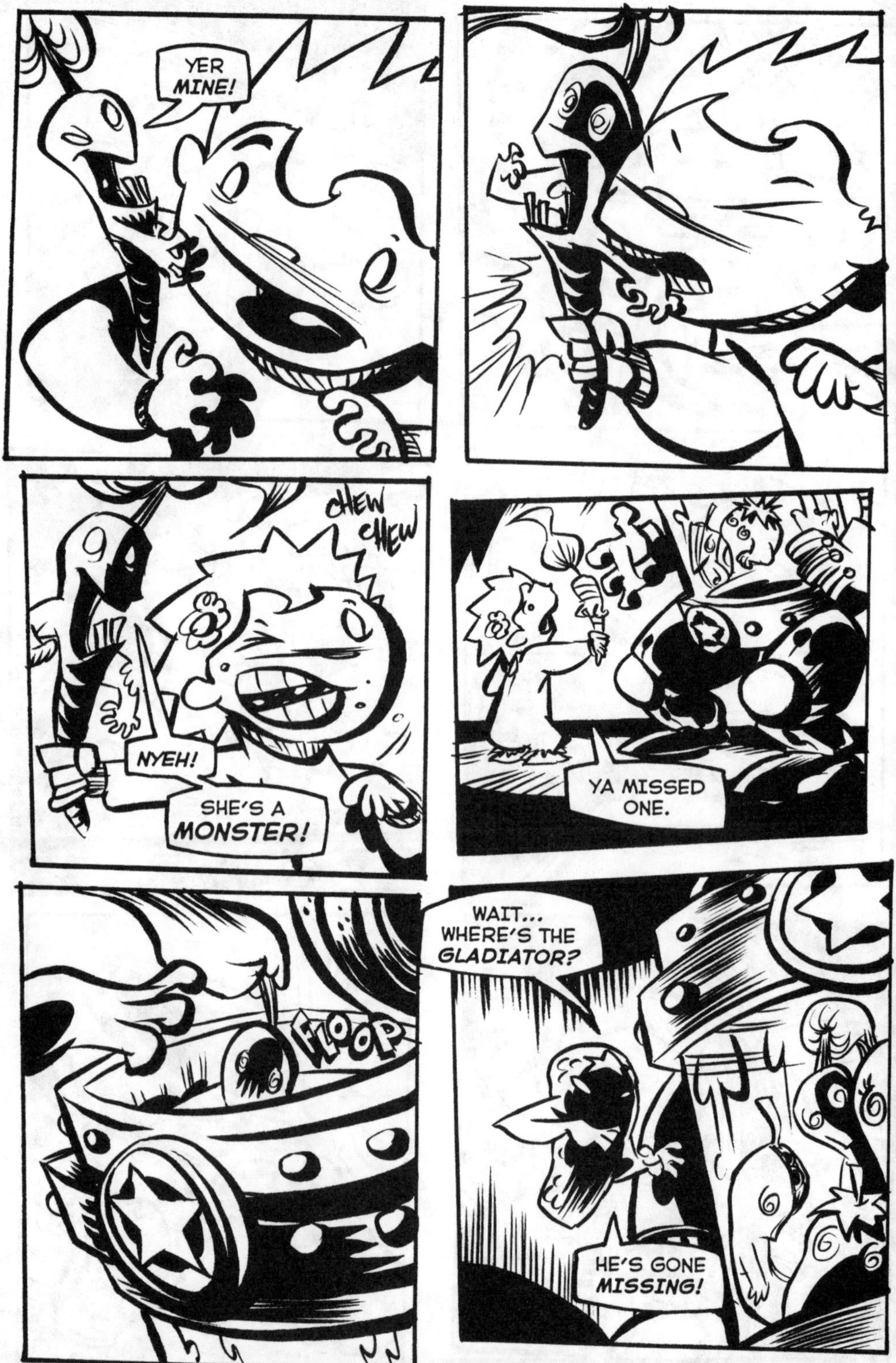
YER MINE!
CHEW CHEW
NYEH!
SHE'S A MONSTER!
YA MISSED ONE.
FLOOP
WAIT... WHERE'S THE GLADIATOR?
HE'S GONE MISSING!

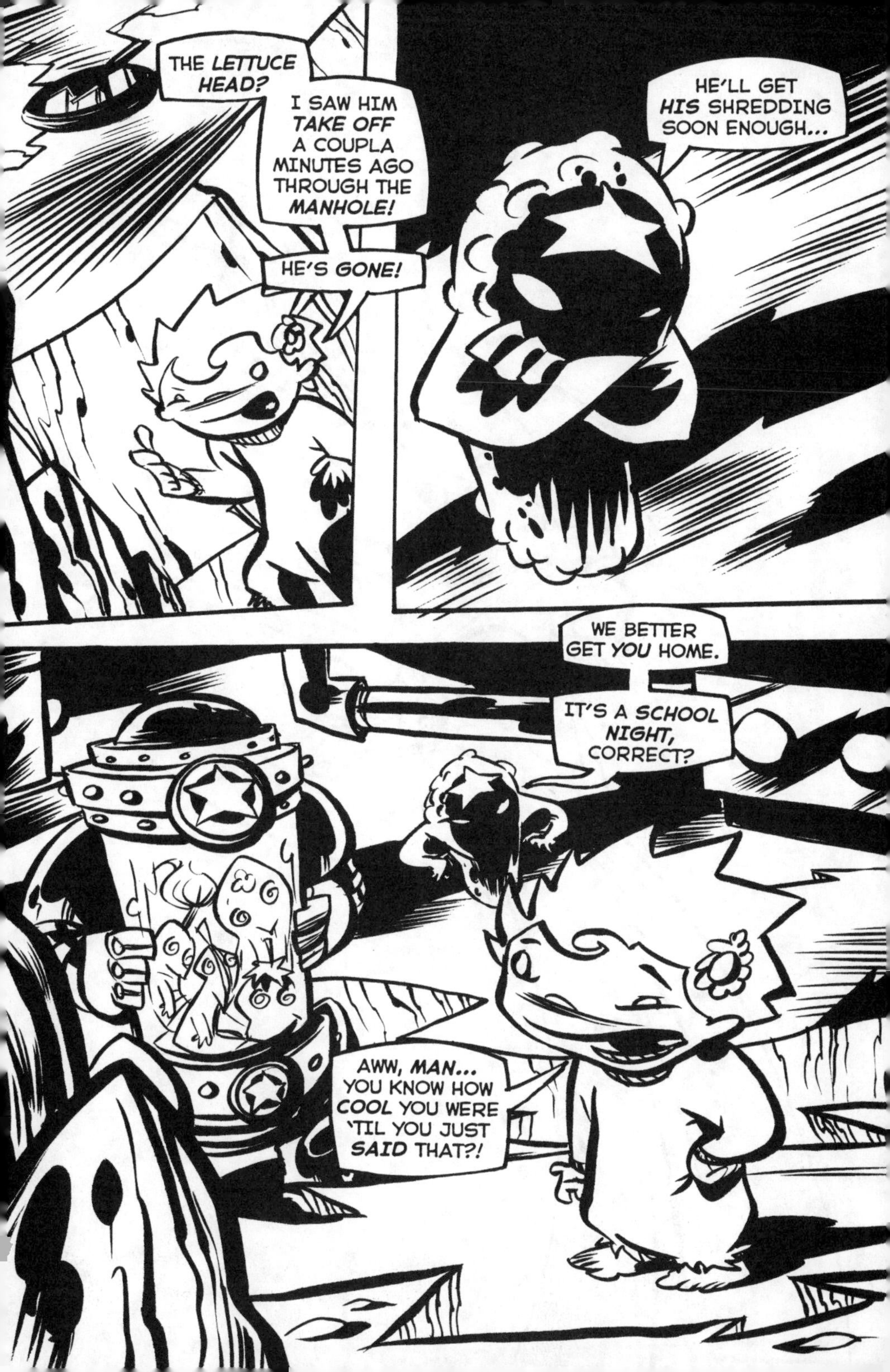
THE LETTUCE HEAD?
I SAW HIM TAKE OFF A COUPLA MINUTES AGO THROUGH THE MANHOLE!
HE'S GONE!
HE'LL GET HIS SHREDDING SOON ENOUGH...
WE BETTER GET YOU HOME.
IT'S A SCHOOL NIGHT, CORRECT?
AWW, MAN... YOU KNOW HOW COOL YOU WERE 'TIL YOU JUST SAID THAT?!

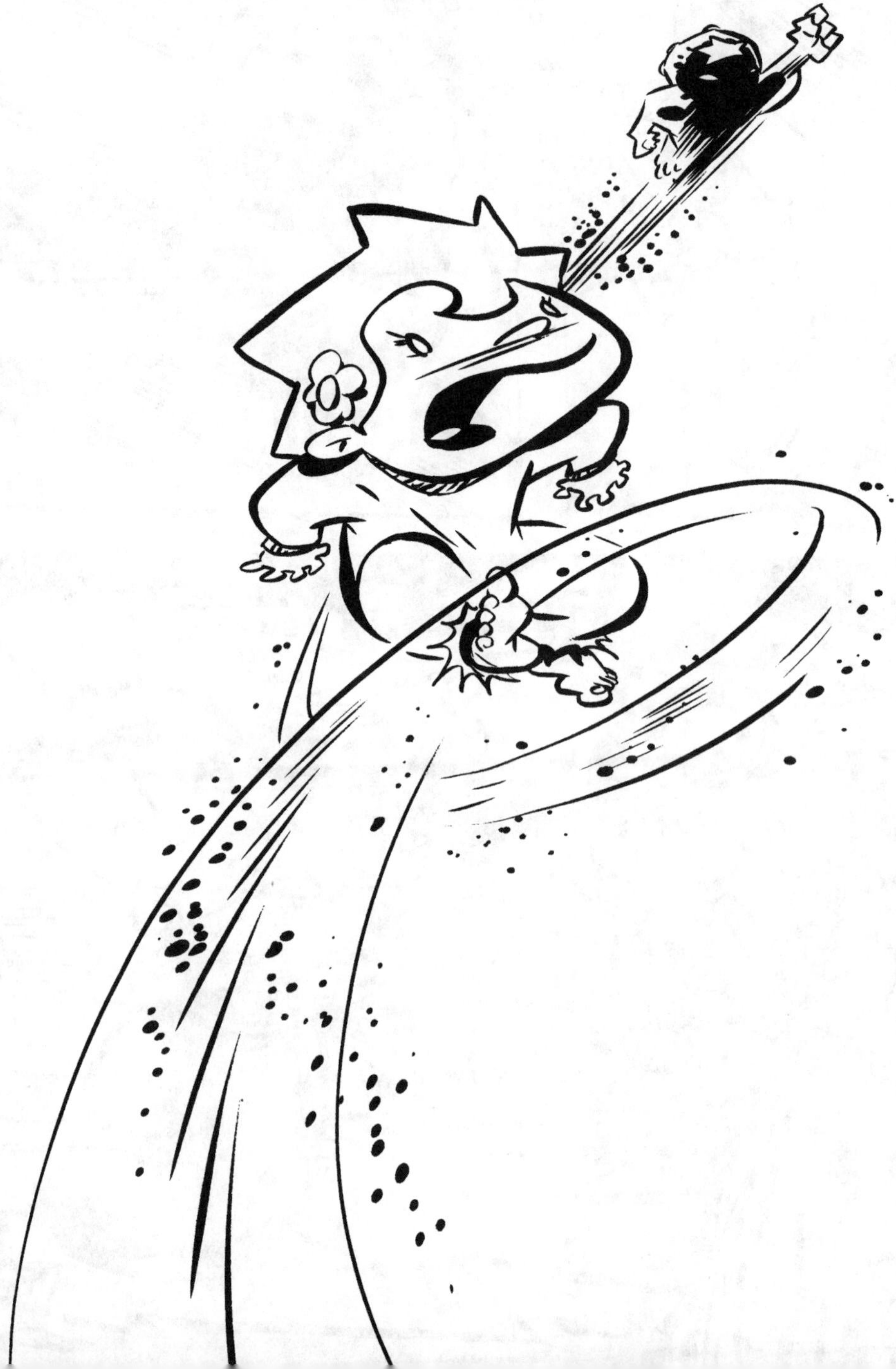

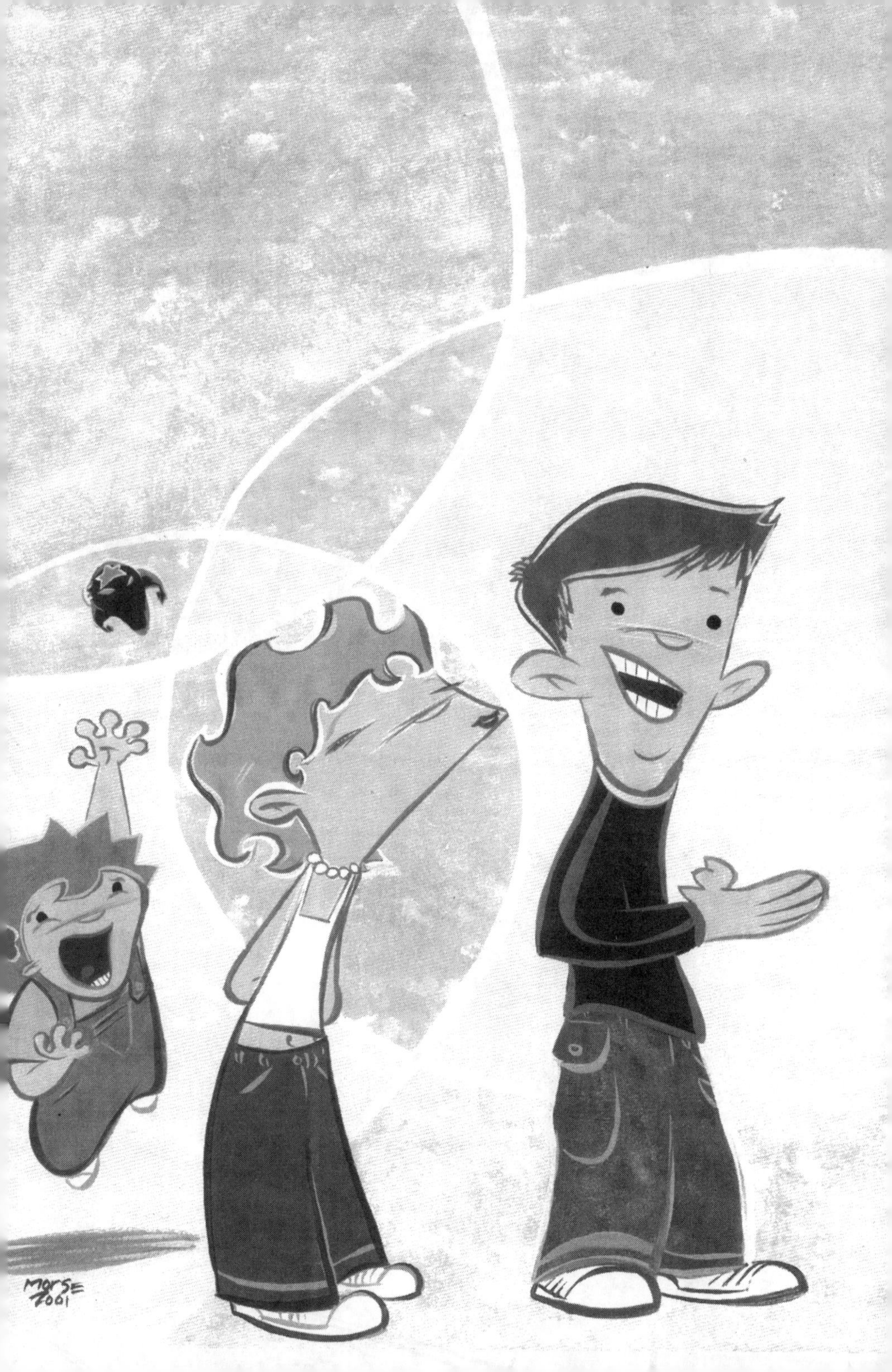
MORSE
2001

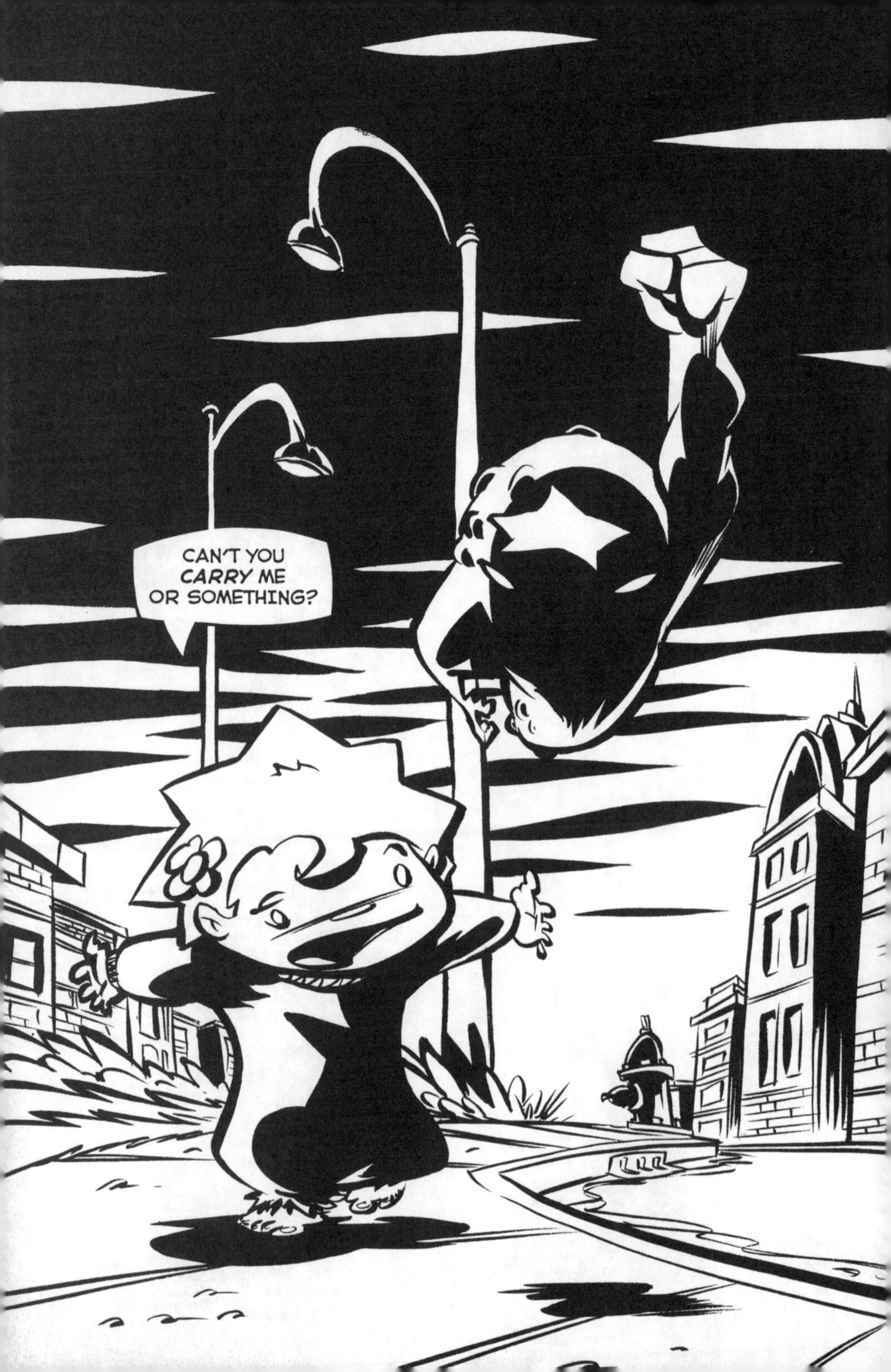
CAN'T YOU CARRY ME OR SOMETHING?

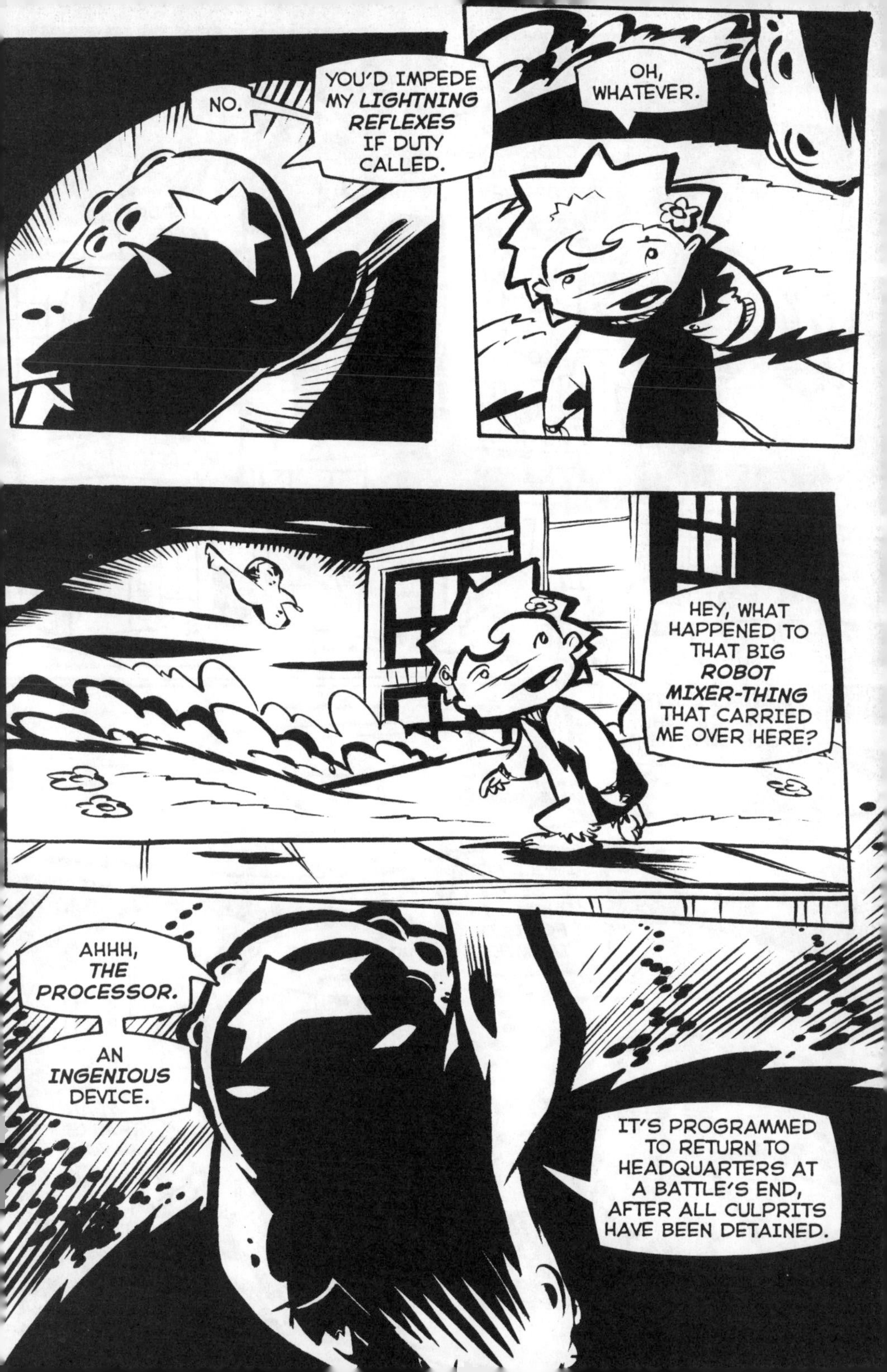
NO.
YOU'D IMPEDE MY *LIGHTNING REFLEXES* IF DUTY CALLED.
OH, WHATEVER.
HEY, WHAT HAPPENED TO THAT BIG *ROBOT MIXER-THING* THAT CARRIED ME OVER HERE?
AHHH, *THE PROCESSOR.*
AN *INGENIOUS* DEVICE.
IT'S PROGRAMMED TO RETURN TO HEADQUARTERS AT A BATTLE'S END, AFTER ALL CULPRITS HAVE BEEN DETAINED.

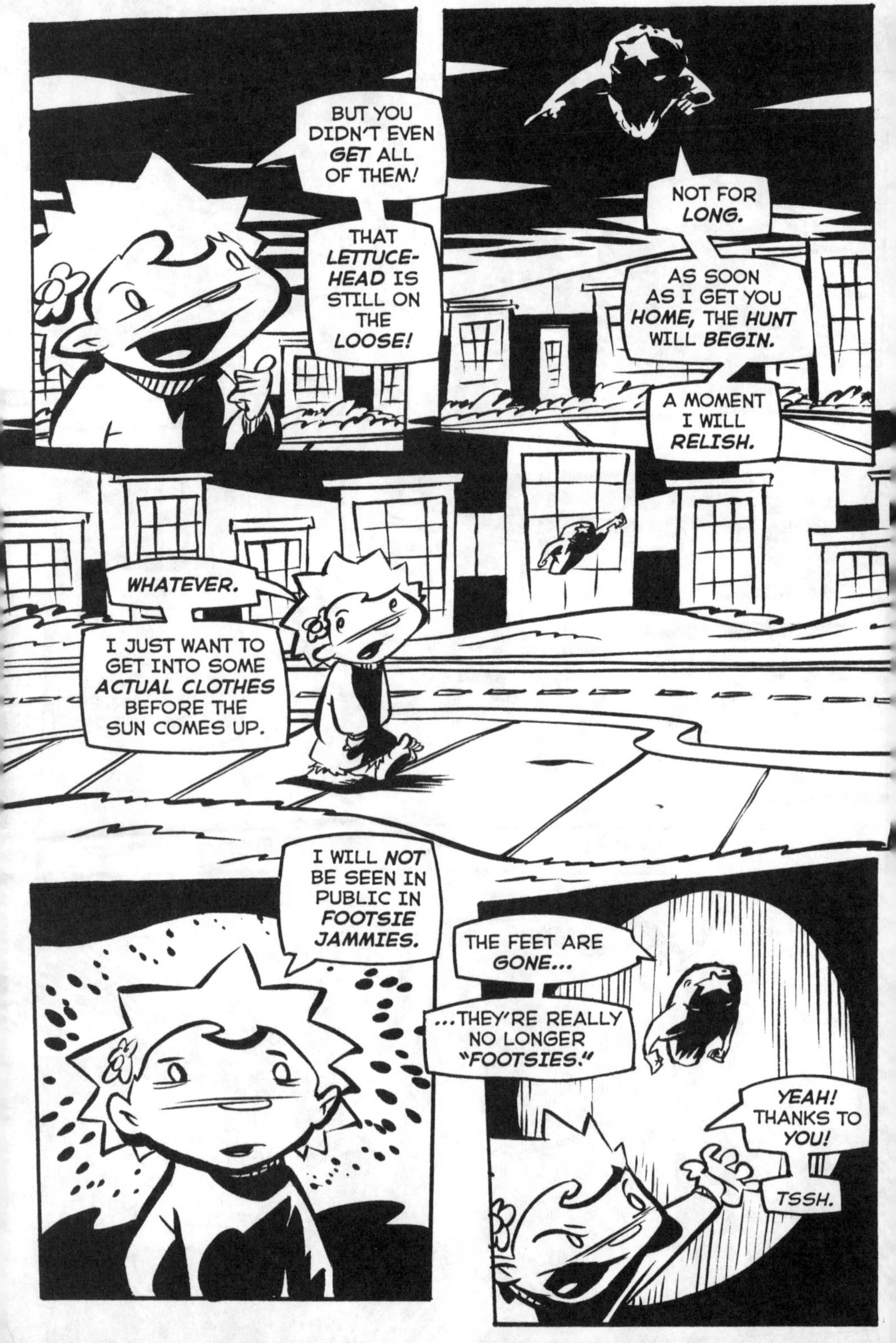

BUT YOU DIDN'T EVEN GET ALL OF THEM!
THAT LETTUCE-HEAD IS STILL ON THE LOOSE!
NOT FOR LONG.
AS SOON AS I GET YOU HOME, THE HUNT WILL BEGIN.
A MOMENT I WILL RELISH.
WHATEVER.
I JUST WANT TO GET INTO SOME ACTUAL CLOTHES BEFORE THE SUN COMES UP.
I WILL NOT BE SEEN IN PUBLIC IN FOOTSIE JAMMIES.
THE FEET ARE GONE...
...THEY'RE REALLY NO LONGER "FOOTSIES."
YEAH! THANKS TO YOU!
TSSH.

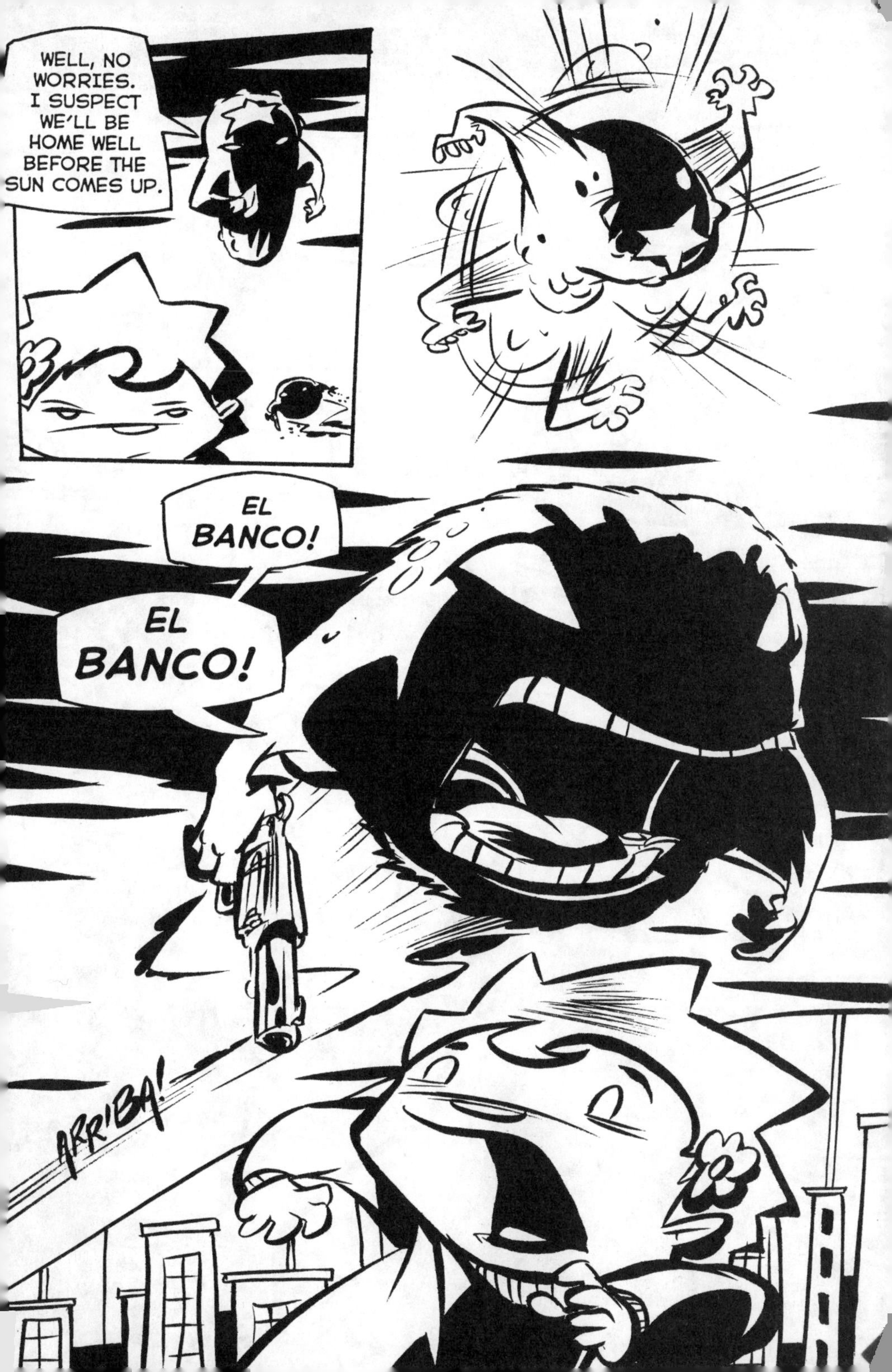
WELL, NO WORRIES. I SUSPECT WE'LL BE HOME WELL BEFORE THE SUN COMES UP.
EL BANCO!
EL BANCO!
ARRIBA!

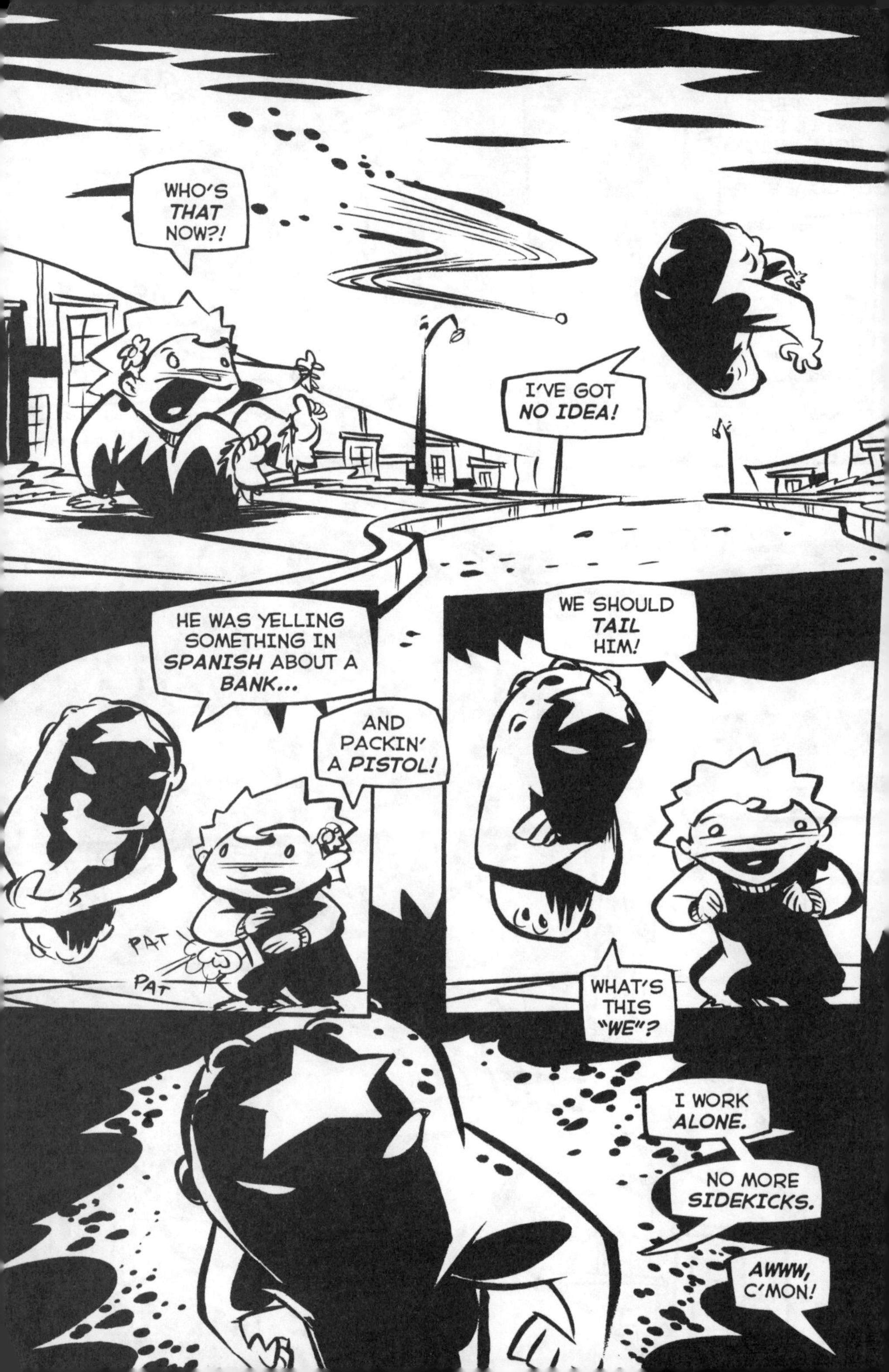
WHO'S THAT NOW?!
I'VE GOT NO IDEA!
HE WAS YELLING SOMETHING IN SPANISH ABOUT A BANK...
AND PACKIN' A PISTOL!
PAT
PAT
WE SHOULD TAIL HIM!
WHAT'S THIS "WE"?
I WORK ALONE.
NO MORE SIDEKICKS.
AWWW, C'MON!

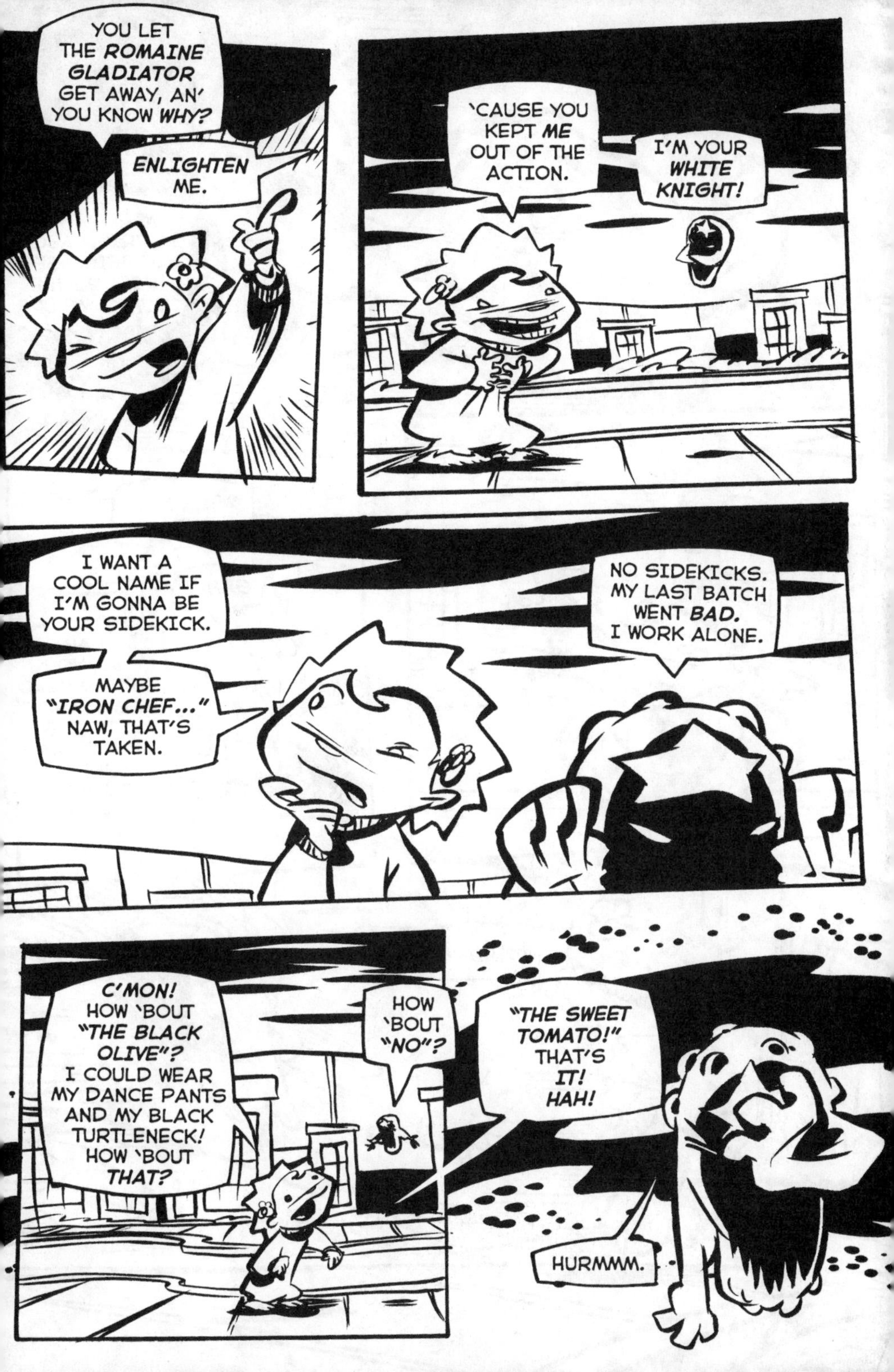

YOU LET THE *ROMAINE GLADIATOR* GET AWAY, AN' YOU KNOW *WHY?*
ENLIGHTEN ME.
'CAUSE YOU KEPT *ME* OUT OF THE ACTION.
I'M YOUR *WHITE KNIGHT!*
I WANT A COOL NAME IF I'M GONNA BE YOUR SIDEKICK.
MAYBE *"IRON CHEF..."* NAW, THAT'S TAKEN.
NO SIDEKICKS. MY LAST BATCH WENT *BAD.* I WORK ALONE.
C'MON! HOW 'BOUT *"THE BLACK OLIVE"?* I COULD WEAR MY DANCE PANTS AND MY BLACK TURTLENECK! HOW 'BOUT *THAT?*
HOW 'BOUT *"NO"?*
"THE SWEET TOMATO!" THAT'S *IT! HAH!*
HURMMM.

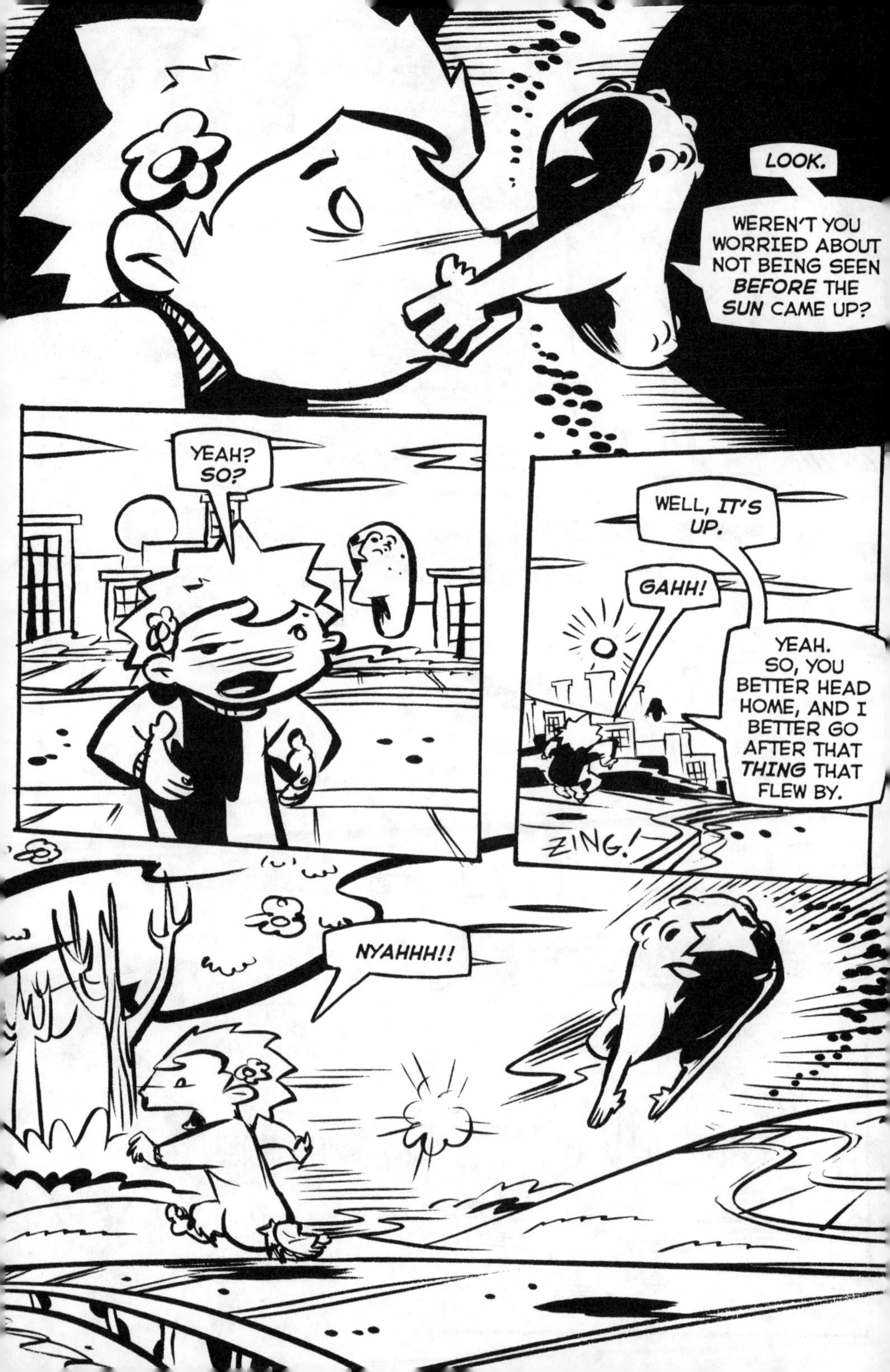
LOOK.
WEREN'T YOU WORRIED ABOUT NOT BEING SEEN *BEFORE* THE *SUN* CAME UP?
YEAH? SO?
WELL, *IT'S* UP.
GAHH!
YEAH. SO, YOU BETTER HEAD HOME, AND I BETTER GO AFTER THAT *THING* THAT FLEW BY.
ZING!
NYAHHH!!

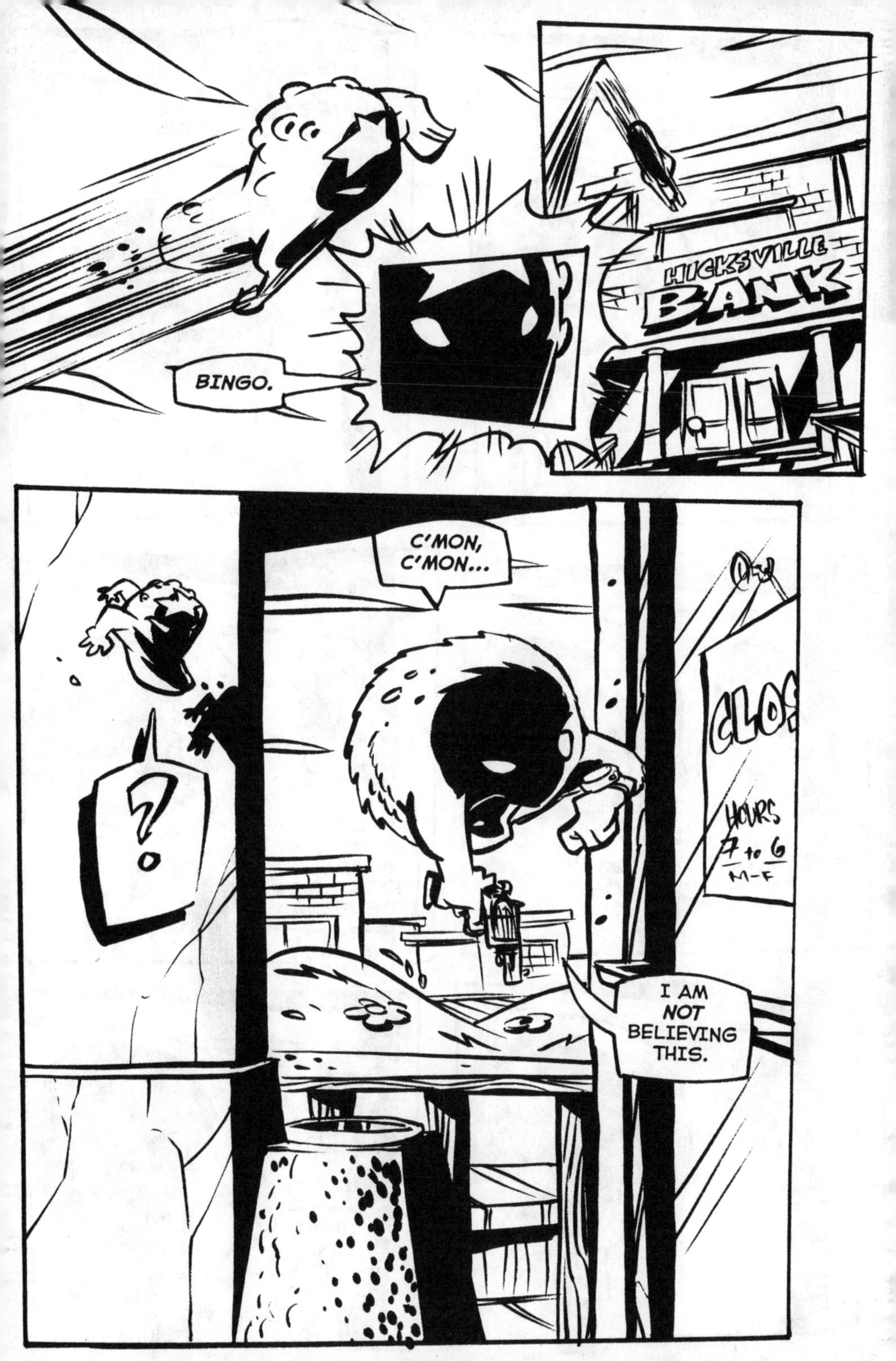
HICKSVILLE BANK
BINGO.
C'MON, C'MON...
?
CLOS
HOURS 7 to 6 M-F
I AM *NOT* BELIEVING THIS.

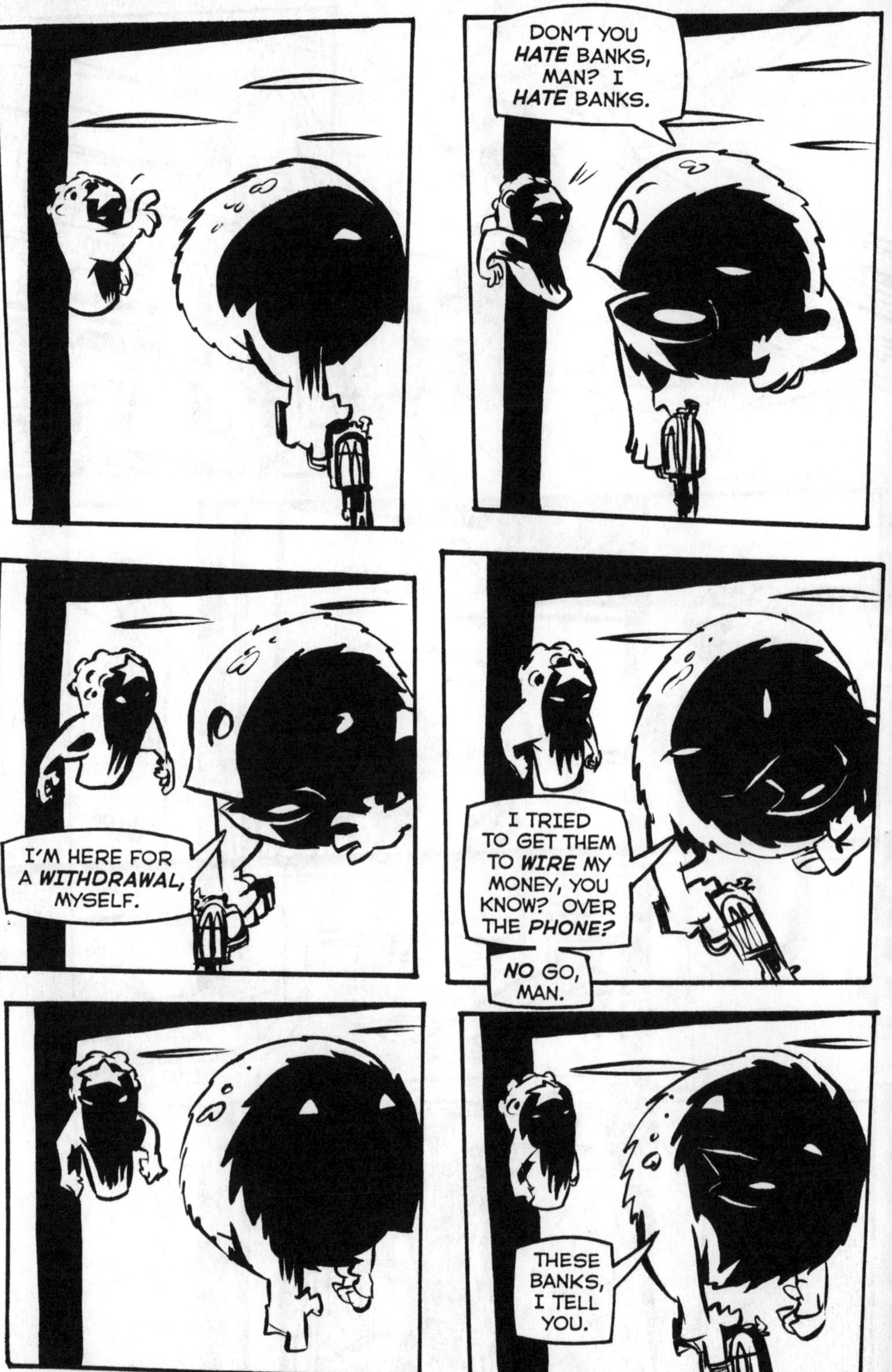
DON'T YOU HATE BANKS, MAN? I HATE BANKS.
I'M HERE FOR A WITHDRAWAL, MYSELF.
I TRIED TO GET THEM TO WIRE MY MONEY, YOU KNOW? OVER THE PHONE?
NO GO, MAN.
THESE BANKS, I TELL YOU.

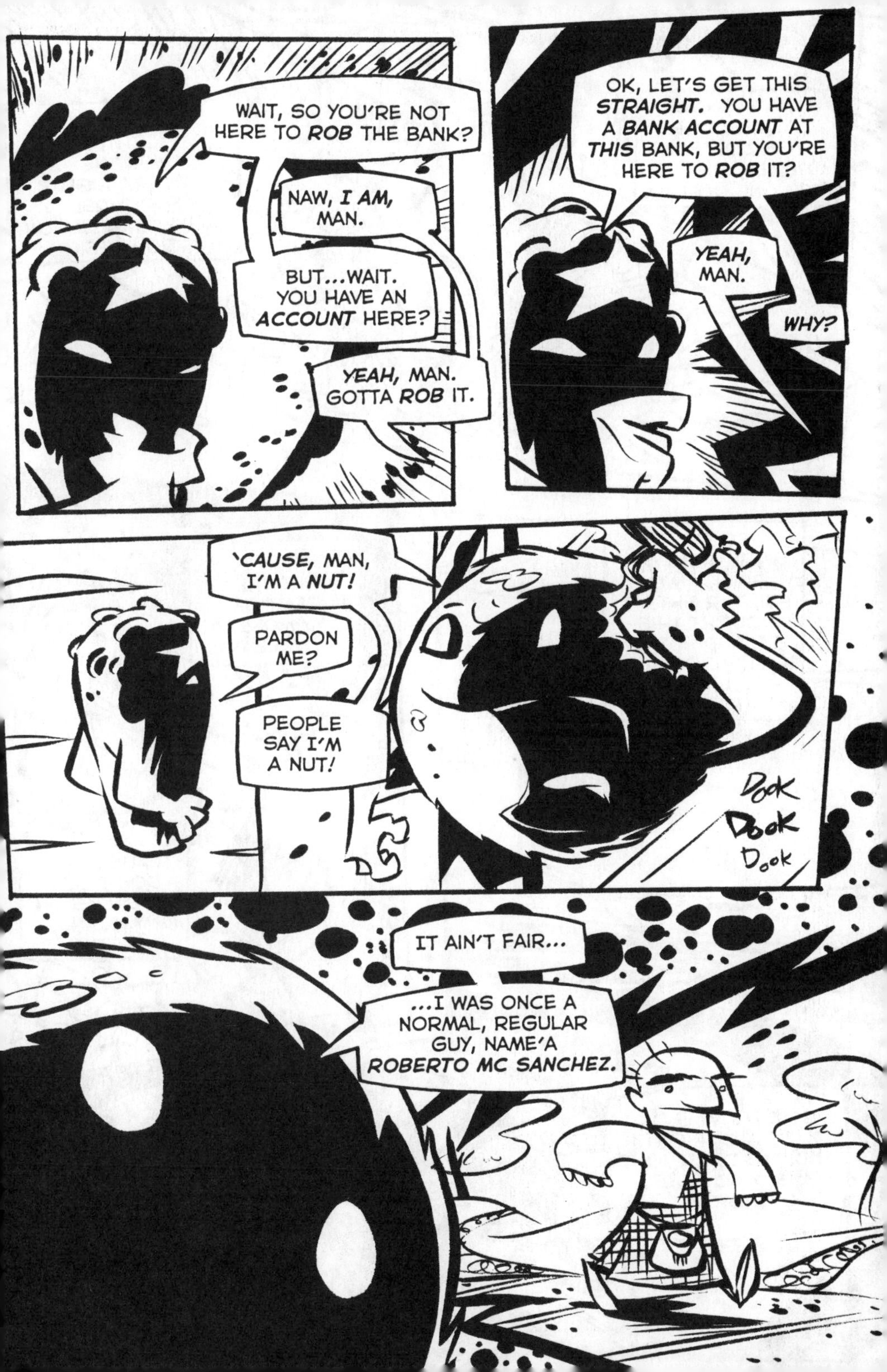
WAIT, SO YOU'RE NOT HERE TO ROB THE BANK?
NAW, I AM, MAN.
BUT...WAIT. YOU HAVE AN ACCOUNT HERE?
YEAH, MAN. GOTTA ROB IT.
OK, LET'S GET THIS STRAIGHT. YOU HAVE A BANK ACCOUNT AT THIS BANK, BUT YOU'RE HERE TO ROB IT?
YEAH, MAN.
WHY?
'CAUSE, MAN, I'M A NUT!
PARDON ME?
PEOPLE SAY I'M A NUT!
DOOK
DOOK
DOOK
IT AIN'T FAIR...
...I WAS ONCE A NORMAL, REGULAR GUY, NAME'A ROBERTO MC SANCHEZ.

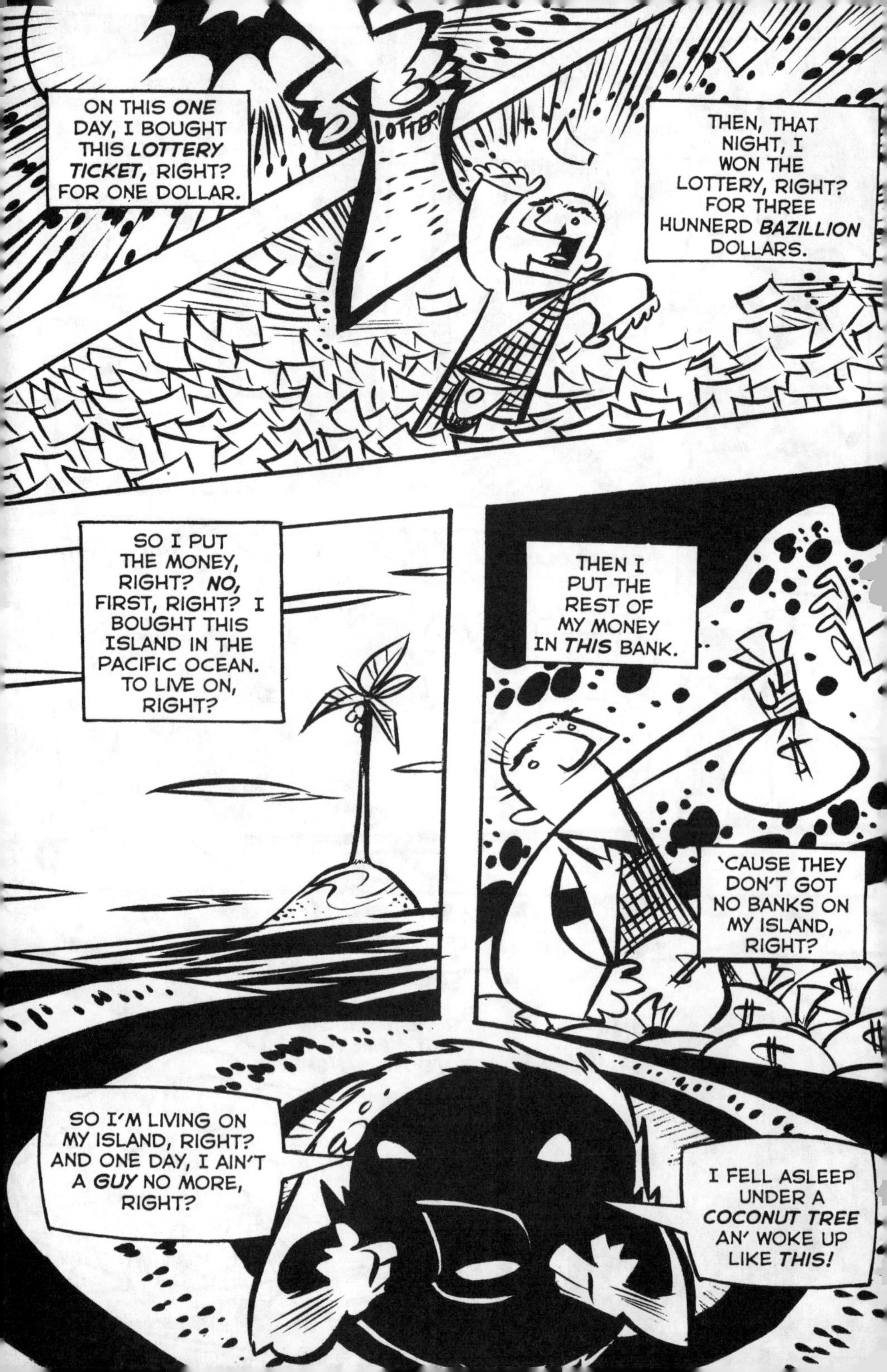
ON THIS ONE DAY, I BOUGHT THIS LOTTERY TICKET, RIGHT? FOR ONE DOLLAR.
LOTTERY
THEN, THAT NIGHT, I WON THE LOTTERY, RIGHT? FOR THREE HUNNERD BAZILLION DOLLARS.
SO I PUT THE MONEY, RIGHT? NO, FIRST, RIGHT? I BOUGHT THIS ISLAND IN THE PACIFIC OCEAN. TO LIVE ON, RIGHT?
THEN I PUT THE REST OF MY MONEY IN THIS BANK.
'CAUSE THEY DON'T GOT NO BANKS ON MY ISLAND, RIGHT?
SO I'M LIVING ON MY ISLAND, RIGHT? AND ONE DAY, I AIN'T A GUY NO MORE, RIGHT?
I FELL ASLEEP UNDER A COCONUT TREE AN' WOKE UP LIKE THIS!

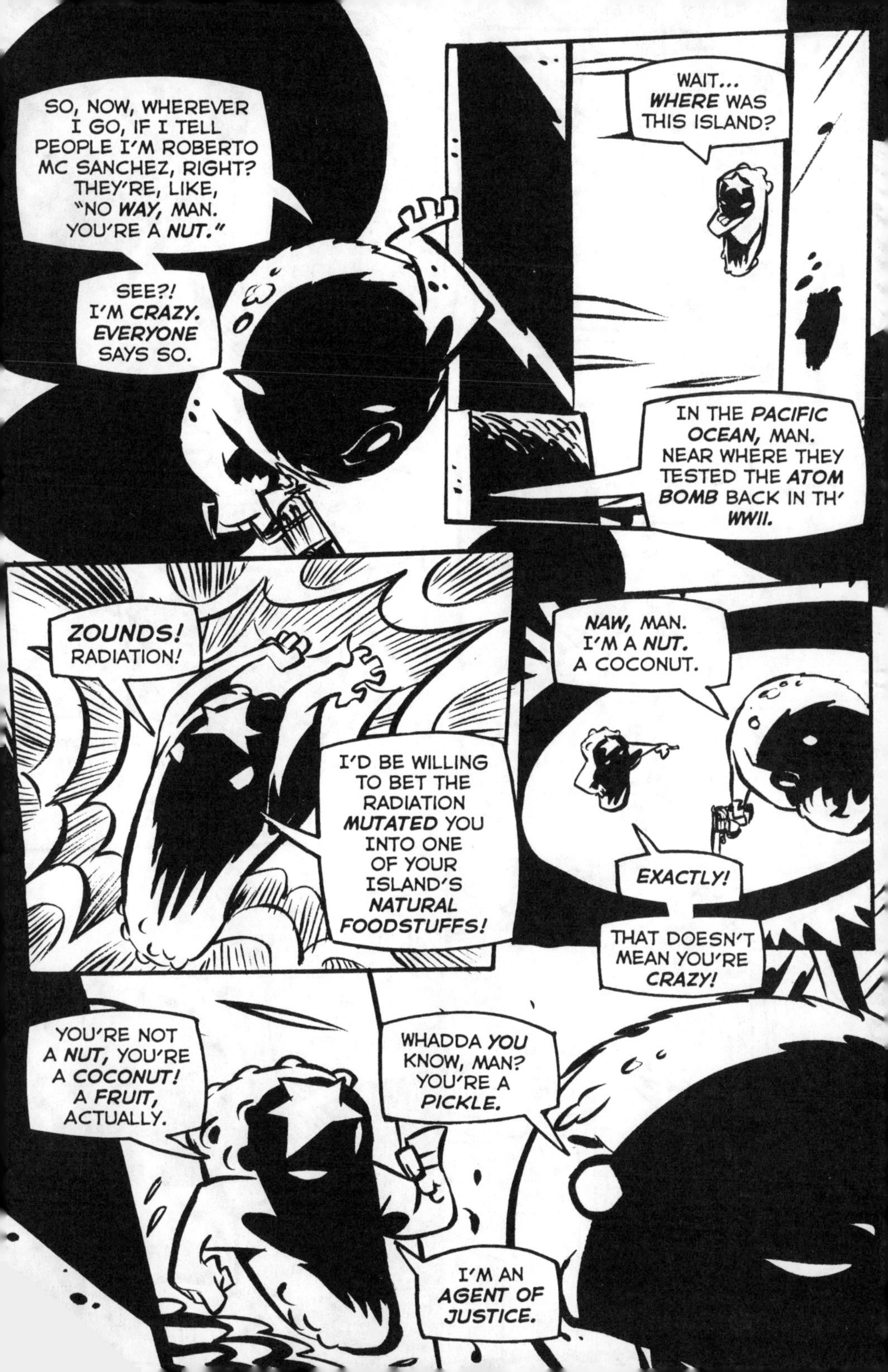
SO, NOW, WHEREVER I GO, IF I TELL PEOPLE I'M ROBERTO MC SANCHEZ, RIGHT? THEY'RE, LIKE, "NO WAY, MAN. YOU'RE A NUT."
SEE?! I'M CRAZY. EVERYONE SAYS SO.
WAIT... WHERE WAS THIS ISLAND?
IN THE PACIFIC OCEAN, MAN. NEAR WHERE THEY TESTED THE ATOM BOMB BACK IN TH' WWII.
ZOUNDS! RADIATION!
I'D BE WILLING TO BET THE RADIATION MUTATED YOU INTO ONE OF YOUR ISLAND'S NATURAL FOODSTUFFS!
NAW, MAN. I'M A NUT. A COCONUT.
EXACTLY!
THAT DOESN'T MEAN YOU'RE CRAZY!
YOU'RE NOT A NUT, YOU'RE A COCONUT! A FRUIT, ACTUALLY.
WHADDA YOU KNOW, MAN? YOU'RE A PICKLE.
I'M AN AGENT OF JUSTICE.

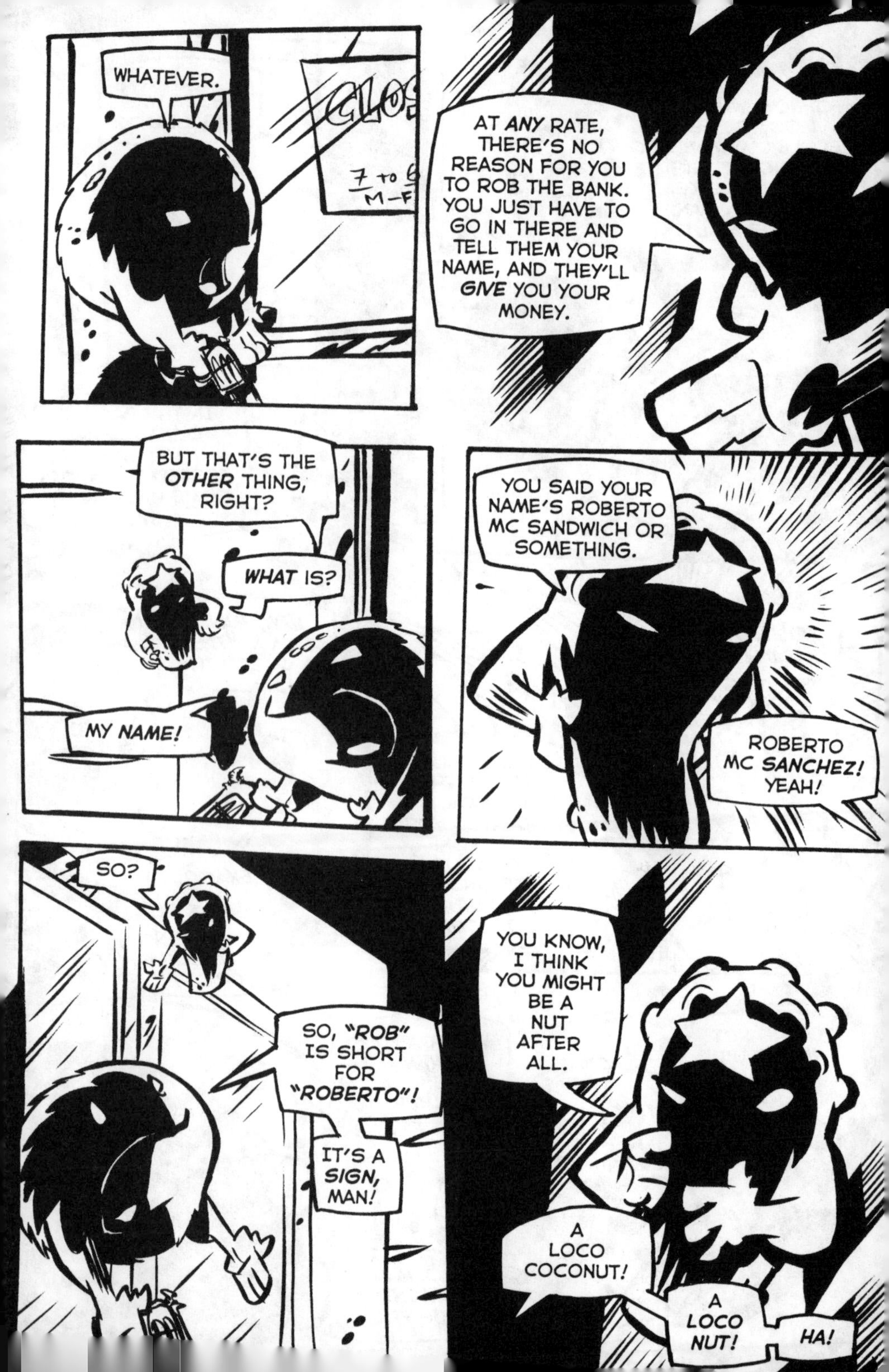
WHATEVER.
CLOS
7 to 6
M-F
AT *ANY* RATE, THERE'S NO REASON FOR YOU TO ROB THE BANK. YOU JUST HAVE TO GO IN THERE AND TELL THEM YOUR NAME, AND THEY'LL *GIVE* YOU YOUR MONEY.
BUT THAT'S THE *OTHER* THING, RIGHT?
WHAT IS?
MY *NAME*!
YOU SAID YOUR NAME'S ROBERTO MC SANDWICH OR SOMETHING.
ROBERTO MC *SANCHEZ*! YEAH!
SO?
SO, *"ROB"* IS SHORT FOR *"ROBERTO"*!
IT'S A *SIGN*, MAN!
YOU KNOW, I THINK YOU MIGHT BE A NUT AFTER ALL.
A LOCO COCONUT!
A *LOCO NUT*!
HA!

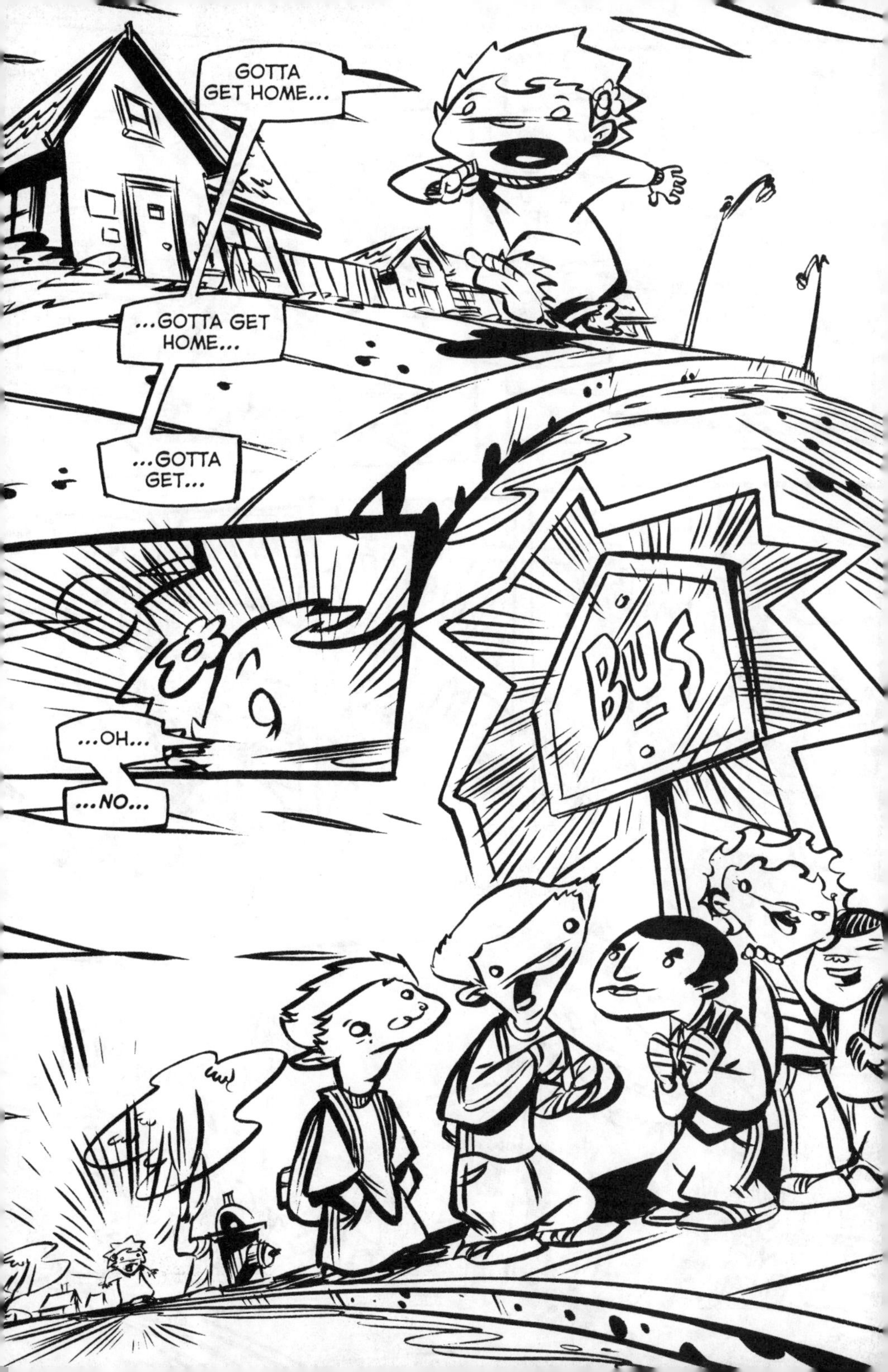
GOTTA GET HOME...
...GOTTA GET HOME...
...GOTTA GET...
...OH...
...NO...
BUS

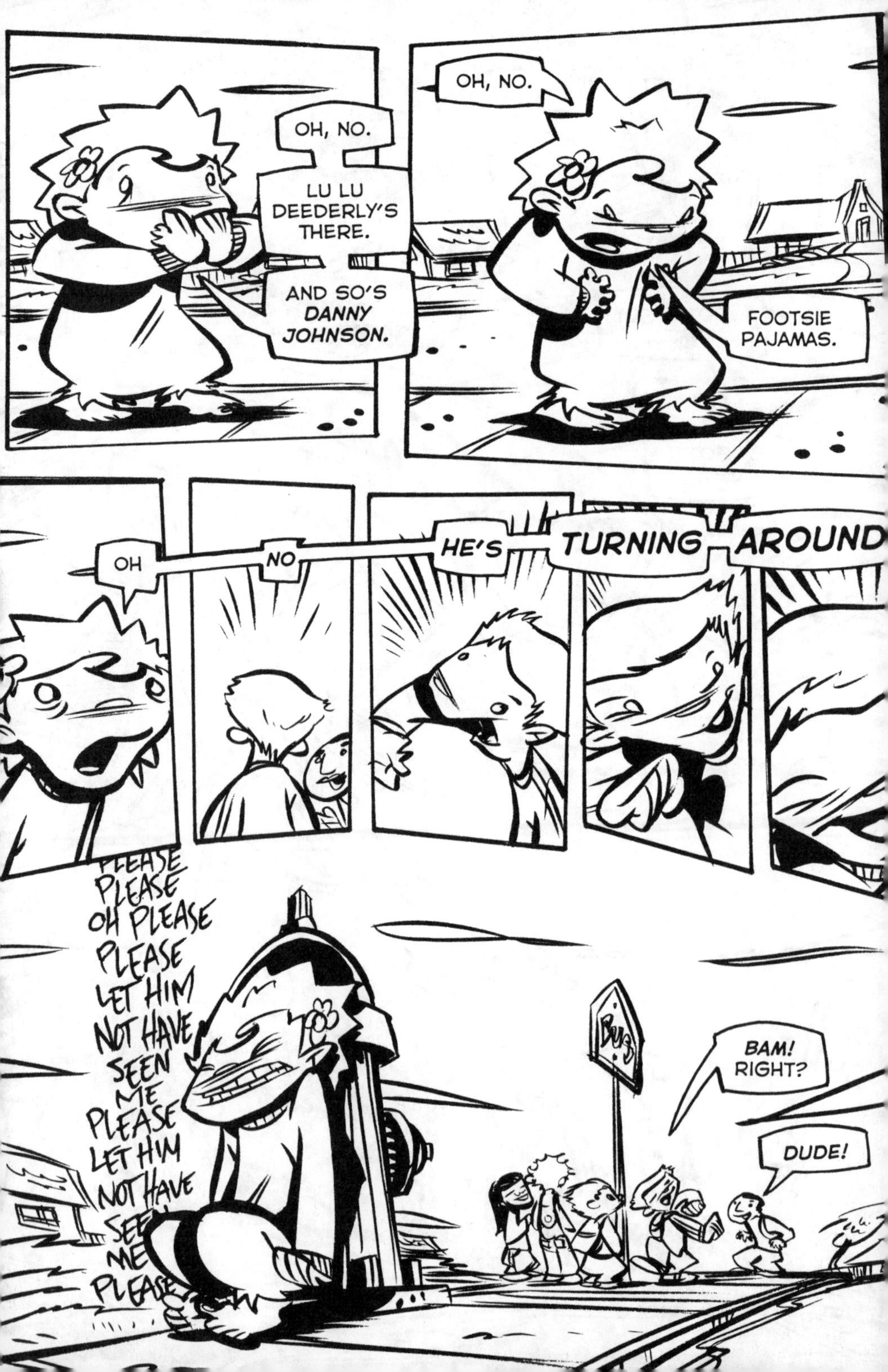

OH, NO.
LU LU DEEDERLY'S THERE.
AND SO'S *DANNY JOHNSON.*
OH, NO.
FOOTSIE PAJAMAS.
OH
NO
HE'S
TURNING
AROUND
PLEASE PLEASE OH PLEASE PLEASE LET HIM NOT HAVE SEEN ME PLEASE LET HIM NOT HAVE SEEN ME PLEASE
BAM! RIGHT?
DUDE!

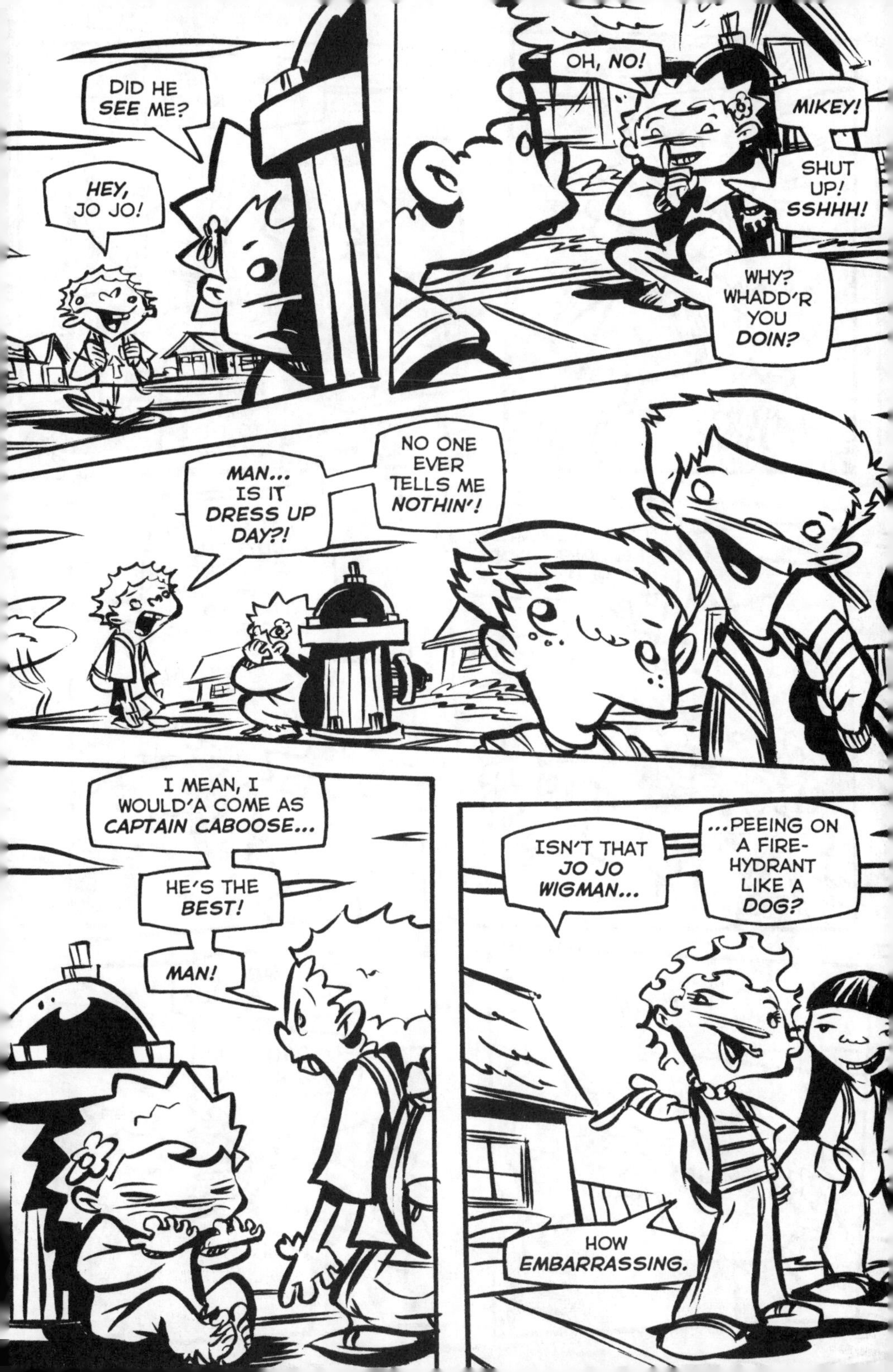
DID HE SEE ME?
HEY, JO JO!
OH, NO!
MIKEY!
SHUT UP! SSHHH!
WHY? WHADD'R YOU DOIN?
MAN... IS IT DRESS UP DAY?!
NO ONE EVER TELLS ME NOTHIN'!
I MEAN, I WOULD'A COME AS CAPTAIN CABOOSE...
HE'S THE BEST!
MAN!
ISN'T THAT JO JO WIGMAN...
...PEEING ON A FIRE-HYDRANT LIKE A DOG?
HOW EMBARRASSING.

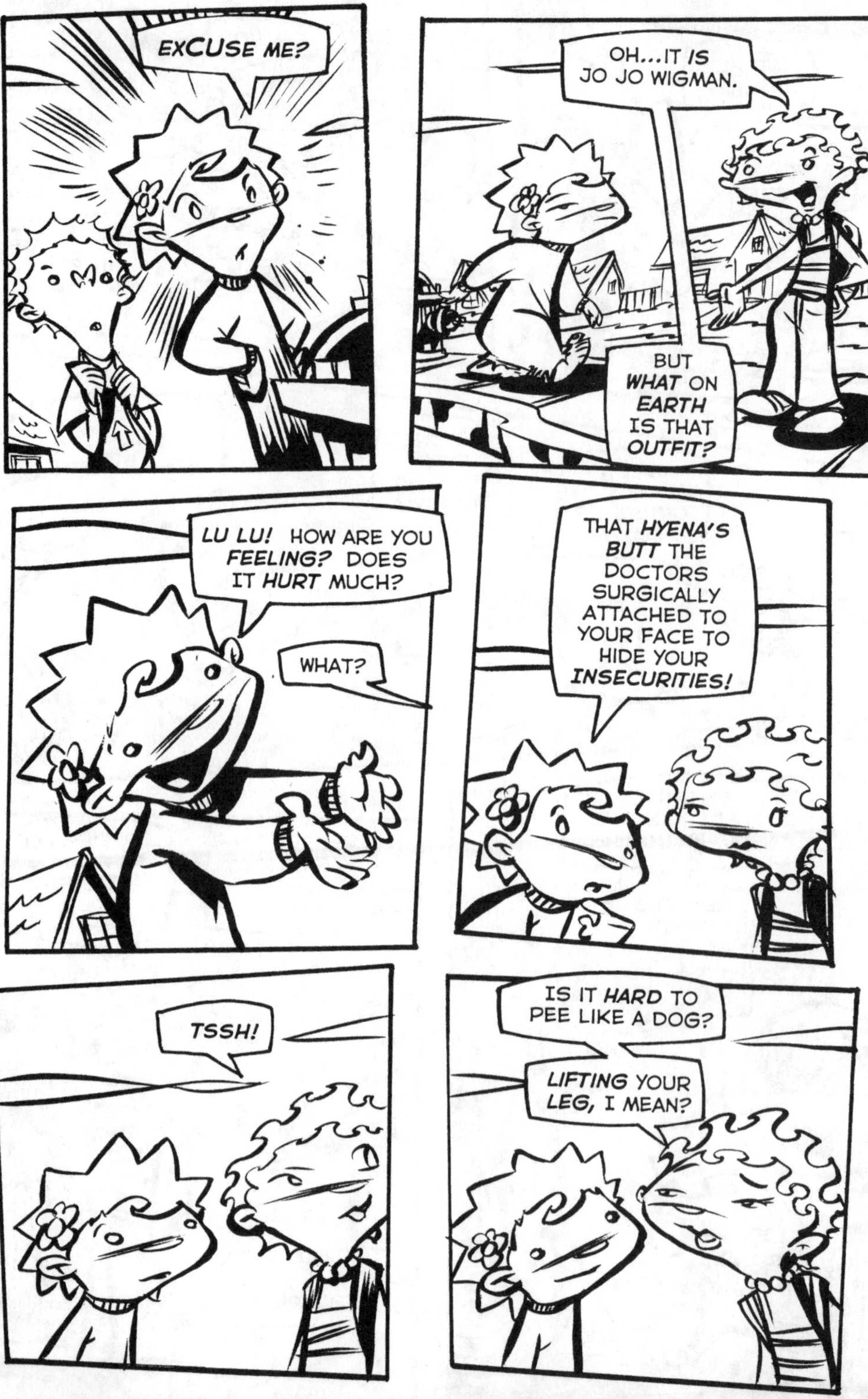
EXCUSE ME?
OH...IT IS JO JO WIGMAN.
BUT WHAT ON EARTH IS THAT OUTFIT?
LU LU! HOW ARE YOU FEELING? DOES IT HURT MUCH?
WHAT?
THAT HYENA'S BUTT THE DOCTORS SURGICALLY ATTACHED TO YOUR FACE TO HIDE YOUR INSECURITIES!
TSSH!
IS IT HARD TO PEE LIKE A DOG?
LIFTING YOUR LEG, I MEAN?

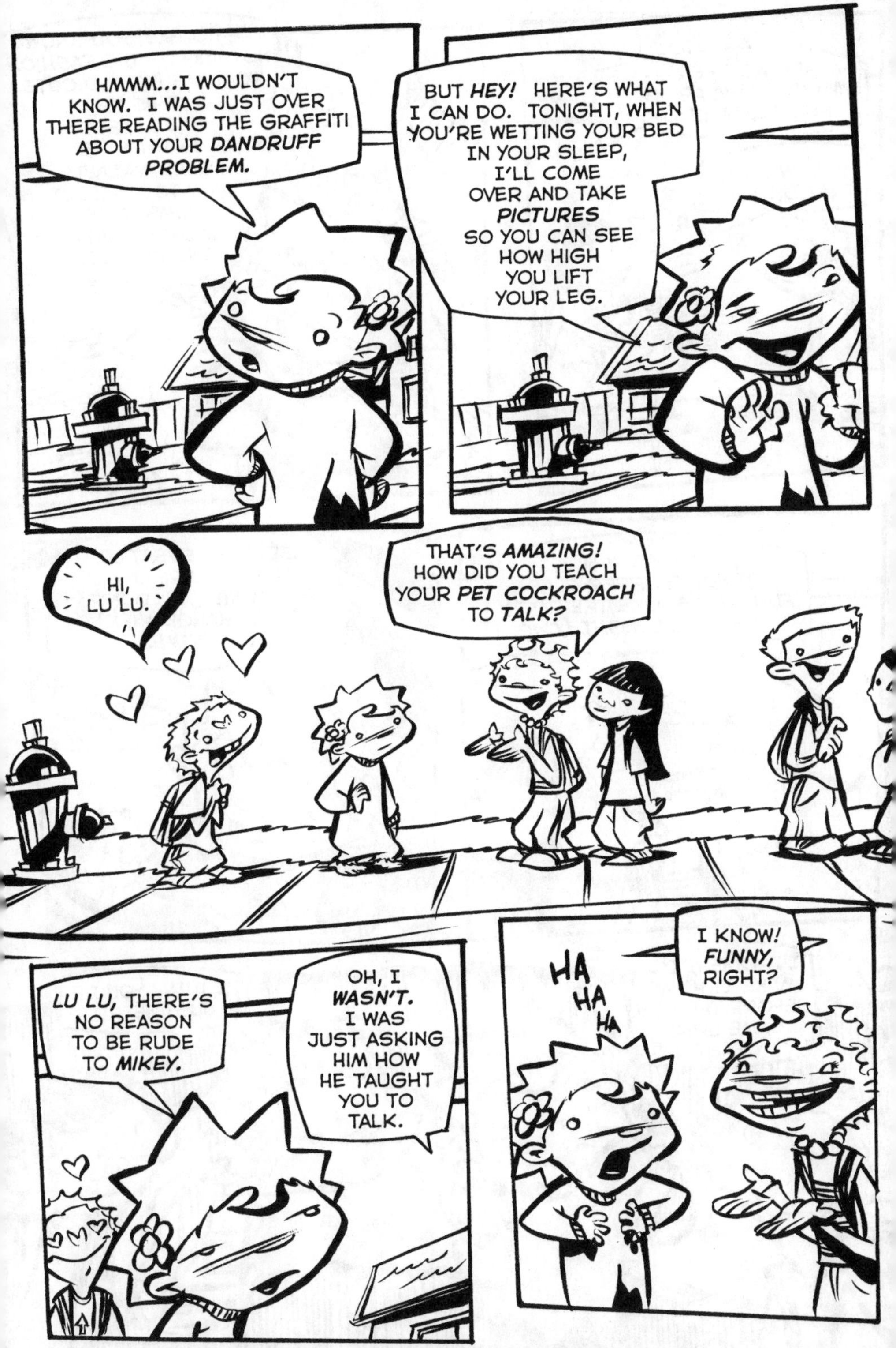
HMMM...I WOULDN'T KNOW. I WAS JUST OVER THERE READING THE GRAFFITI ABOUT YOUR DANDRUFF PROBLEM.
BUT HEY! HERE'S WHAT I CAN DO. TONIGHT, WHEN YOU'RE WETTING YOUR BED IN YOUR SLEEP, I'LL COME OVER AND TAKE PICTURES SO YOU CAN SEE HOW HIGH YOU LIFT YOUR LEG.
HI, LU LU.
THAT'S AMAZING! HOW DID YOU TEACH YOUR PET COCKROACH TO TALK?
LU LU, THERE'S NO REASON TO BE RUDE TO MIKEY.
OH, I WASN'T. I WAS JUST ASKING HIM HOW HE TAUGHT YOU TO TALK.
HA HA HA
I KNOW! FUNNY, RIGHT?

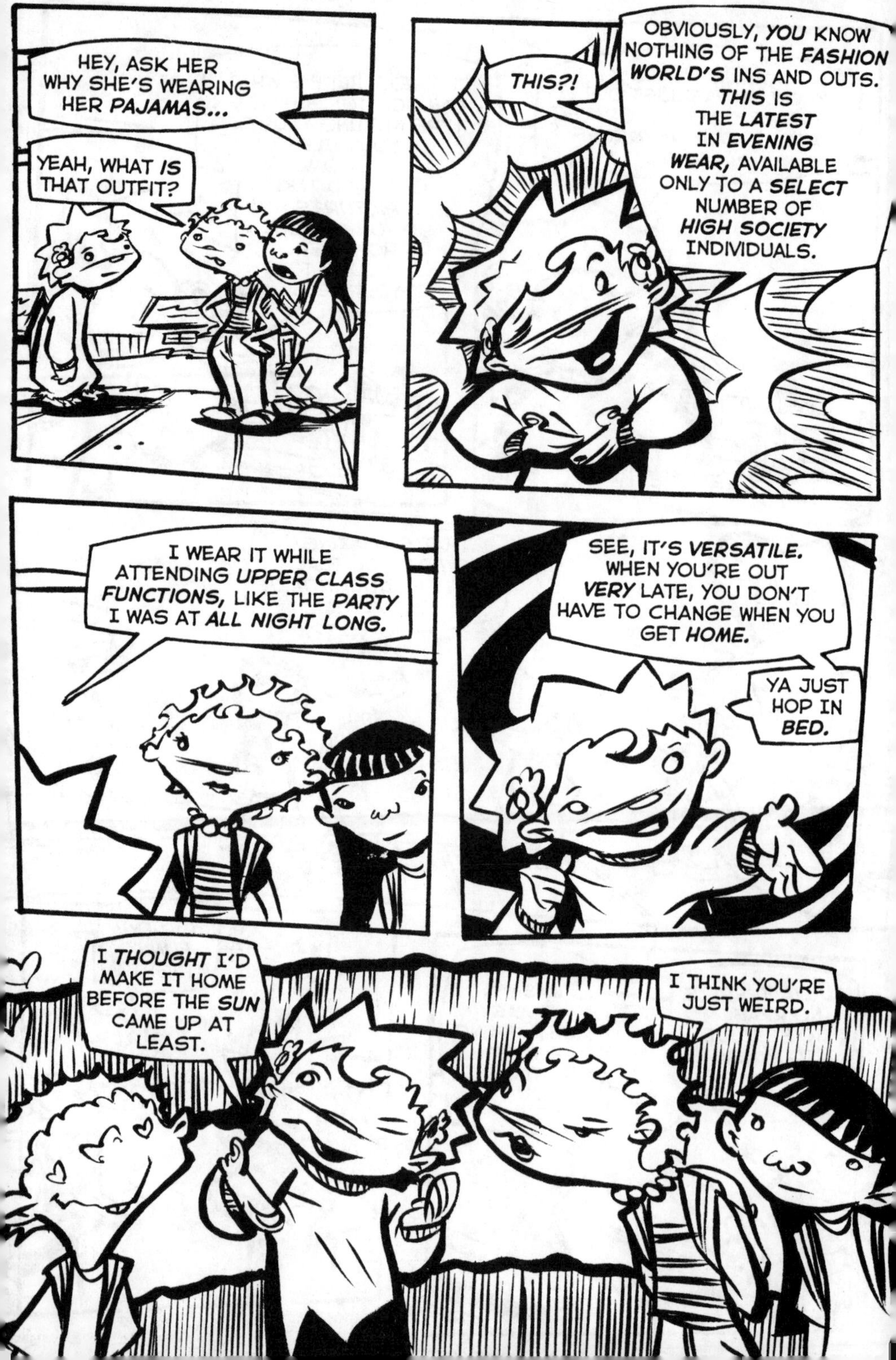
HEY, ASK HER WHY SHE'S WEARING HER PAJAMAS...
YEAH, WHAT IS THAT OUTFIT?
THIS?!
OBVIOUSLY, YOU KNOW NOTHING OF THE FASHION WORLD'S INS AND OUTS. THIS IS THE LATEST IN EVENING WEAR, AVAILABLE ONLY TO A SELECT NUMBER OF HIGH SOCIETY INDIVIDUALS.
I WEAR IT WHILE ATTENDING UPPER CLASS FUNCTIONS, LIKE THE PARTY I WAS AT ALL NIGHT LONG.
SEE, IT'S VERSATILE. WHEN YOU'RE OUT VERY LATE, YOU DON'T HAVE TO CHANGE WHEN YOU GET HOME.
YA JUST HOP IN BED.
I THOUGHT I'D MAKE IT HOME BEFORE THE SUN CAME UP AT LEAST.
I THINK YOU'RE JUST WEIRD.

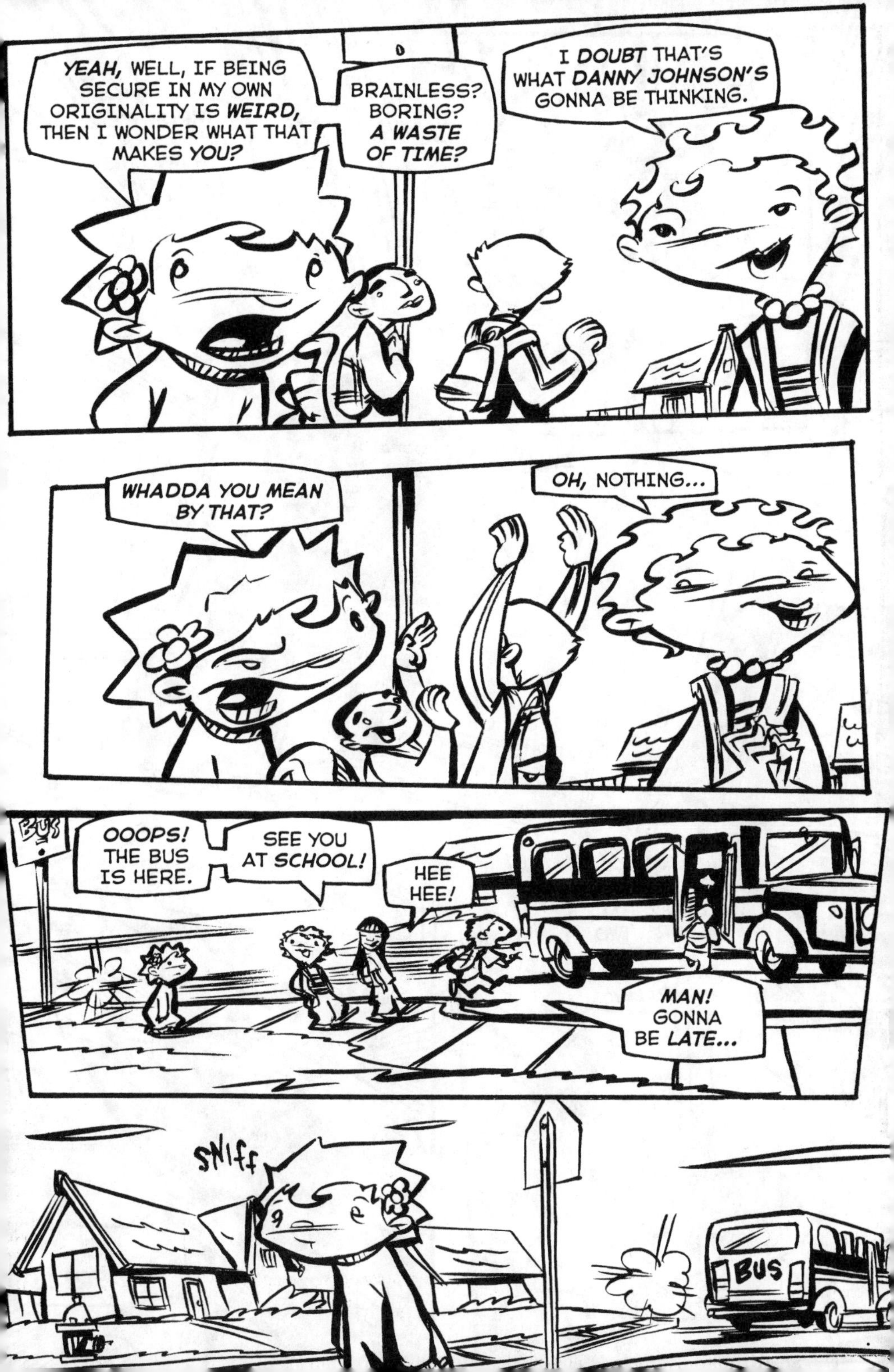
YEAH, WELL, IF BEING SECURE IN MY OWN ORIGINALITY IS WEIRD, THEN I WONDER WHAT THAT MAKES YOU?
BRAINLESS? BORING? A WASTE OF TIME?
I DOUBT THAT'S WHAT DANNY JOHNSON'S GONNA BE THINKING.
WHADDA YOU MEAN BY THAT?
OH, NOTHING...
BUS
OOOPS! THE BUS IS HERE.
SEE YOU AT SCHOOL!
HEE HEE!
MAN! GONNA BE LATE...
SNIFF
BUS

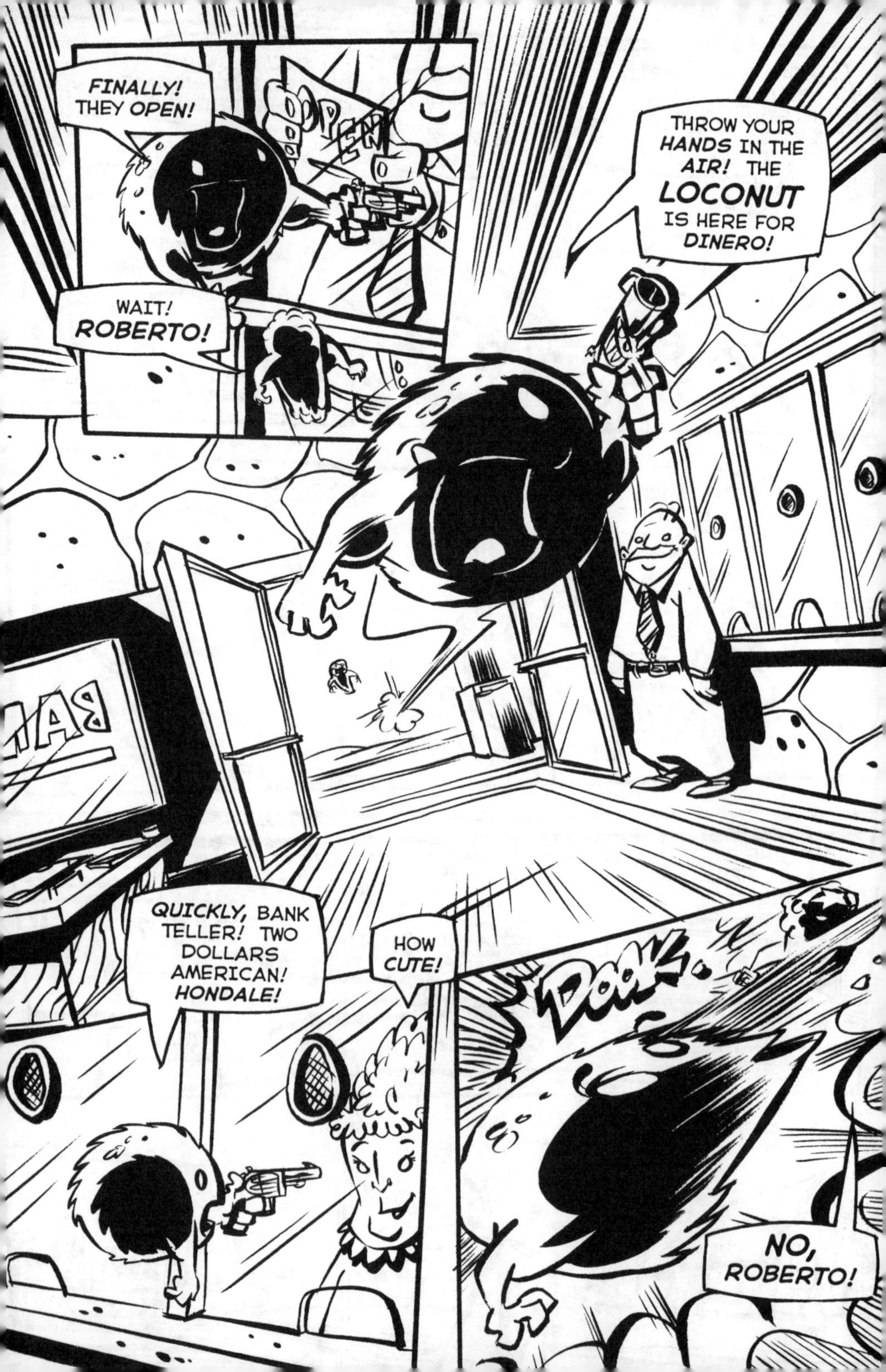
FINALLY! THEY OPEN!
OPEN
THROW YOUR HANDS IN THE AIR! THE LOCONUT IS HERE FOR DINERO!
WAIT! ROBERTO!
QUICKLY, BANK TELLER! TWO DOLLARS AMERICAN! HONDALE!
HOW CUTE!
DOOK!
NO, ROBERTO!

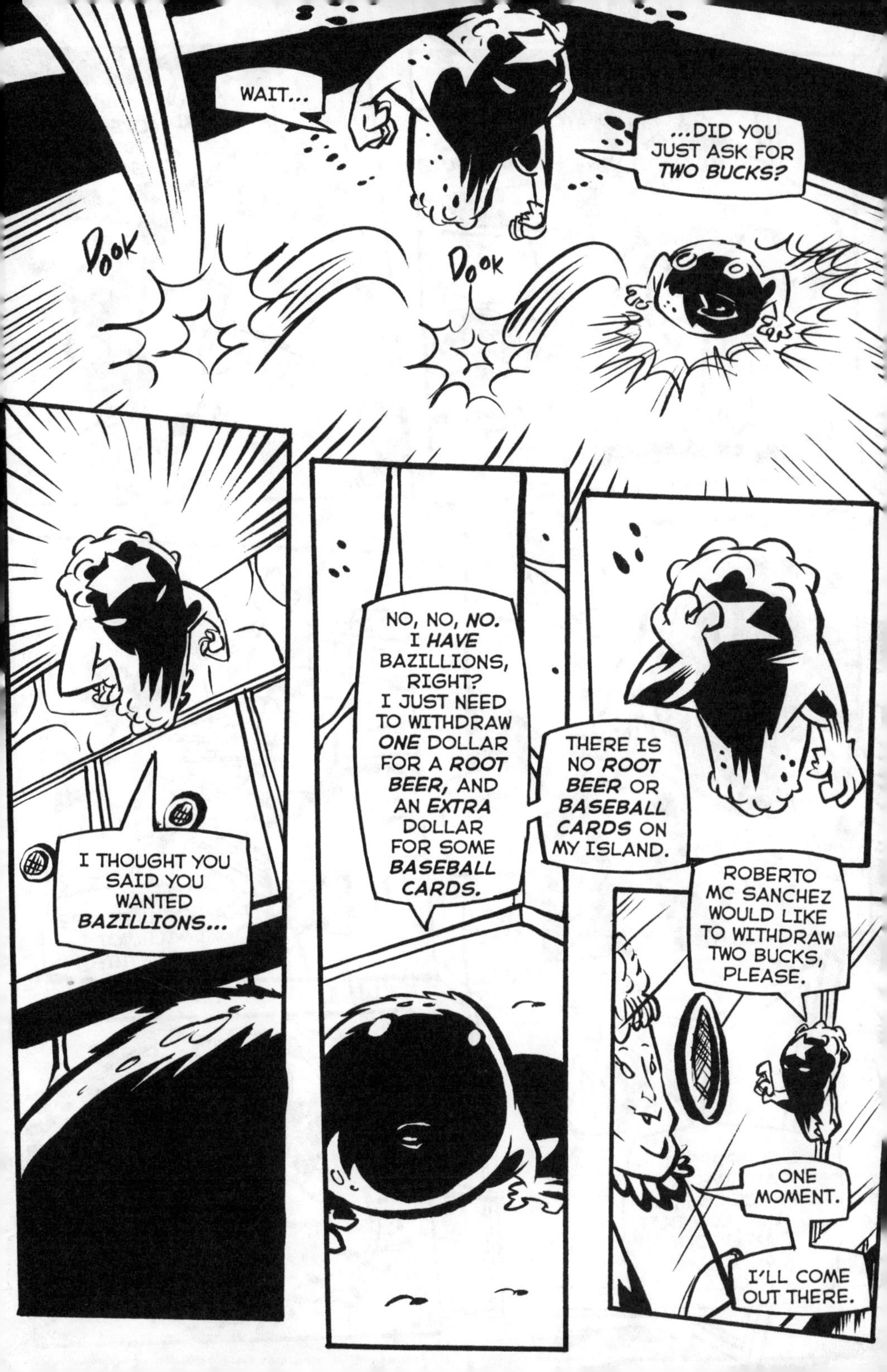
WAIT...
...DID YOU JUST ASK FOR *TWO BUCKS?*
DOOK
DOOK
I THOUGHT YOU SAID YOU WANTED *BAZILLIONS...*
NO, NO, *NO.* I *HAVE* BAZILLIONS, RIGHT? I JUST NEED TO WITHDRAW *ONE* DOLLAR FOR A *ROOT BEER,* AND AN *EXTRA* DOLLAR FOR SOME *BASEBALL CARDS.*
THERE IS NO *ROOT BEER* OR *BASEBALL CARDS* ON MY ISLAND.
ROBERTO MC SANCHEZ WOULD LIKE TO WITHDRAW TWO BUCKS, PLEASE.
ONE MOMENT.
I'LL COME OUT THERE.

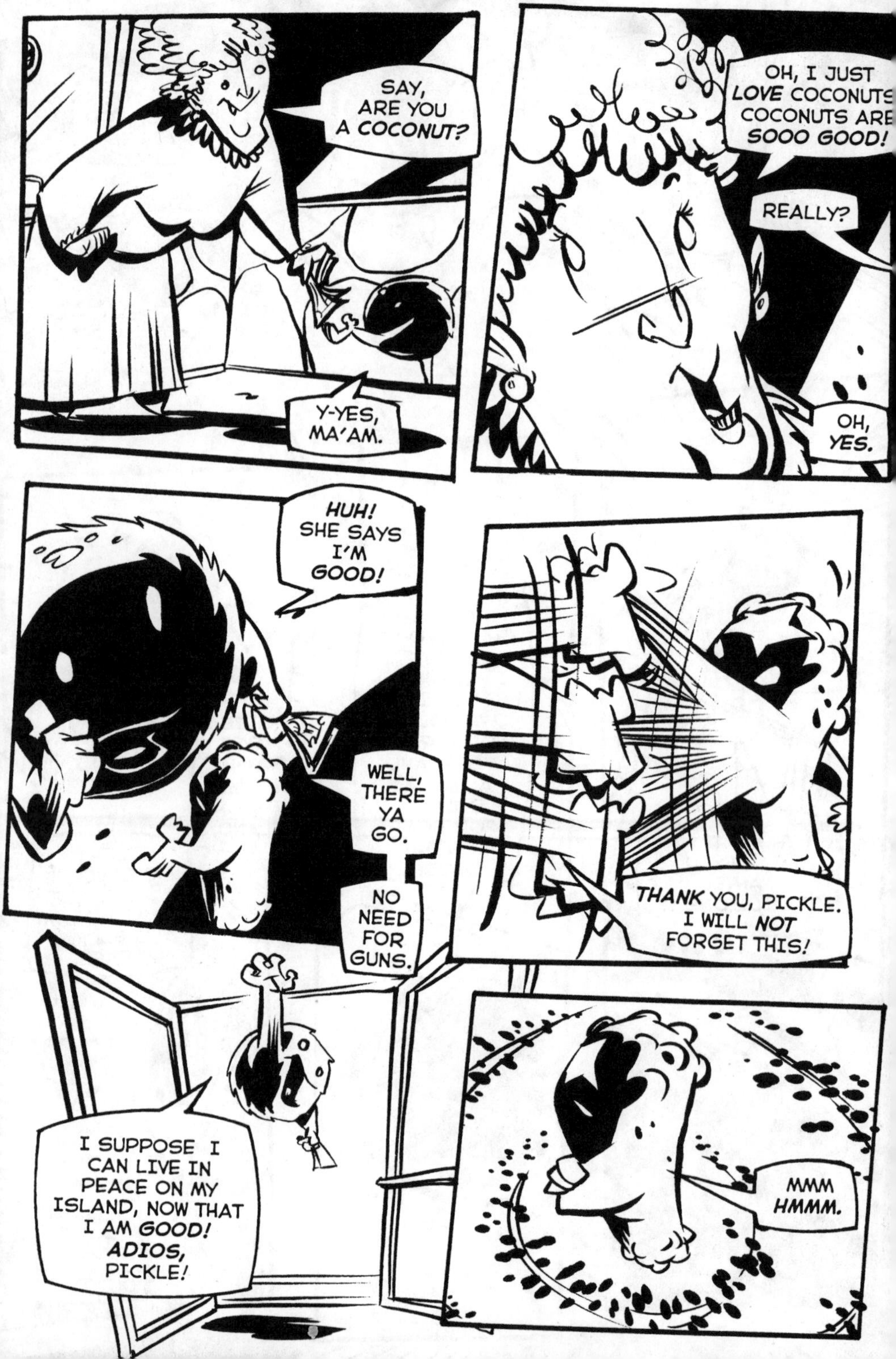

SAY, ARE YOU A COCONUT?
Y-YES, MA'AM.
OH, I JUST LOVE COCONUTS COCONUTS ARE SOOO GOOD!
REALLY?
OH, YES.
HUH! SHE SAYS I'M GOOD!
WELL, THERE YA GO.
NO NEED FOR GUNS.
THANK YOU, PICKLE. I WILL NOT FORGET THIS!
I SUPPOSE I CAN LIVE IN PEACE ON MY ISLAND, NOW THAT I AM GOOD! ADIOS, PICKLE!
MMM HMMM.

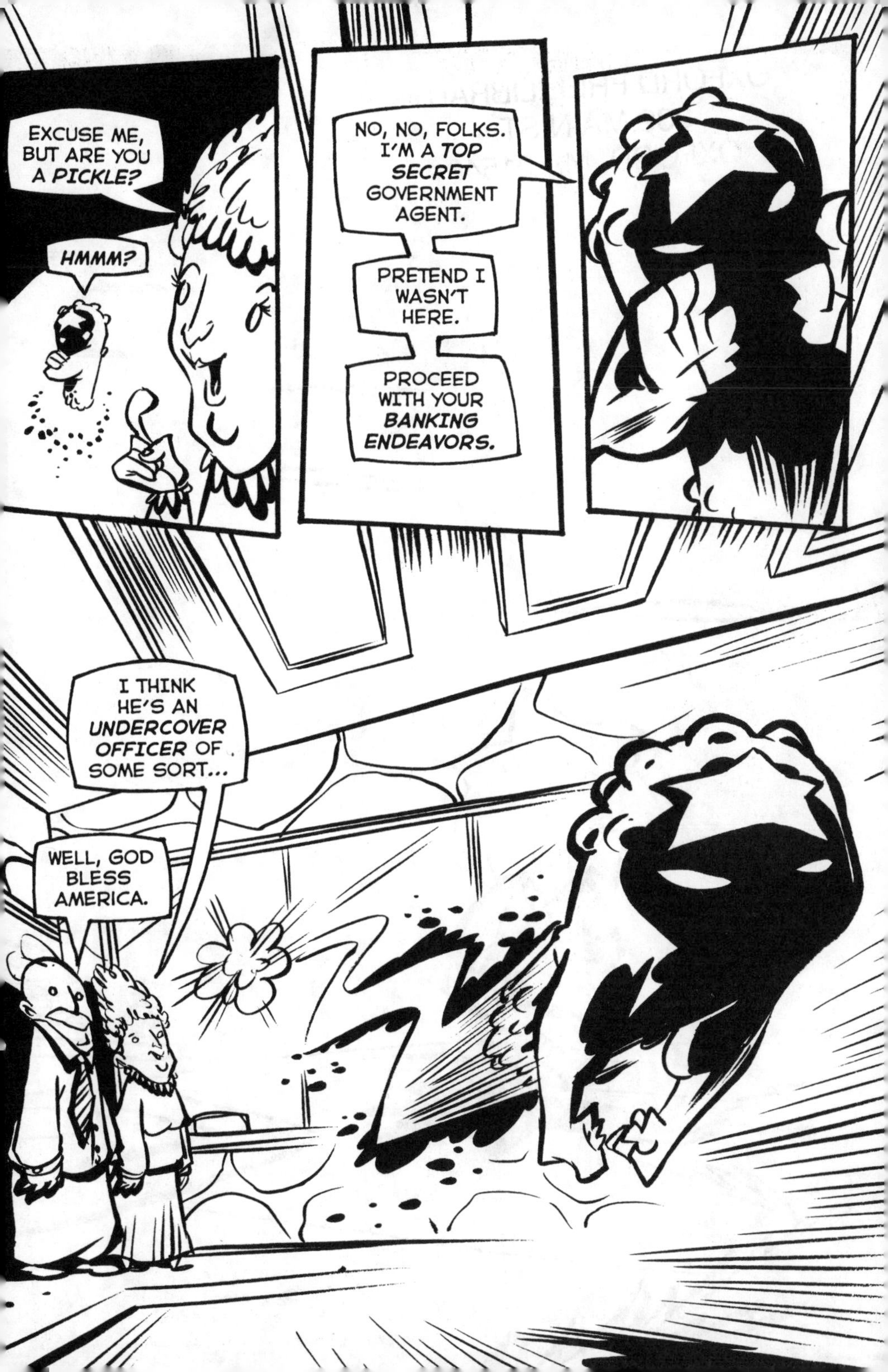
EXCUSE ME, BUT ARE YOU A *PICKLE?*
HMMM?
NO, NO, FOLKS. I'M A *TOP SECRET* GOVERNMENT AGENT.
PRETEND I WASN'T HERE.
PROCEED WITH YOUR *BANKING ENDEAVORS.*
I THINK HE'S AN *UNDERCOVER OFFICER* OF SOME SORT...
WELL, GOD BLESS AMERICA.

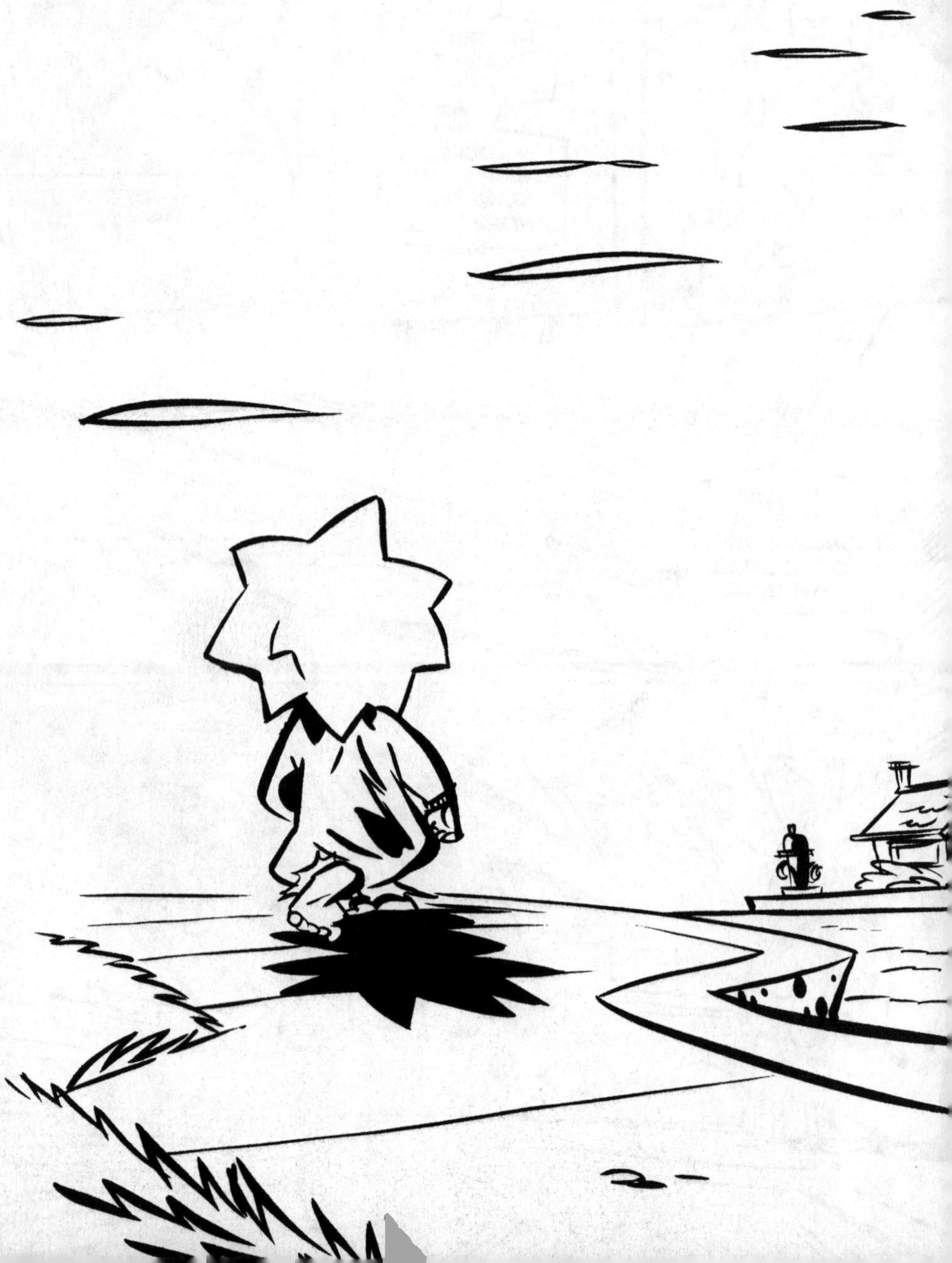

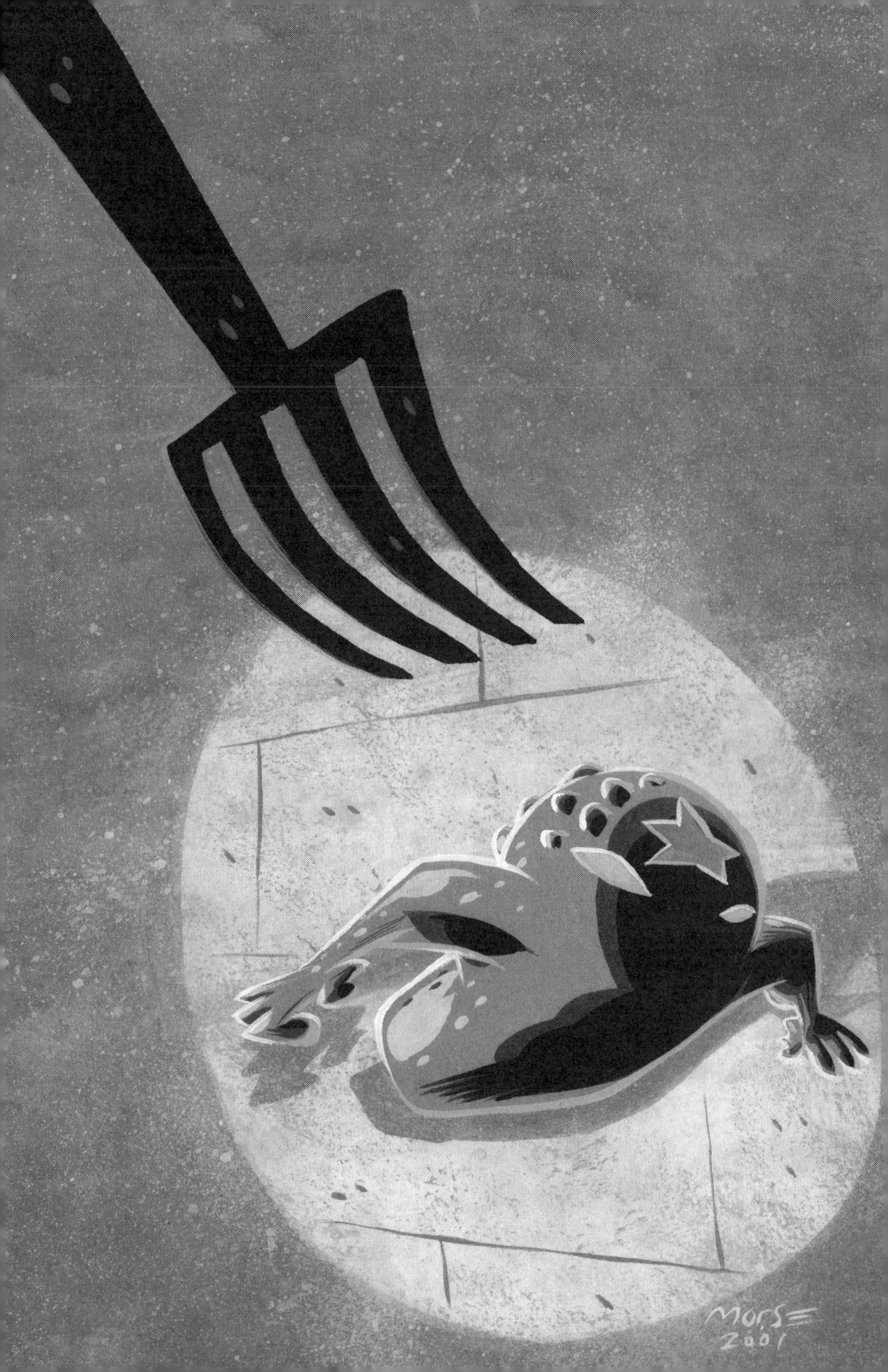
MORSE
2001

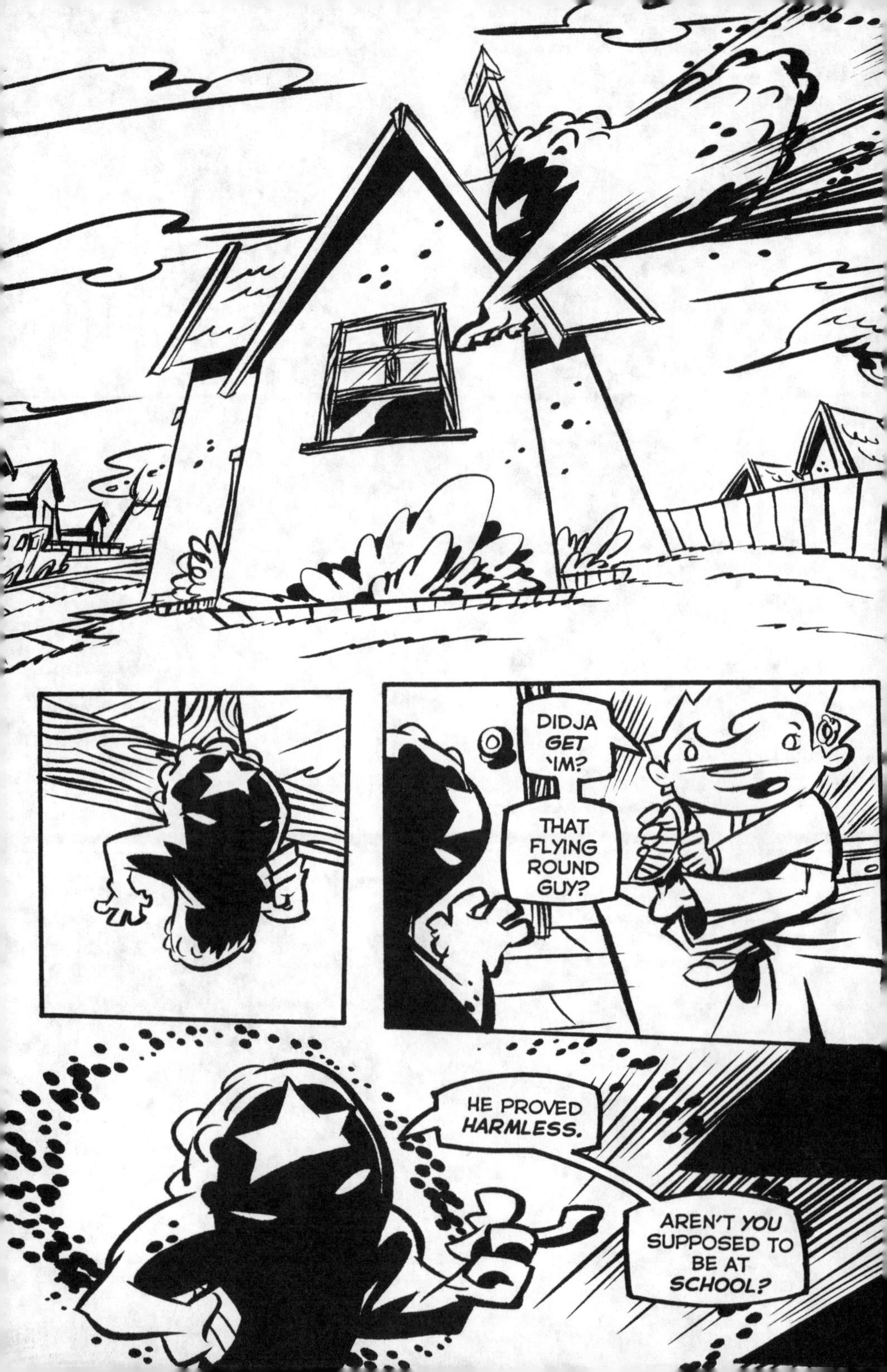
DIDJA GET 'IM?
THAT FLYING ROUND GUY?
HE PROVED HARMLESS.
AREN'T YOU SUPPOSED TO BE AT SCHOOL?

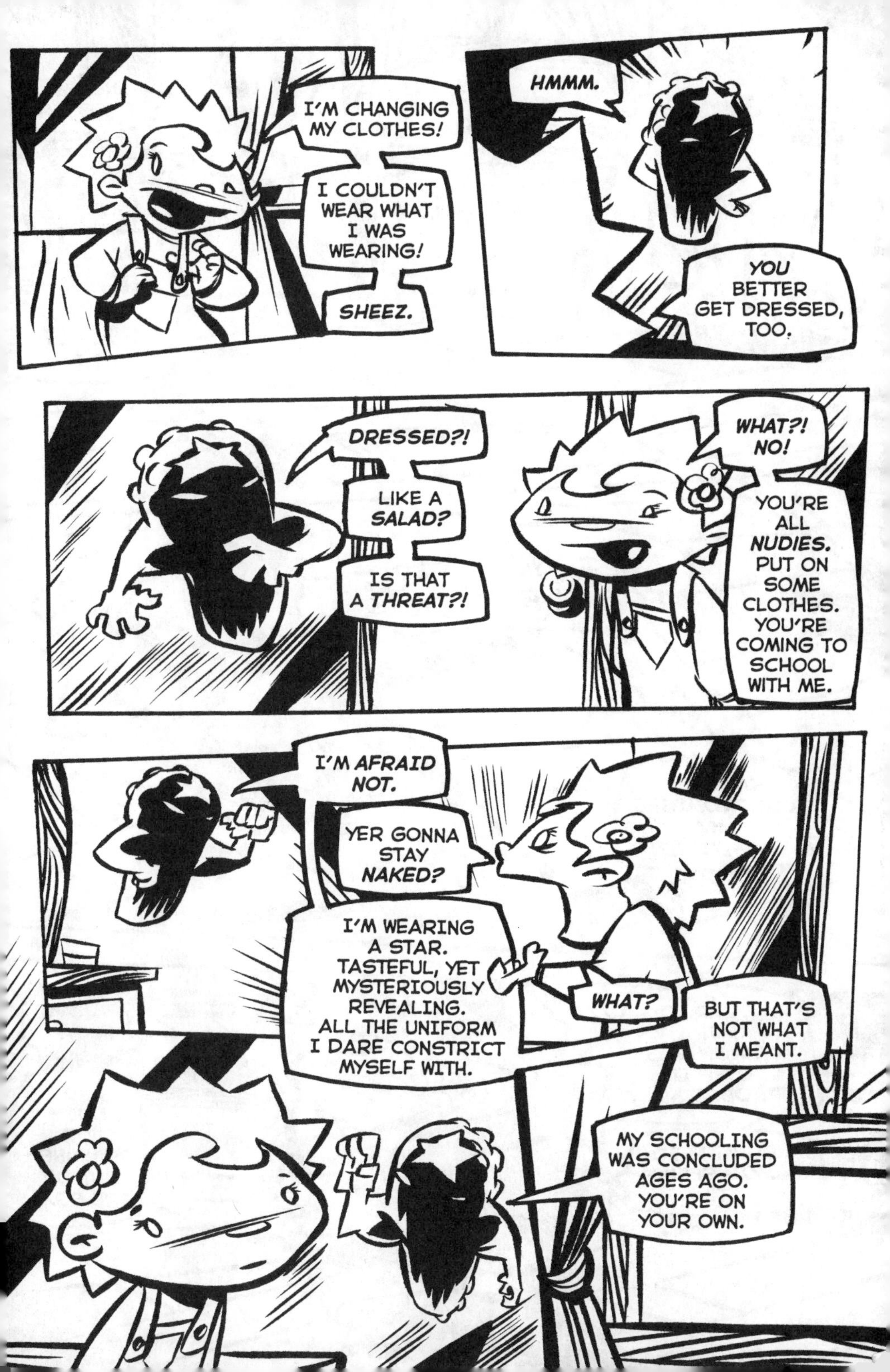
I'M CHANGING MY CLOTHES!
I COULDN'T WEAR WHAT I WAS WEARING!
SHEEZ.
HMMM.
YOU BETTER GET DRESSED, TOO.
DRESSED?!
LIKE A SALAD?
IS THAT A THREAT?!
WHAT?! NO!
YOU'RE ALL NUDIES. PUT ON SOME CLOTHES. YOU'RE COMING TO SCHOOL WITH ME.
I'M AFRAID NOT.
YER GONNA STAY NAKED?
I'M WEARING A STAR. TASTEFUL, YET MYSTERIOUSLY REVEALING. ALL THE UNIFORM I DARE CONSTRICT MYSELF WITH.
WHAT?
BUT THAT'S NOT WHAT I MEANT.
MY SCHOOLING WAS CONCLUDED AGES AGO. YOU'RE ON YOUR OWN.

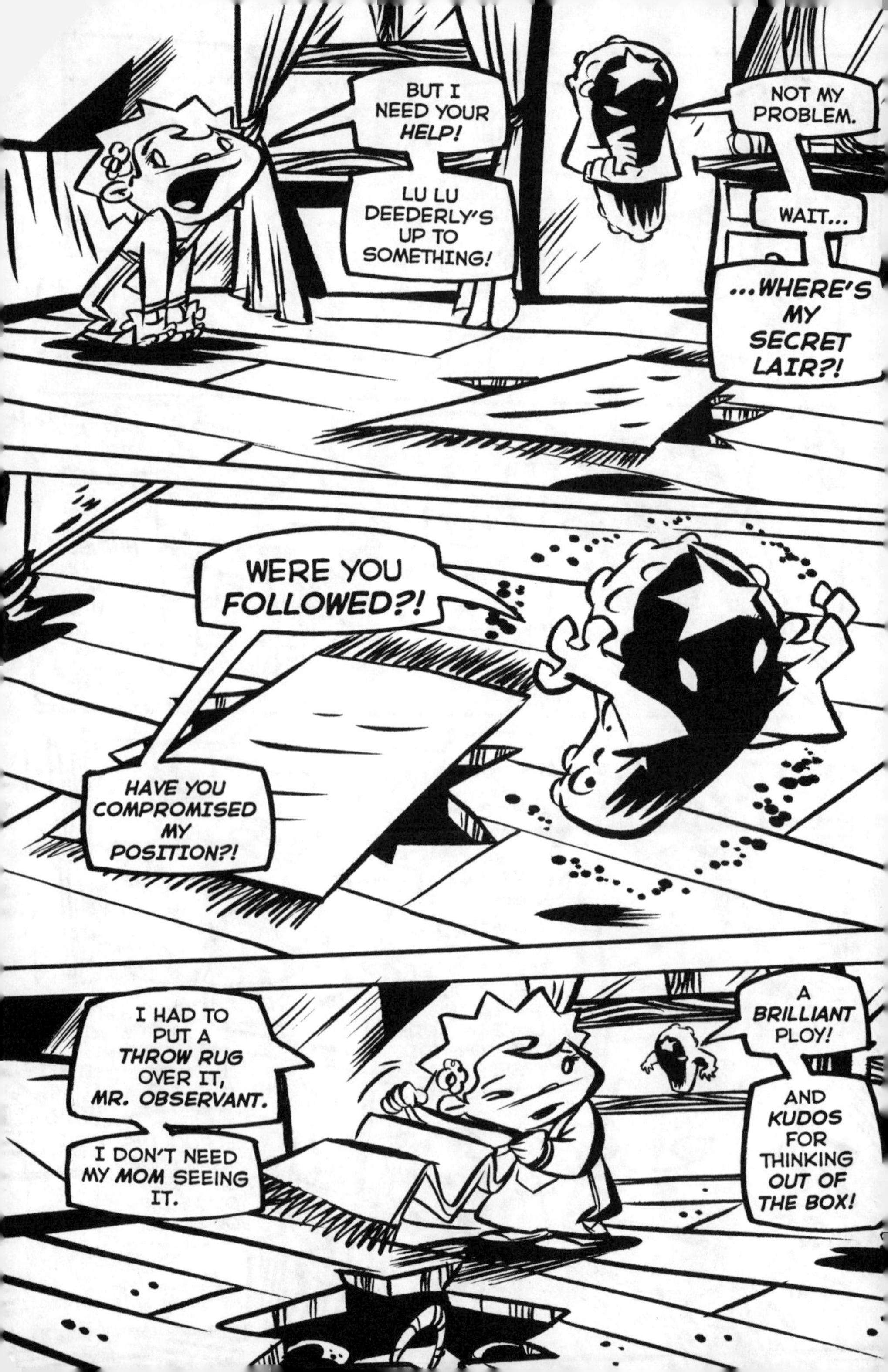
BUT I NEED YOUR HELP!
LU LU DEEDERLY'S UP TO SOMETHING!
NOT MY PROBLEM.
WAIT...
...WHERE'S MY SECRET LAIR?!
WERE YOU FOLLOWED?!
HAVE YOU COMPROMISED MY POSITION?!
I HAD TO PUT A THROW RUG OVER IT, MR. OBSERVANT.
I DON'T NEED MY MOM SEEING IT.
A BRILLIANT PLOY!
AND KUDOS FOR THINKING OUT OF THE BOX!

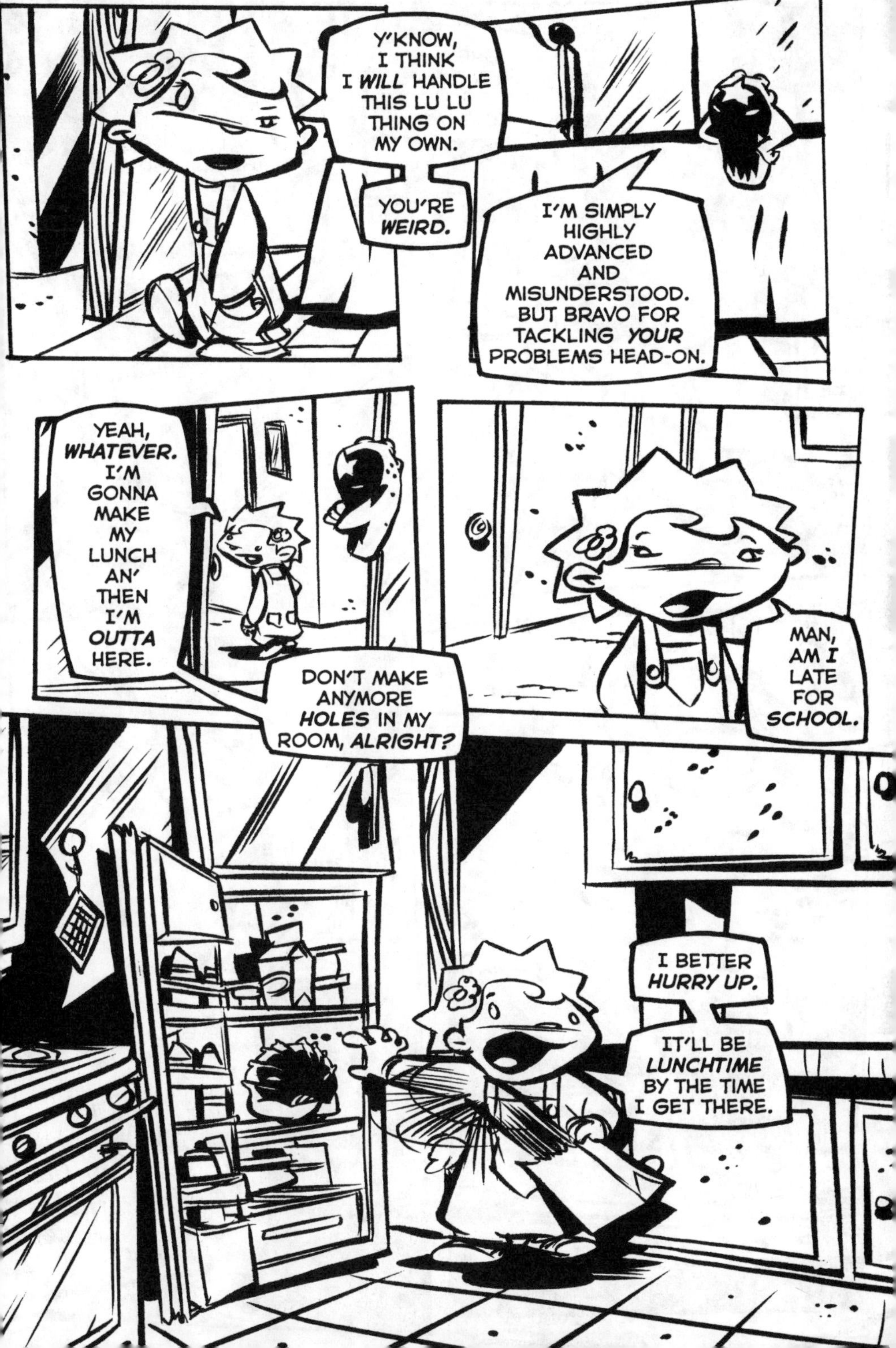
Y'KNOW, I THINK I *WILL* HANDLE THIS LU LU THING ON MY OWN.
YOU'RE *WEIRD.*
I'M SIMPLY HIGHLY ADVANCED AND MISUNDERSTOOD. BUT BRAVO FOR TACKLING *YOUR* PROBLEMS HEAD-ON.
YEAH, *WHATEVER.* I'M GONNA MAKE MY LUNCH AN' THEN I'M *OUTTA* HERE.
DON'T MAKE ANYMORE *HOLES* IN MY ROOM, *ALRIGHT?*
MAN, AM *I* LATE FOR *SCHOOL.*
I BETTER *HURRY UP.*
IT'LL BE *LUNCHTIME* BY THE TIME I GET THERE.

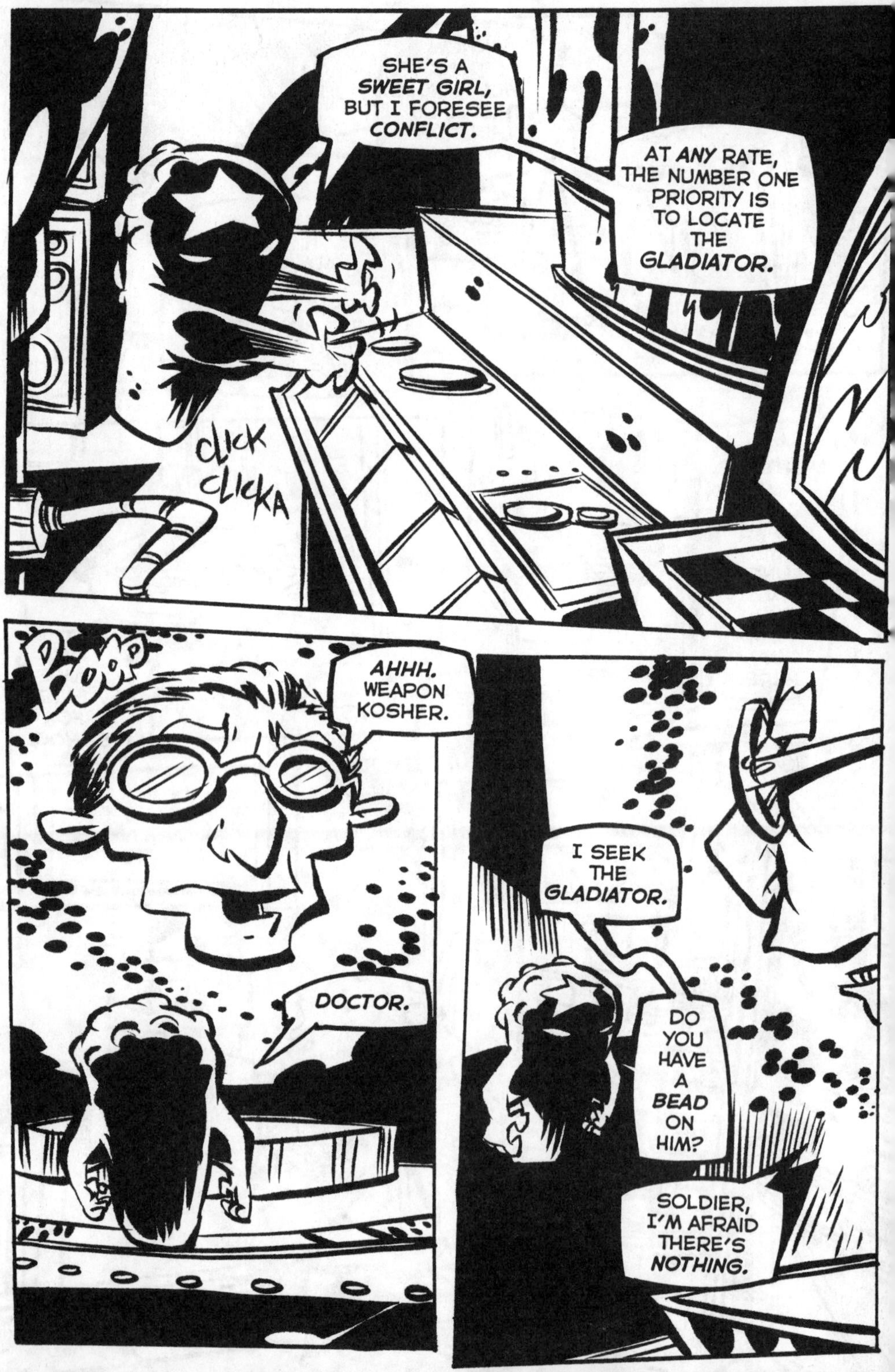
SHE'S A *SWEET GIRL,* BUT I FORESEE *CONFLICT.*
AT *ANY* RATE, THE NUMBER ONE PRIORITY IS TO LOCATE THE *GLADIATOR.*
CLICK CLICKA
BOOP
AHHH. WEAPON KOSHER.
DOCTOR.
I SEEK THE *GLADIATOR.*
DO YOU HAVE A *BEAD* ON HIM?
SOLDIER, I'M AFRAID THERE'S *NOTHING.*

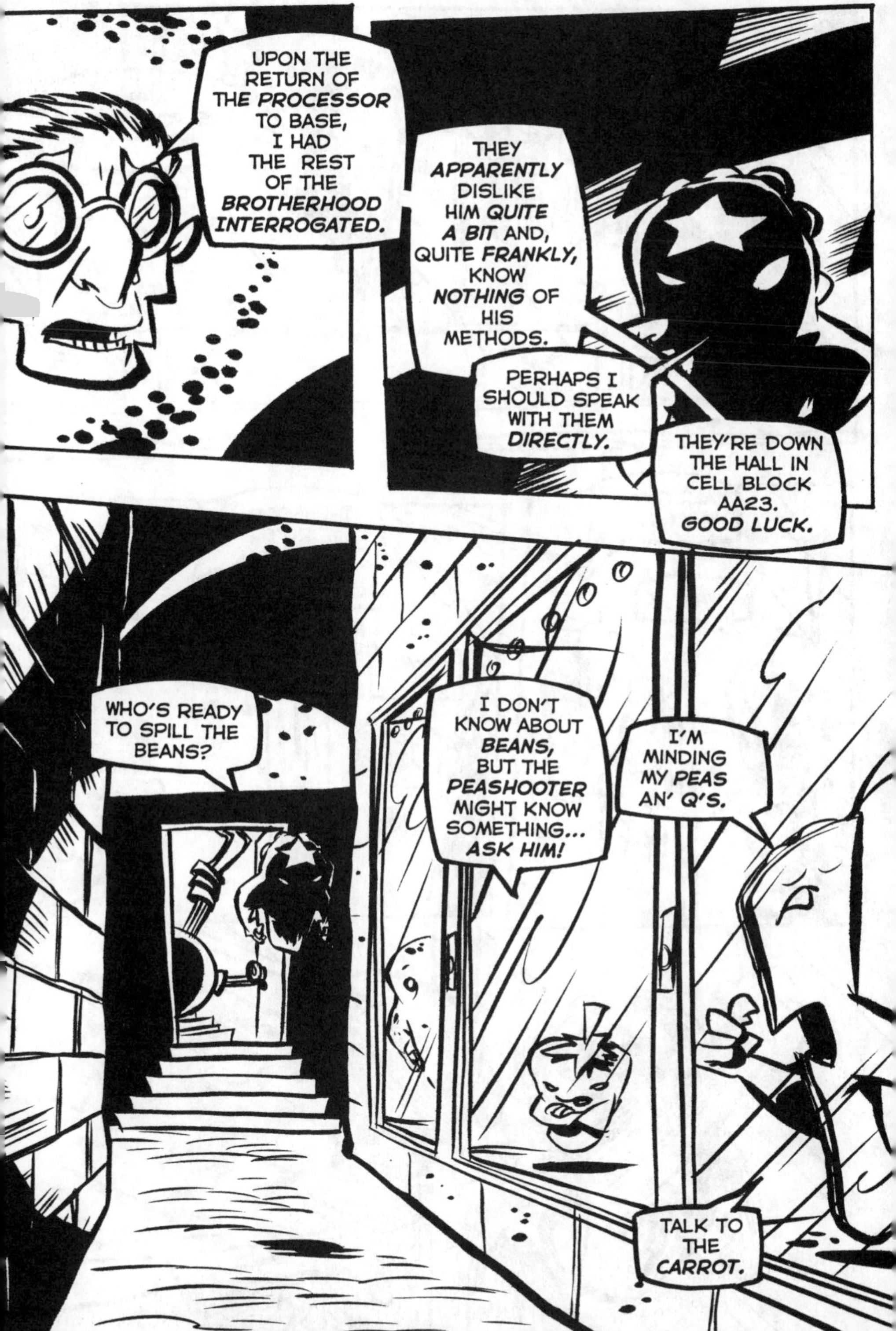
UPON THE RETURN OF THE PROCESSOR TO BASE, I HAD THE REST OF THE BROTHERHOOD INTERROGATED.
THEY APPARENTLY DISLIKE HIM QUITE A BIT AND, QUITE FRANKLY, KNOW NOTHING OF HIS METHODS.
PERHAPS I SHOULD SPEAK WITH THEM DIRECTLY.
THEY'RE DOWN THE HALL IN CELL BLOCK AA23. GOOD LUCK.
WHO'S READY TO SPILL THE BEANS?
I DON'T KNOW ABOUT BEANS, BUT THE PEASHOOTER MIGHT KNOW SOMETHING... ASK HIM!
I'M MINDING MY PEAS AN' Q'S.
TALK TO THE CARROT.

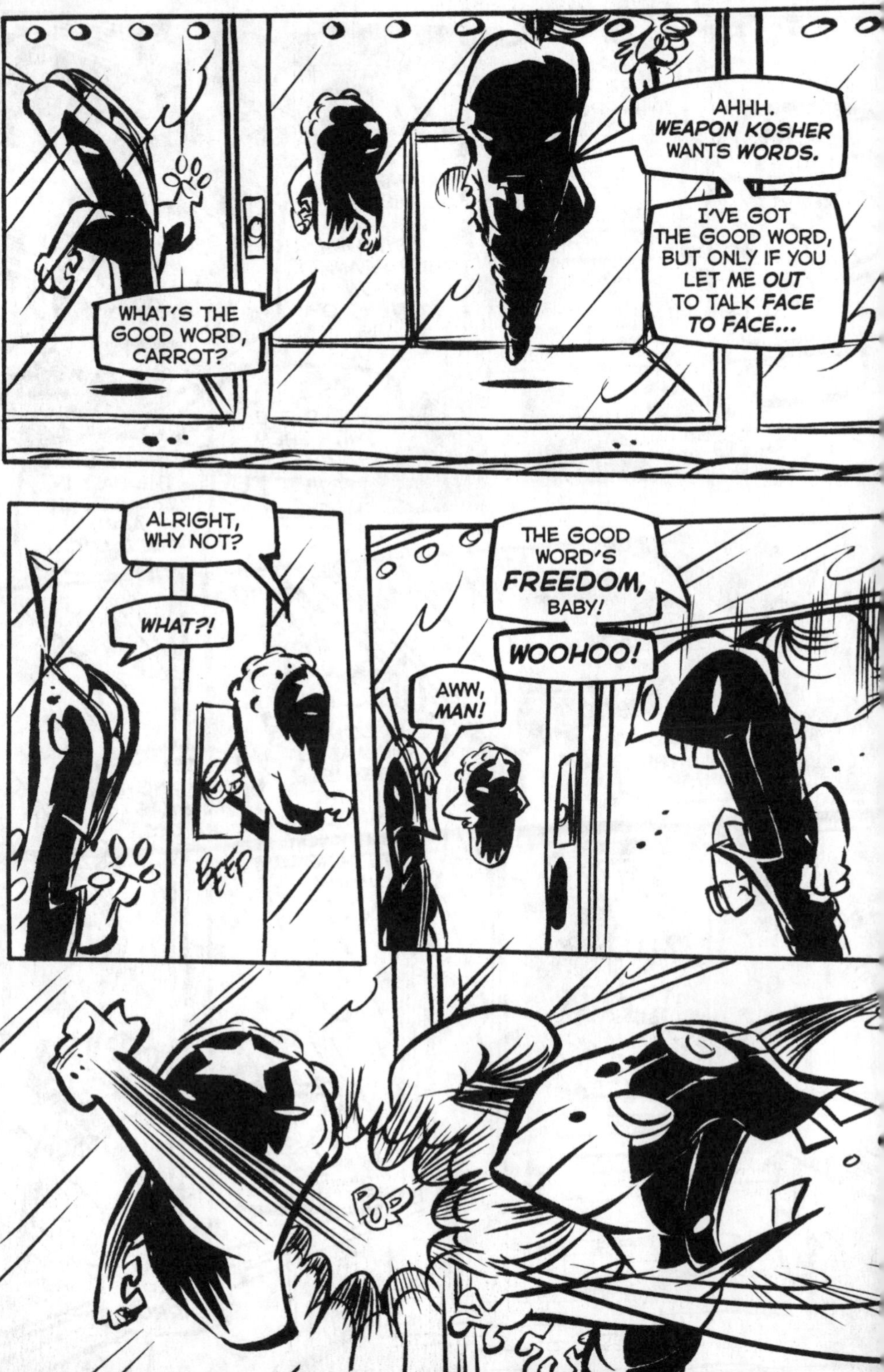
WHAT'S THE GOOD WORD, CARROT?
AHHH. WEAPON KOSHER WANTS WORDS.
I'VE GOT THE GOOD WORD, BUT ONLY IF YOU LET ME OUT TO TALK FACE TO FACE...
ALRIGHT, WHY NOT?
WHAT?!
BEEP
THE GOOD WORD'S FREEDOM, BABY!
WOOHOO!
AWW, MAN!
POP

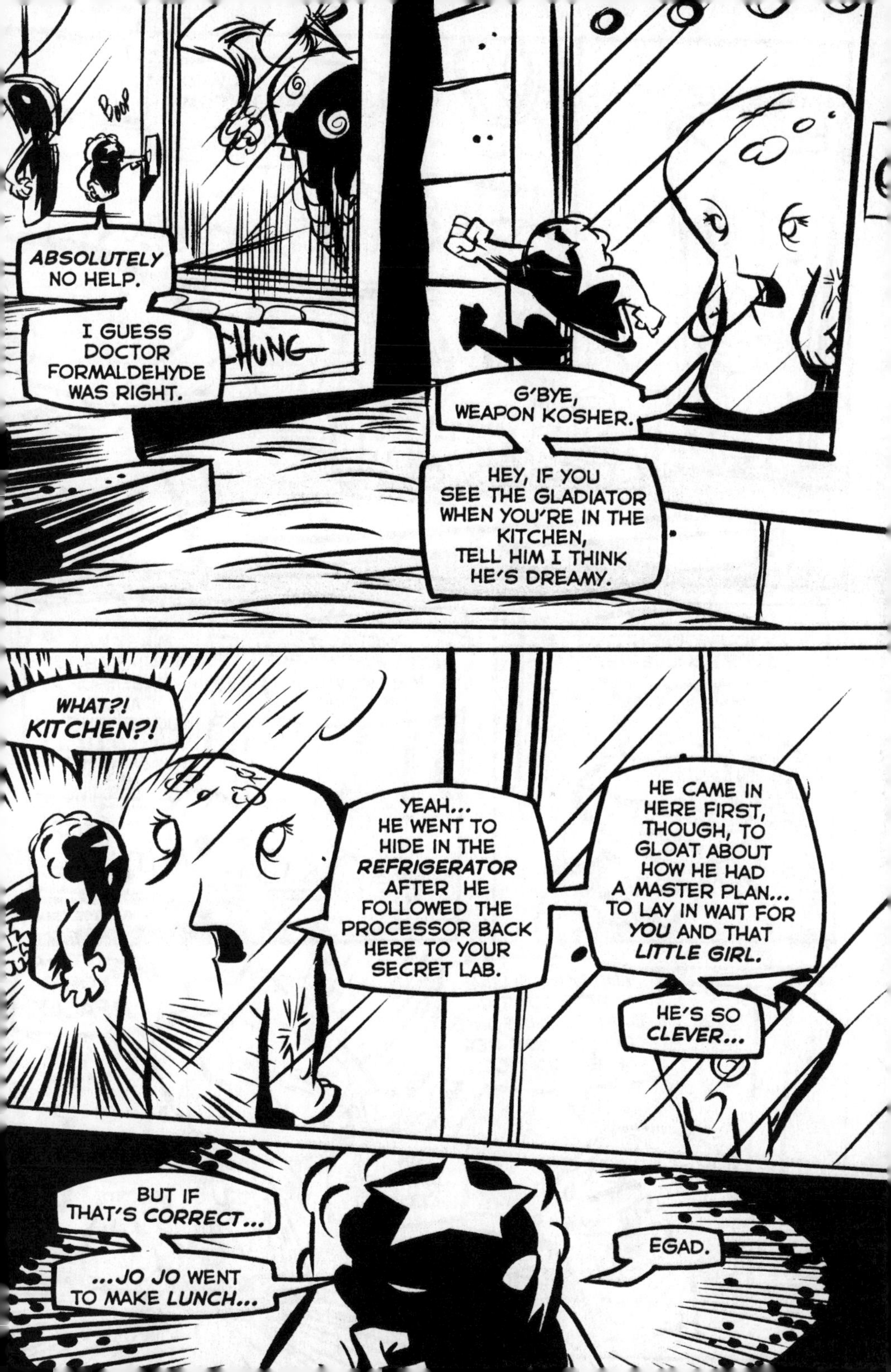
ABSOLUTELY NO HELP.
I GUESS DOCTOR FORMALDEHYDE WAS RIGHT.
CHUNG
G'BYE, WEAPON KOSHER.
HEY, IF YOU SEE THE GLADIATOR WHEN YOU'RE IN THE KITCHEN, TELL HIM I THINK HE'S DREAMY.
WHAT?! KITCHEN?!
YEAH... HE WENT TO HIDE IN THE *REFRIGERATOR* AFTER HE FOLLOWED THE PROCESSOR BACK HERE TO YOUR SECRET LAB.
HE CAME IN HERE FIRST, THOUGH, TO GLOAT ABOUT HOW HE HAD A MASTER PLAN... TO LAY IN WAIT FOR *YOU* AND THAT *LITTLE GIRL*.
HE'S SO *CLEVER*...
BUT IF THAT'S *CORRECT*...
...JO JO WENT TO MAKE *LUNCH*...
EGAD.

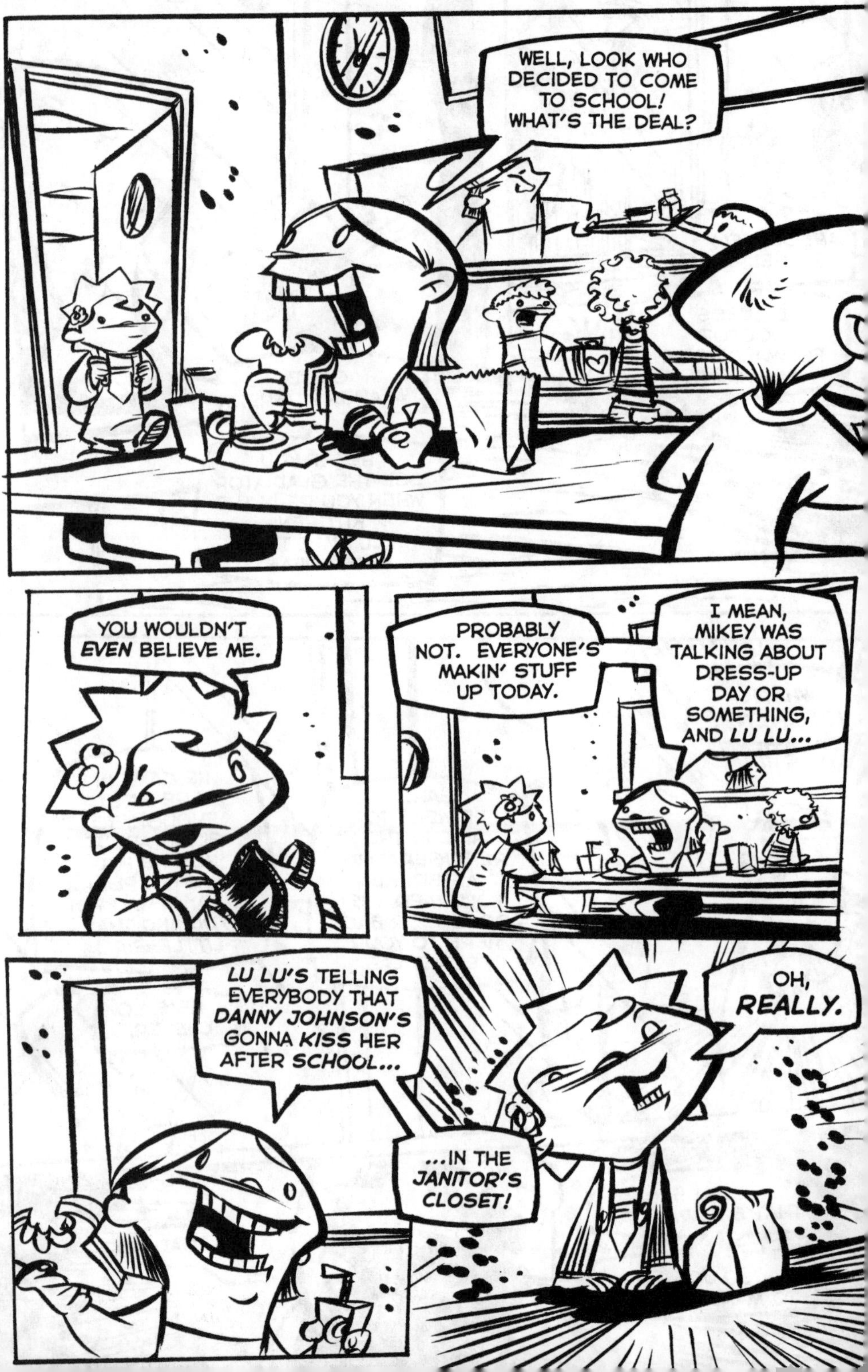
WELL, LOOK WHO DECIDED TO COME TO SCHOOL! WHAT'S THE DEAL?
YOU WOULDN'T *EVEN* BELIEVE ME.
PROBABLY NOT. EVERYONE'S MAKIN' STUFF UP TODAY.
I MEAN, MIKEY WAS TALKING ABOUT DRESS-UP DAY OR SOMETHING, AND *LU LU*...
LU LU'S TELLING EVERYBODY THAT *DANNY JOHNSON'S* GONNA *KISS* HER AFTER *SCHOOL*...
...IN THE *JANITOR'S* *CLOSET!*
OH, *REALLY.*

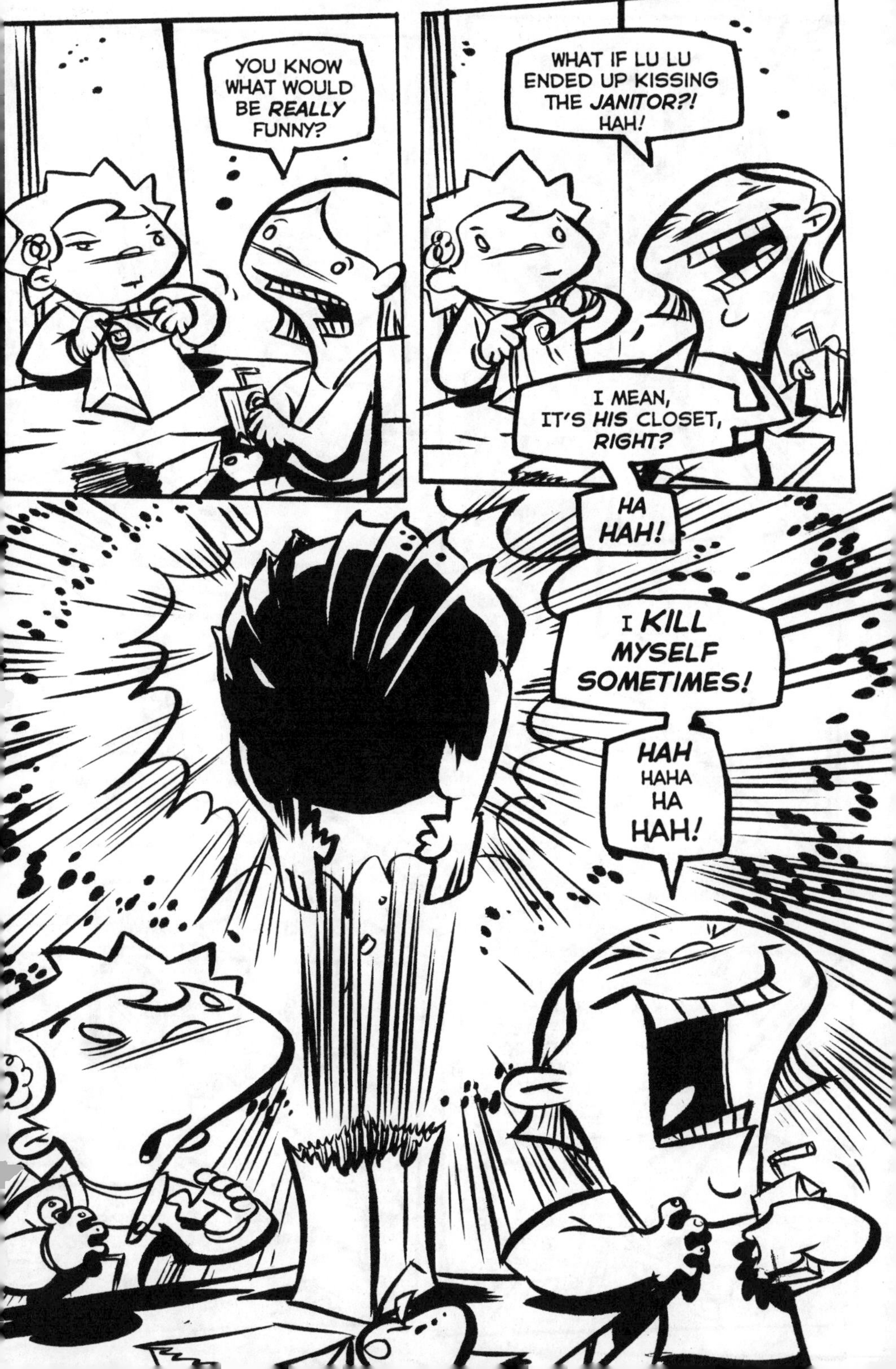
YOU KNOW WHAT WOULD BE *REALLY* FUNNY?
WHAT IF LU LU ENDED UP KISSING THE *JANITOR?!* HAH!
I MEAN, IT'S *HIS* CLOSET, *RIGHT?*
HA HAH!
I **KILL MYSELF SOMETIMES!**
HAH HAHA HA HAH!

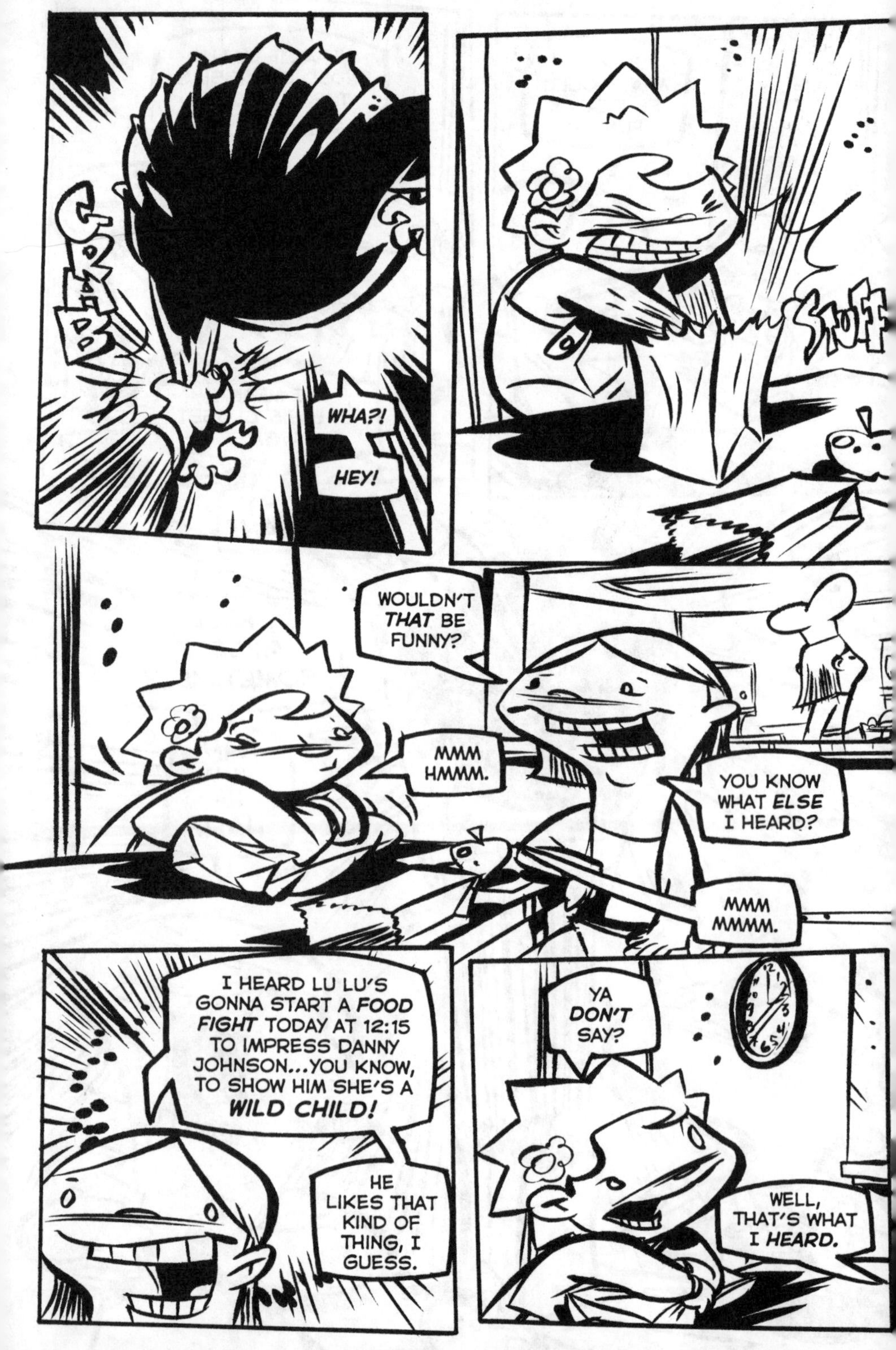
WHA?!
HEY!
STUFF
WOULDN'T THAT BE FUNNY?
MMM HMMM.
YOU KNOW WHAT ELSE I HEARD?
MMM MMMM.
I HEARD LU LU'S GONNA START A FOOD FIGHT TODAY AT 12:15 TO IMPRESS DANNY JOHNSON...YOU KNOW, TO SHOW HIM SHE'S A WILD CHILD!
HE LIKES THAT KIND OF THING, I GUESS.
YA DON'T SAY?
WELL, THAT'S WHAT I HEARD.

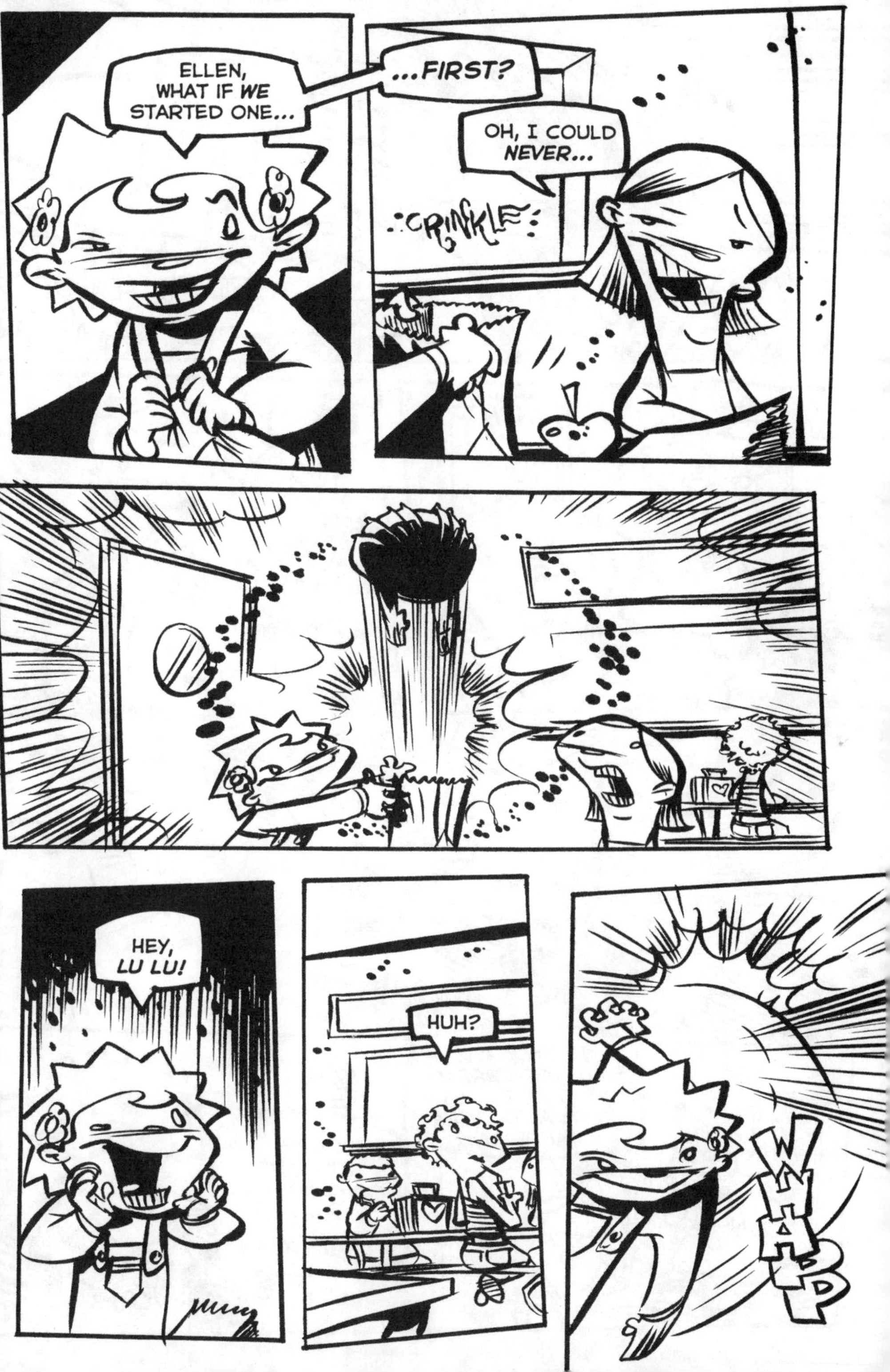
ELLEN, WHAT IF WE STARTED ONE...
...FIRST?
OH, I COULD NEVER...
CRINKLE
HEY, LU LU!
HUH?
WHAP

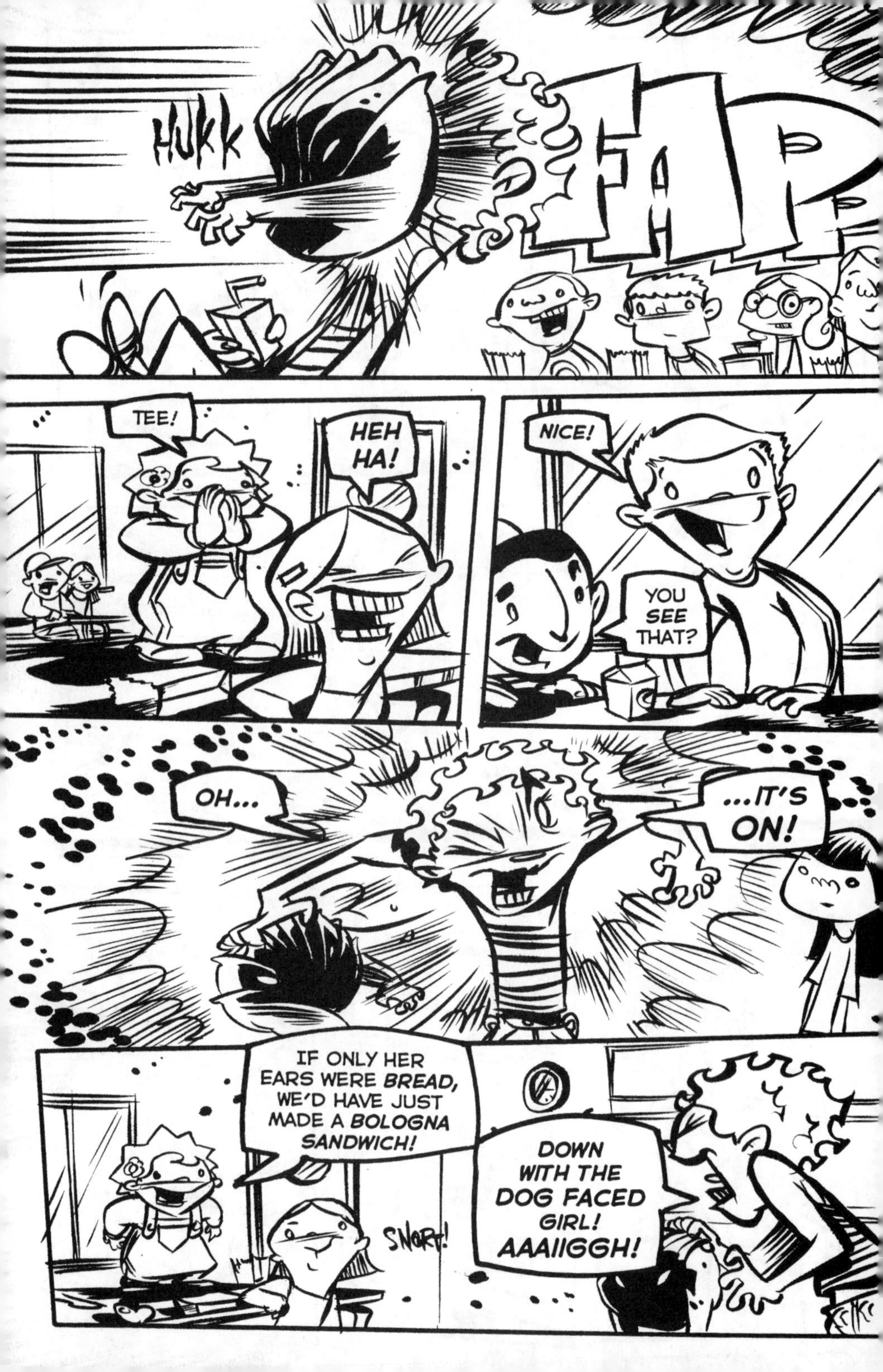
HUKK
FAP
TEE!
HEH HA!
NICE!
YOU SEE THAT?
OH...
...IT'S ON!
IF ONLY HER EARS WERE BREAD, WE'D HAVE JUST MADE A BOLOGNA SANDWICH!
SNORT!
DOWN WITH THE DOG FACED GIRL! AAAIIGGH!

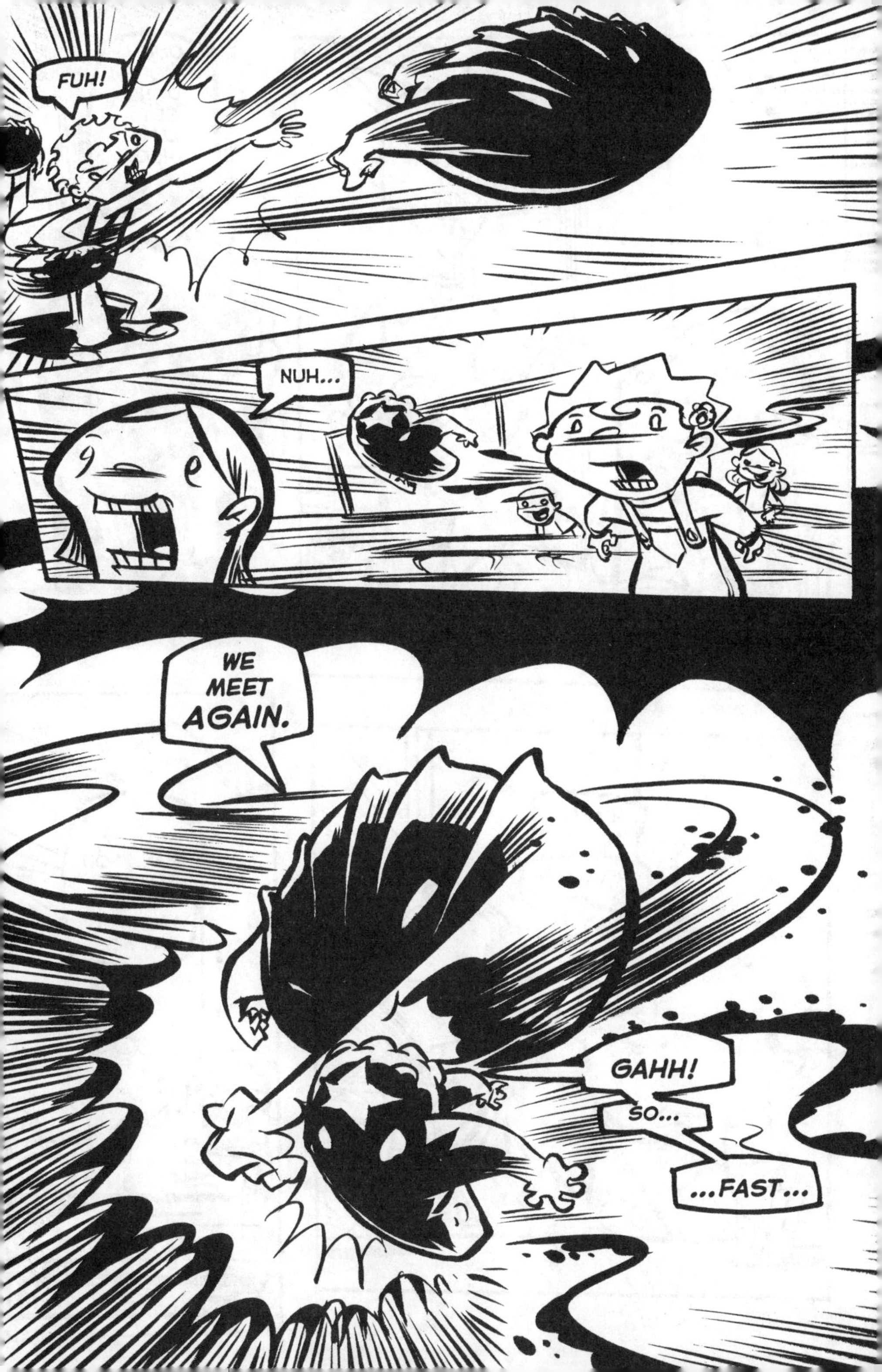
FUH!
NUH...
WE MEET AGAIN.
GAHH!
SO...
...FAST...

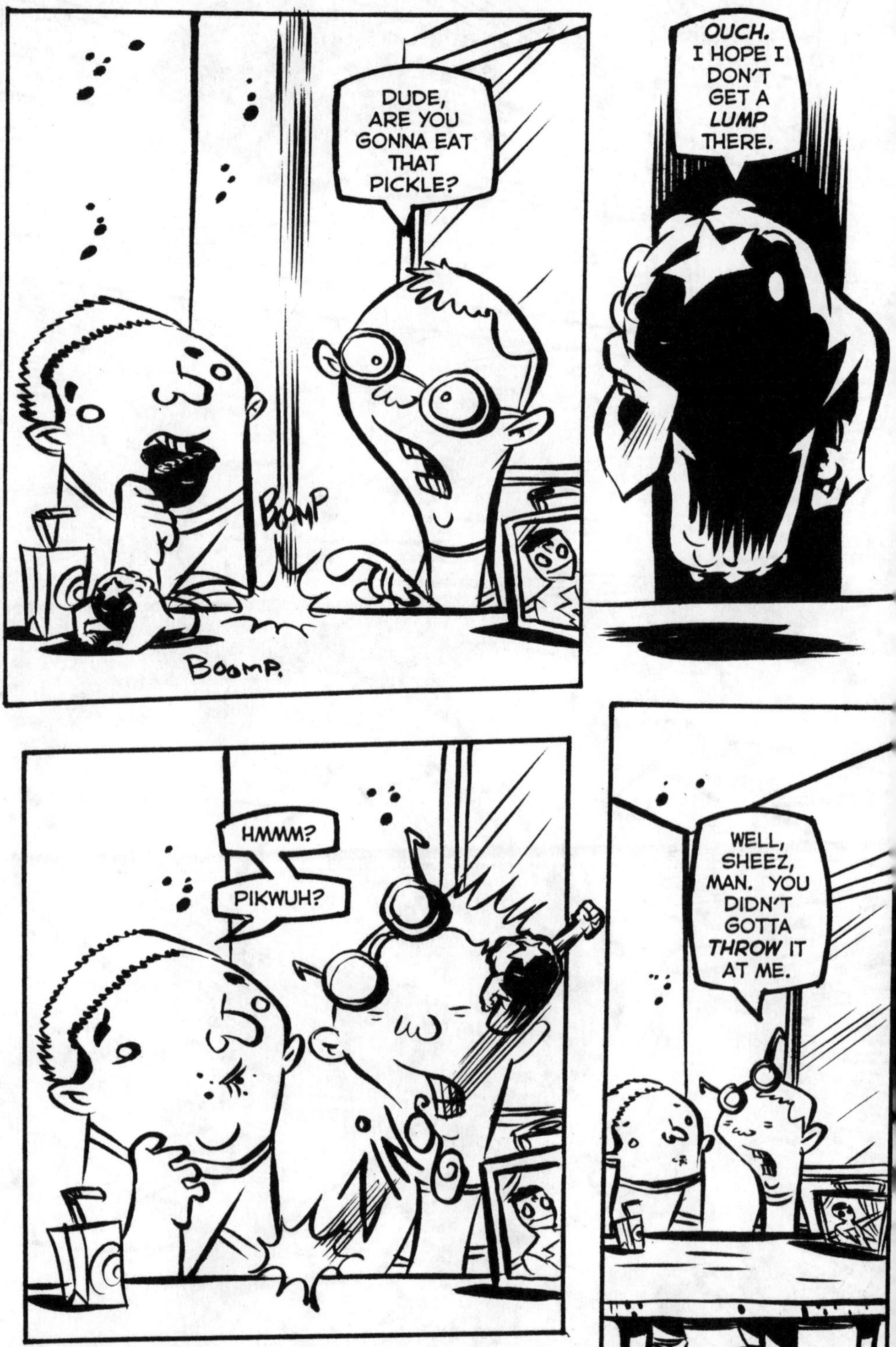
DUDE, ARE YOU GONNA EAT THAT PICKLE?
BOOMP
BOOMP.
OUCH. I HOPE I DON'T GET A LUMP THERE.
HMMM?
PIKWUH?
ZING
WELL, SHEEZ, MAN. YOU DIDN'T GOTTA THROW IT AT ME.

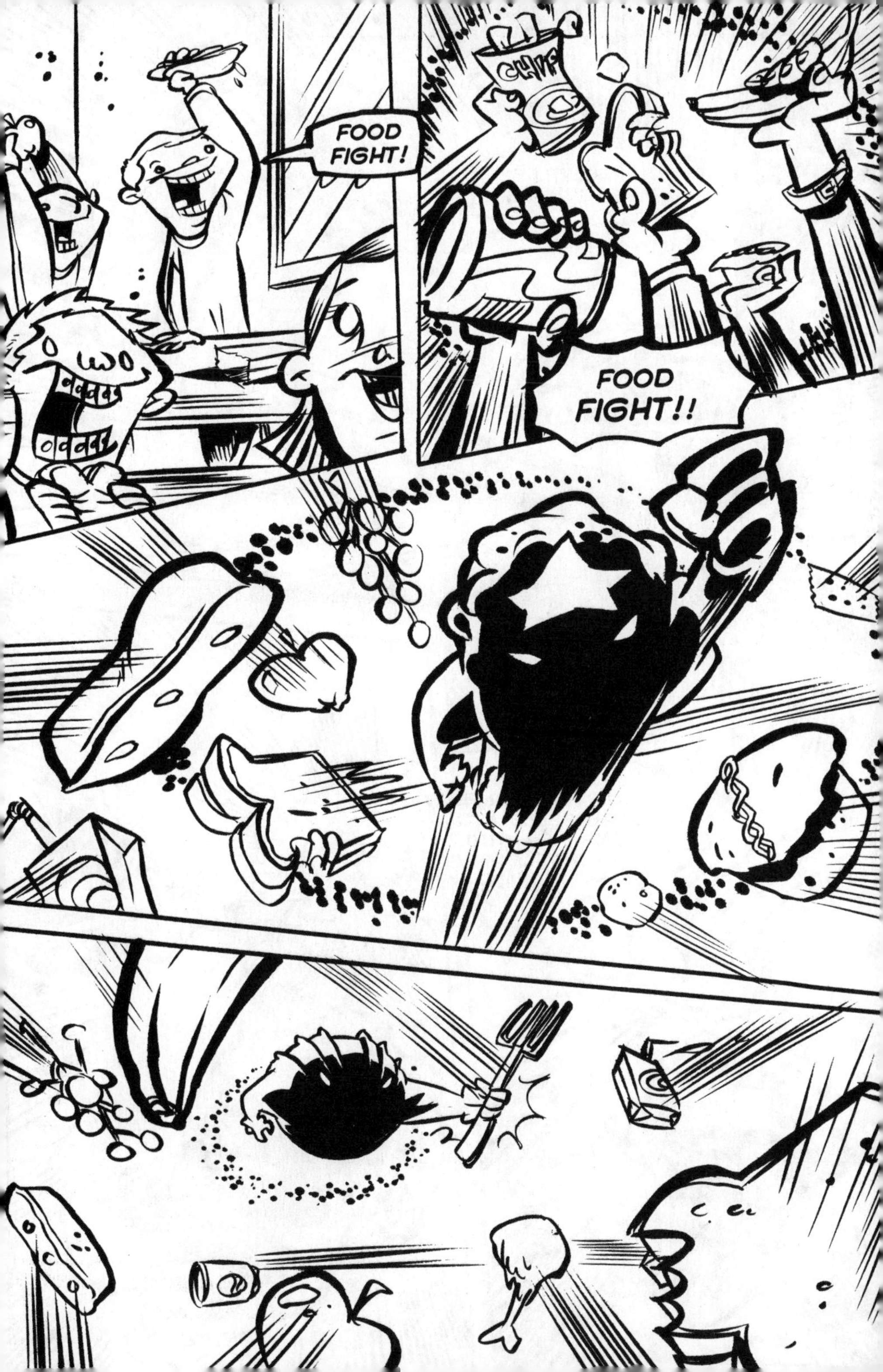
FOOD FIGHT!
FOOD FIGHT!!

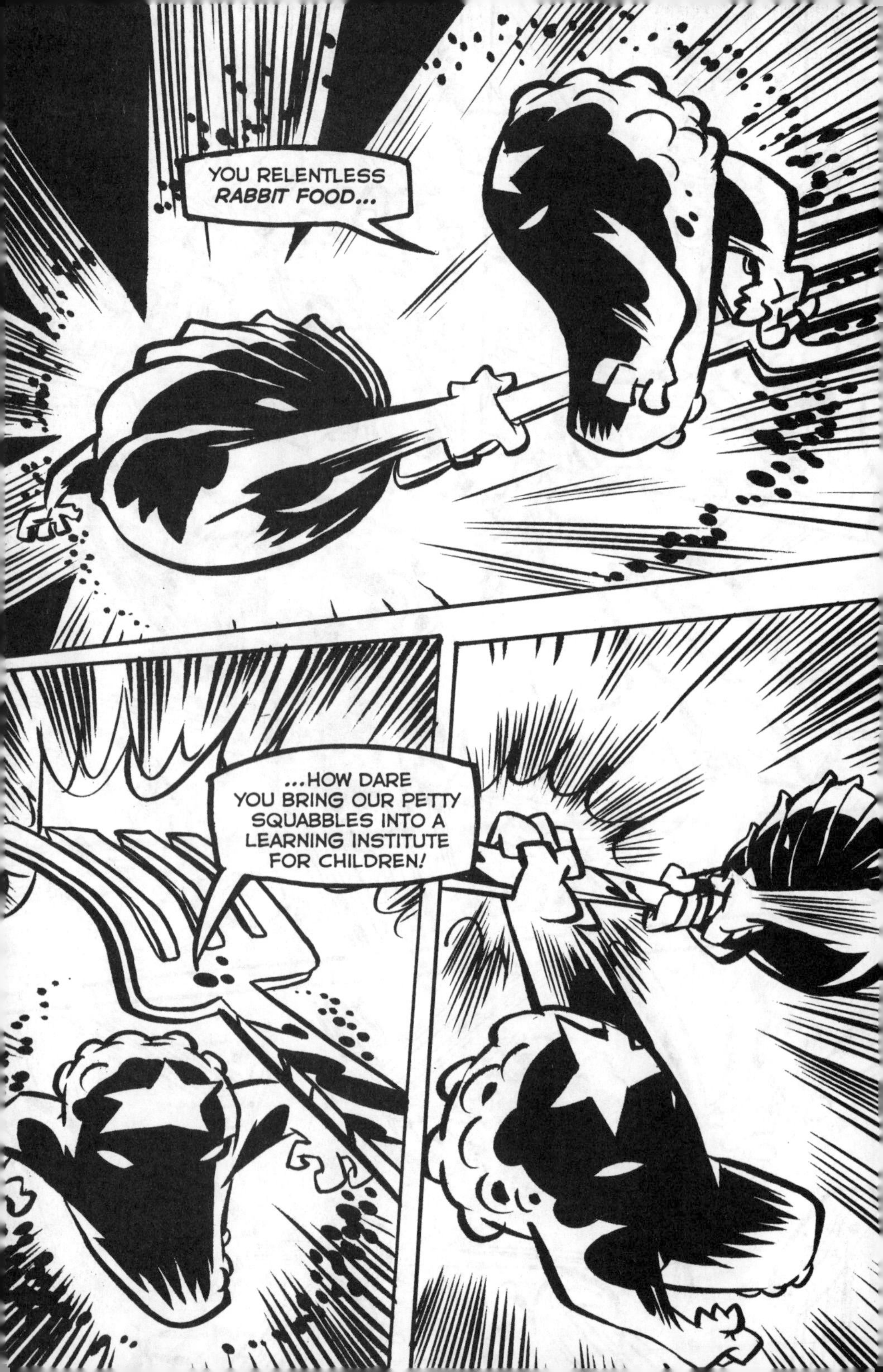

YOU RELENTLESS RABBIT FOOD...
...HOW DARE YOU BRING OUR PETTY SQUABBLES INTO A LEARNING INSTITUTE FOR CHILDREN!

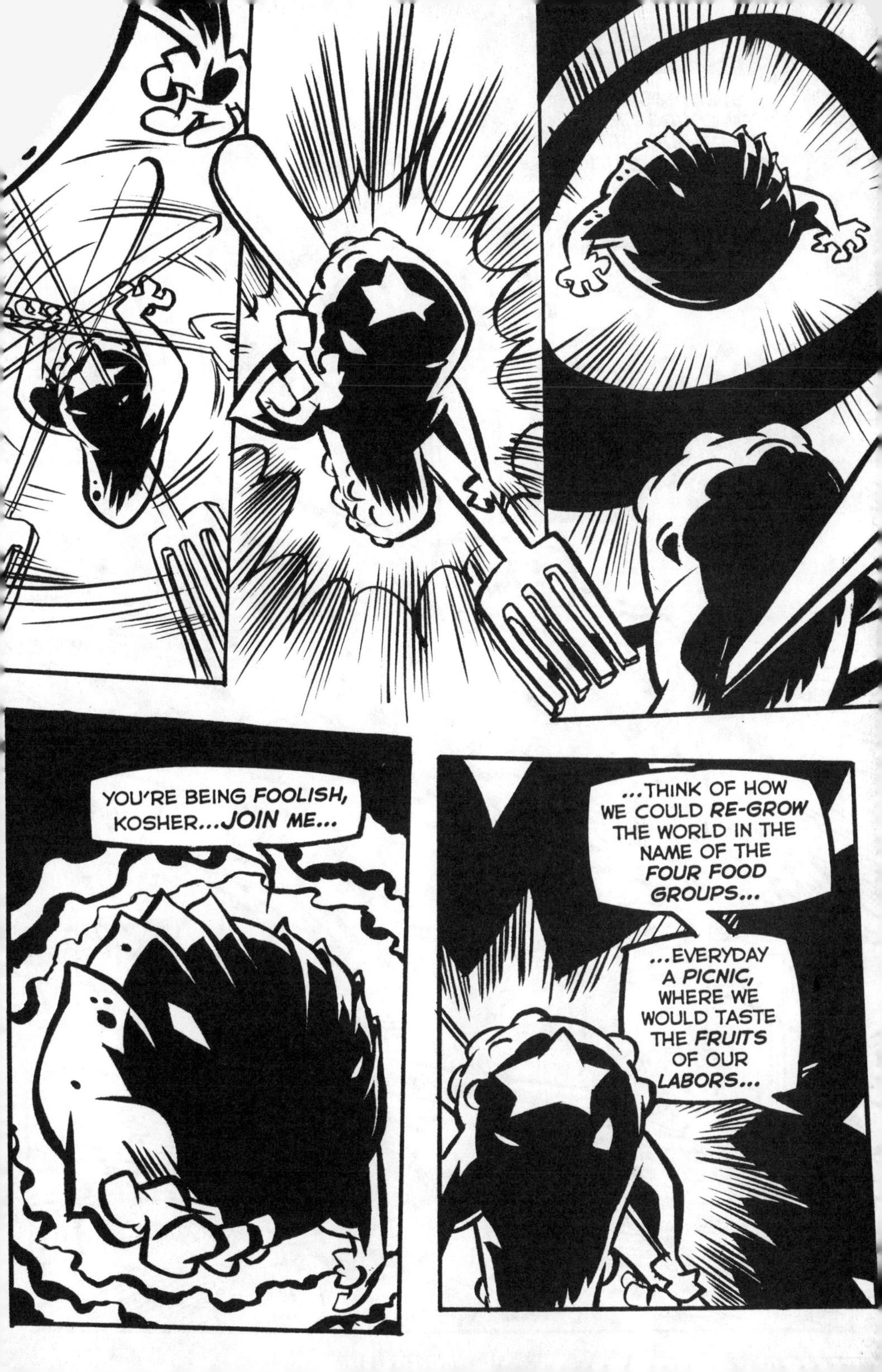
YOU'RE BEING FOOLISH, KOSHER...JOIN ME...
...THINK OF HOW WE COULD RE-GROW THE WORLD IN THE NAME OF THE FOUR FOOD GROUPS...
...EVERYDAY A PICNIC, WHERE WE WOULD TASTE THE FRUITS OF OUR LABORS...

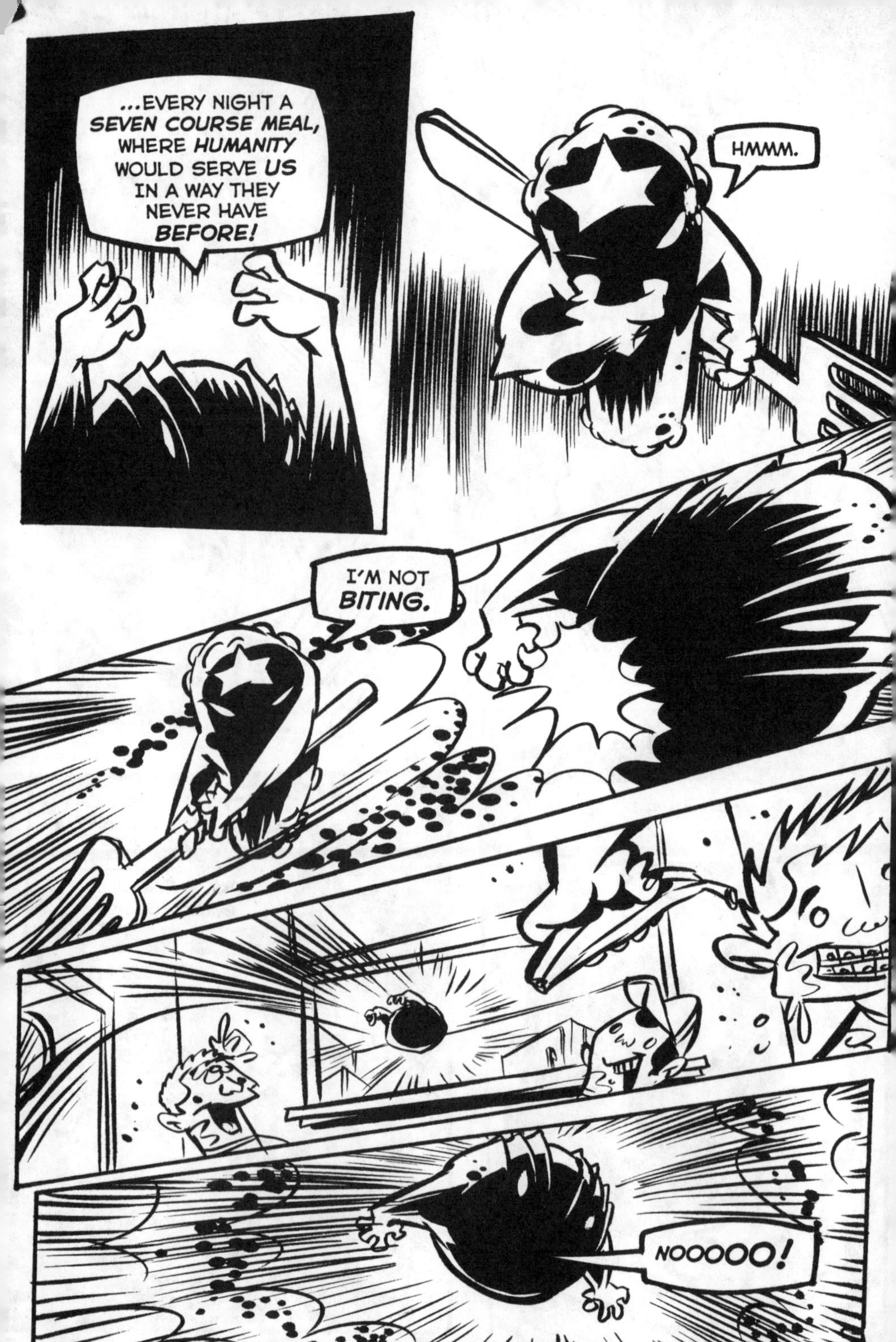
...EVERY NIGHT A SEVEN COURSE MEAL, WHERE HUMANITY WOULD SERVE US IN A WAY THEY NEVER HAVE BEFORE!
HMMM.
I'M NOT BITING.
NOOOOO!

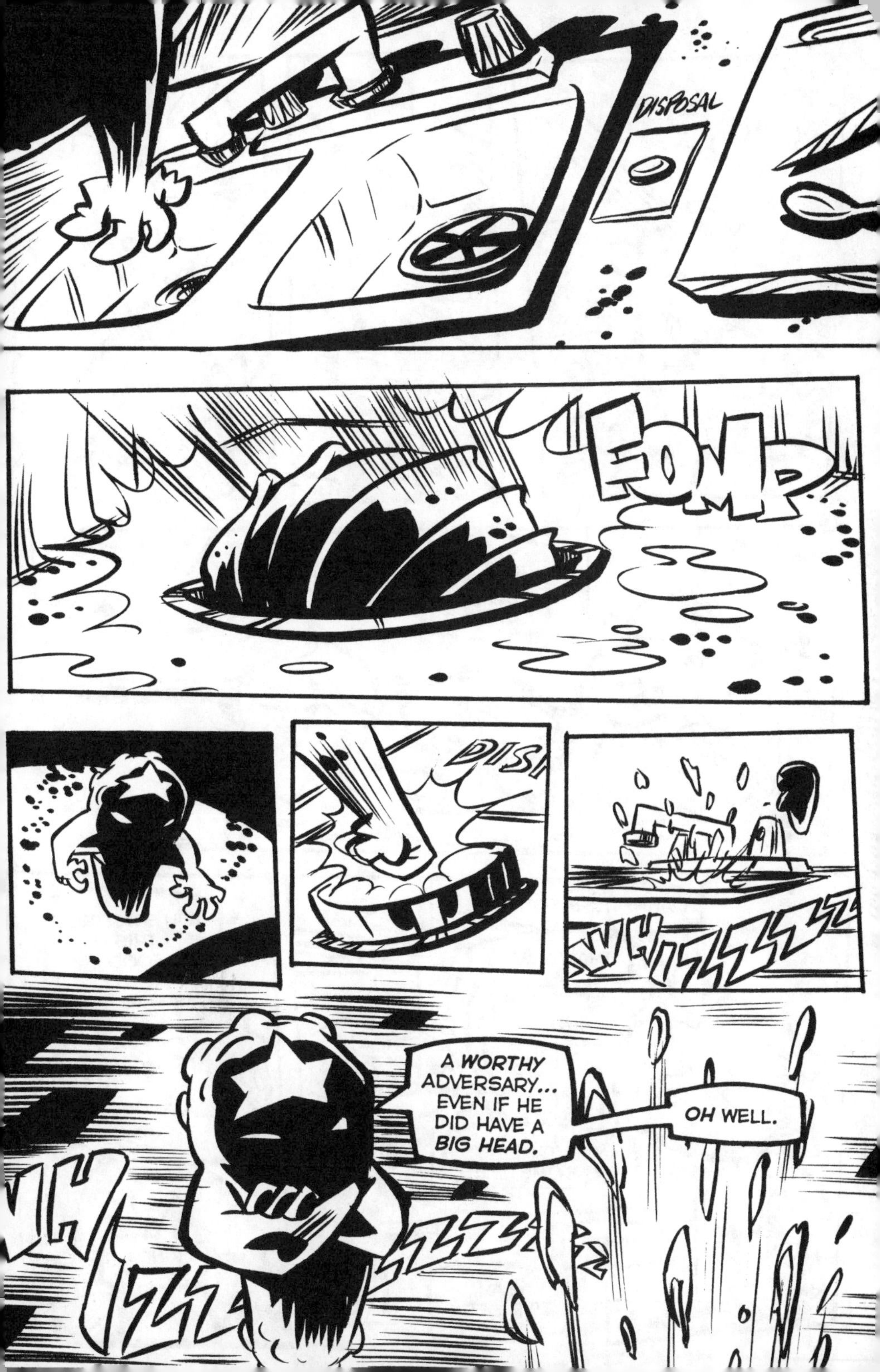
DISPOSAL
FOMP
DISH
WHISSSSS
A WORTHY ADVERSARY... EVEN IF HE DID HAVE A BIG HEAD.
OH WELL.

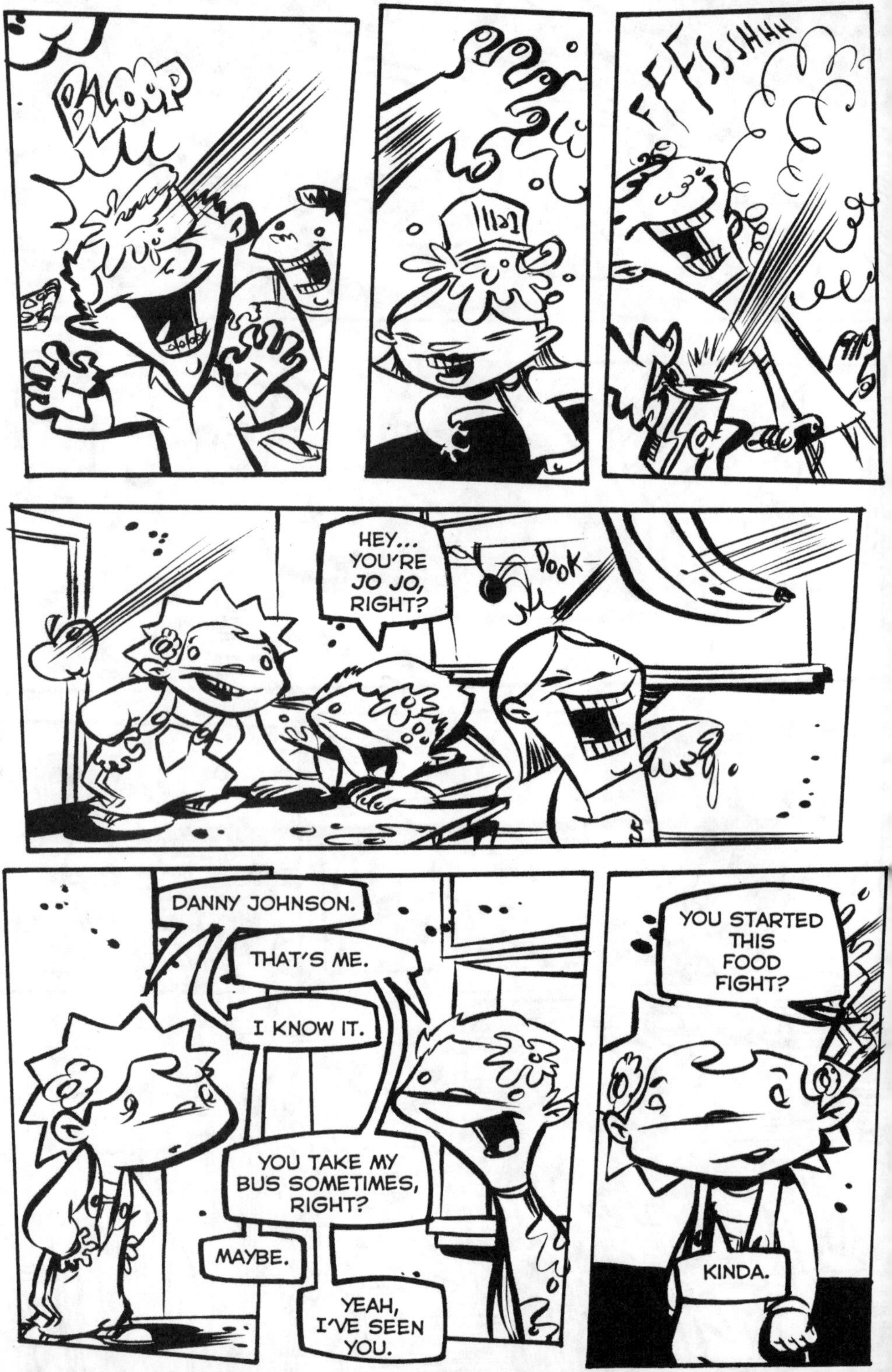
BLOOP
FFFSSSHHH
HEY... YOU'RE JO JO, RIGHT?
POOK
DANNY JOHNSON.
THAT'S ME.
I KNOW IT.
YOU TAKE MY BUS SOMETIMES, RIGHT?
MAYBE.
YEAH, I'VE SEEN YOU.
YOU STARTED THIS FOOD FIGHT?
KINDA.

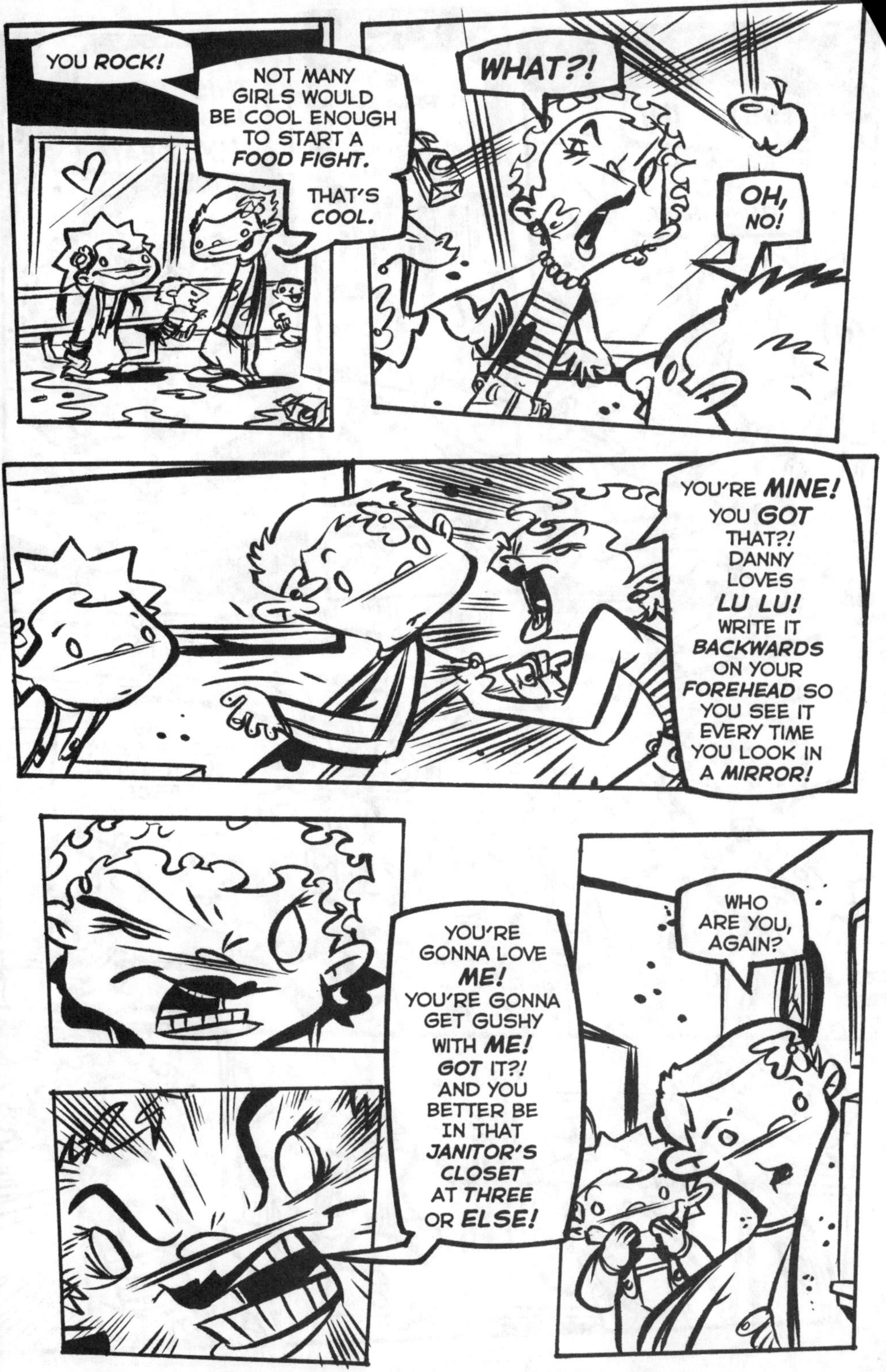
YOU ROCK!
NOT MANY GIRLS WOULD BE COOL ENOUGH TO START A FOOD FIGHT.
THAT'S COOL.
WHAT?!
OH, NO!
YOU'RE MINE! YOU GOT THAT?! DANNY LOVES LU LU! WRITE IT BACKWARDS ON YOUR FOREHEAD SO YOU SEE IT EVERY TIME YOU LOOK IN A MIRROR!
YOU'RE GONNA LOVE ME! YOU'RE GONNA GET GUSHY WITH ME! GOT IT?! AND YOU BETTER BE IN THAT JANITOR'S CLOSET AT THREE OR ELSE!
WHO ARE YOU, AGAIN?

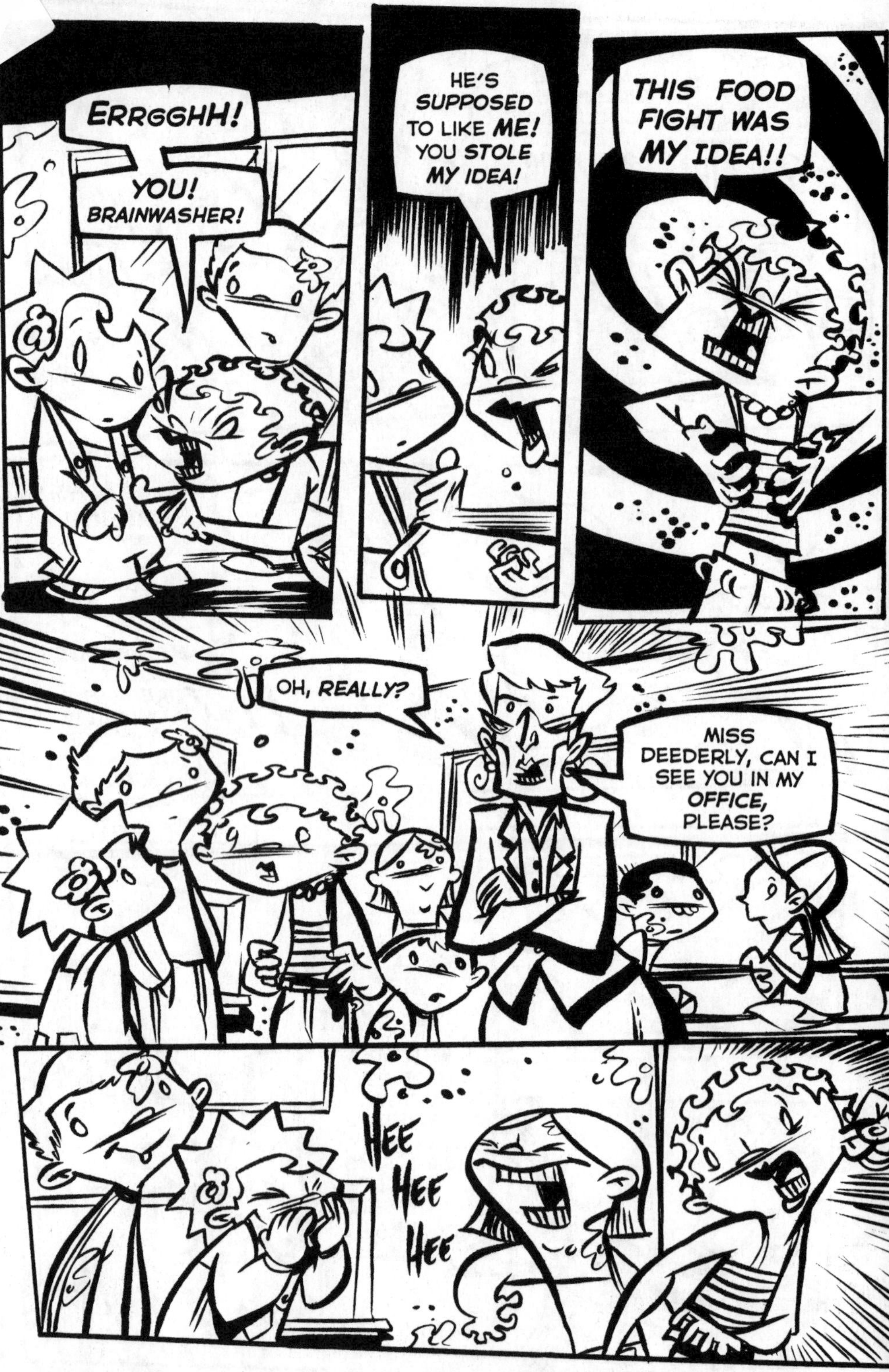
ERRGGHH!
YOU! BRAINWASHER!
HE'S SUPPOSED TO LIKE ME! YOU STOLE MY IDEA!
THIS FOOD FIGHT WAS MY IDEA!!
OH, REALLY?
MISS DEEDERLY, CAN I SEE YOU IN MY OFFICE, PLEASE?
HEE HEE HEE

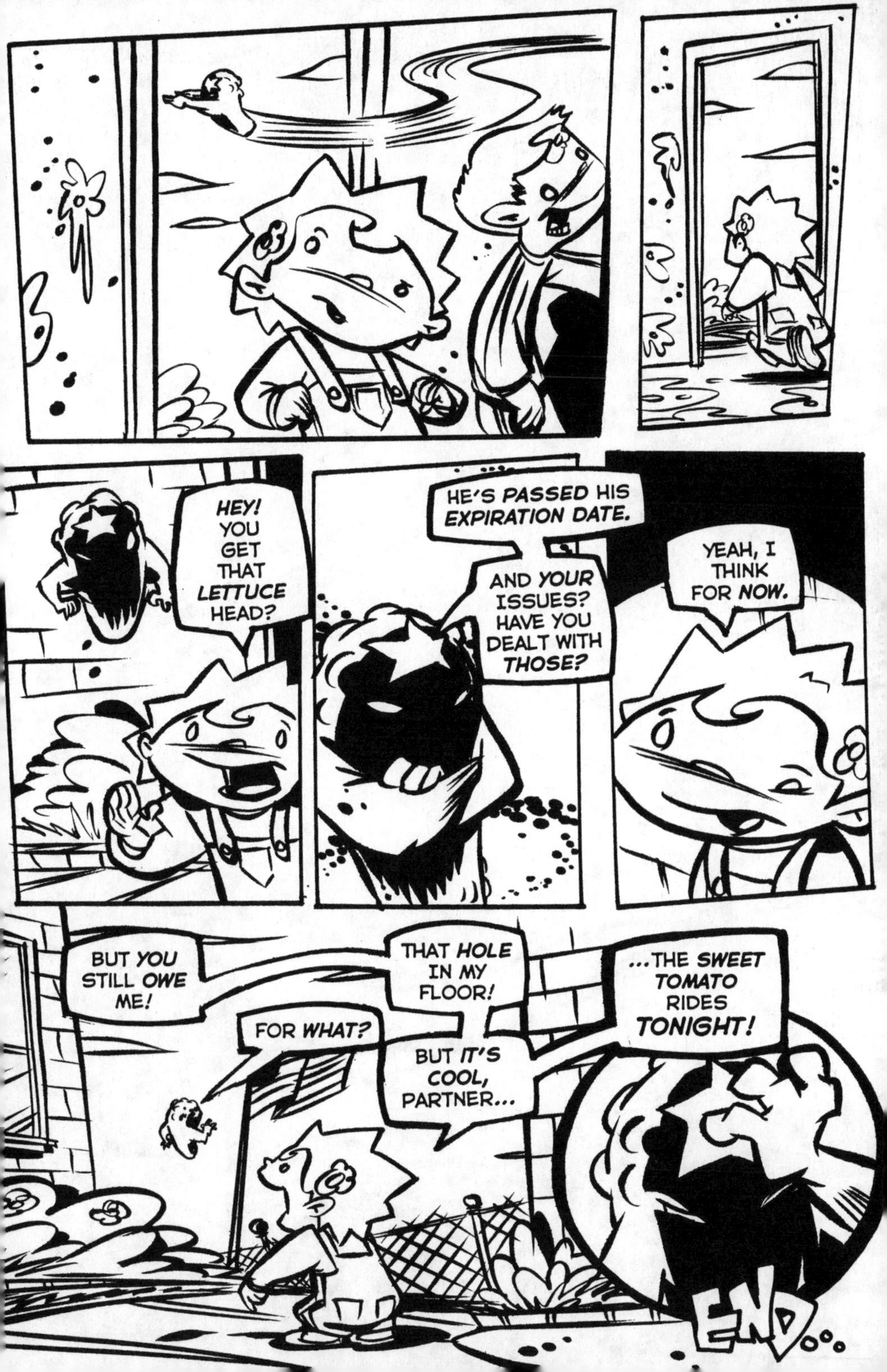
HEY! YOU GET THAT LETTUCE HEAD?
HE'S PASSED HIS EXPIRATION DATE.
AND YOUR ISSUES? HAVE YOU DEALT WITH THOSE?
YEAH, I THINK FOR NOW.
BUT YOU STILL OWE ME!
FOR WHAT?
THAT HOLE IN MY FLOOR!
BUT IT'S COOL, PARTNER...
...THE SWEET TOMATO RIDES TONIGHT!
END...

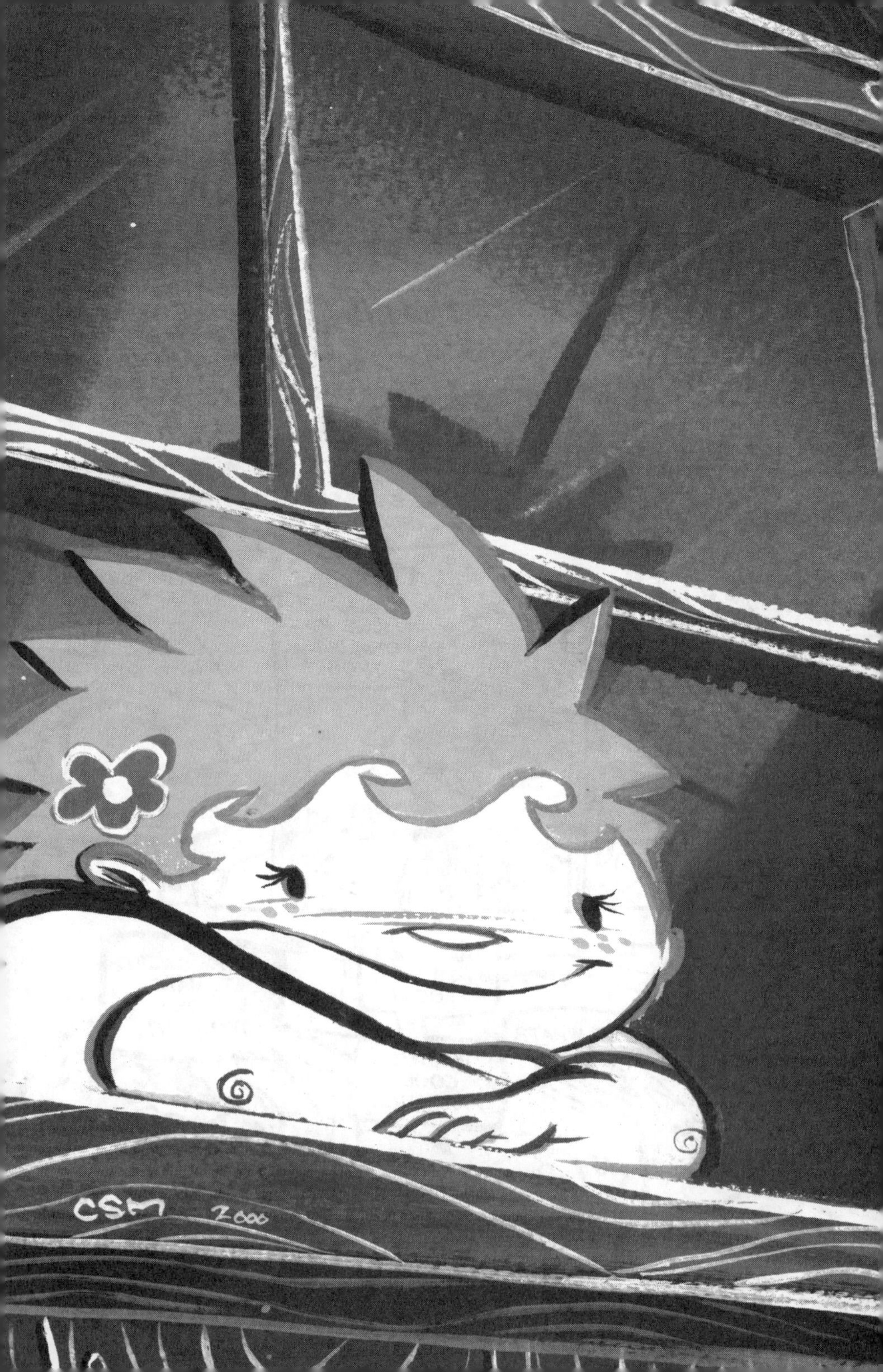
CSM 2000

WHAT ARE FOLKS SAYING ABOUT

the MAGIC PICKLE?

LET'S HEAR FROM SOME **EXPERTS...**

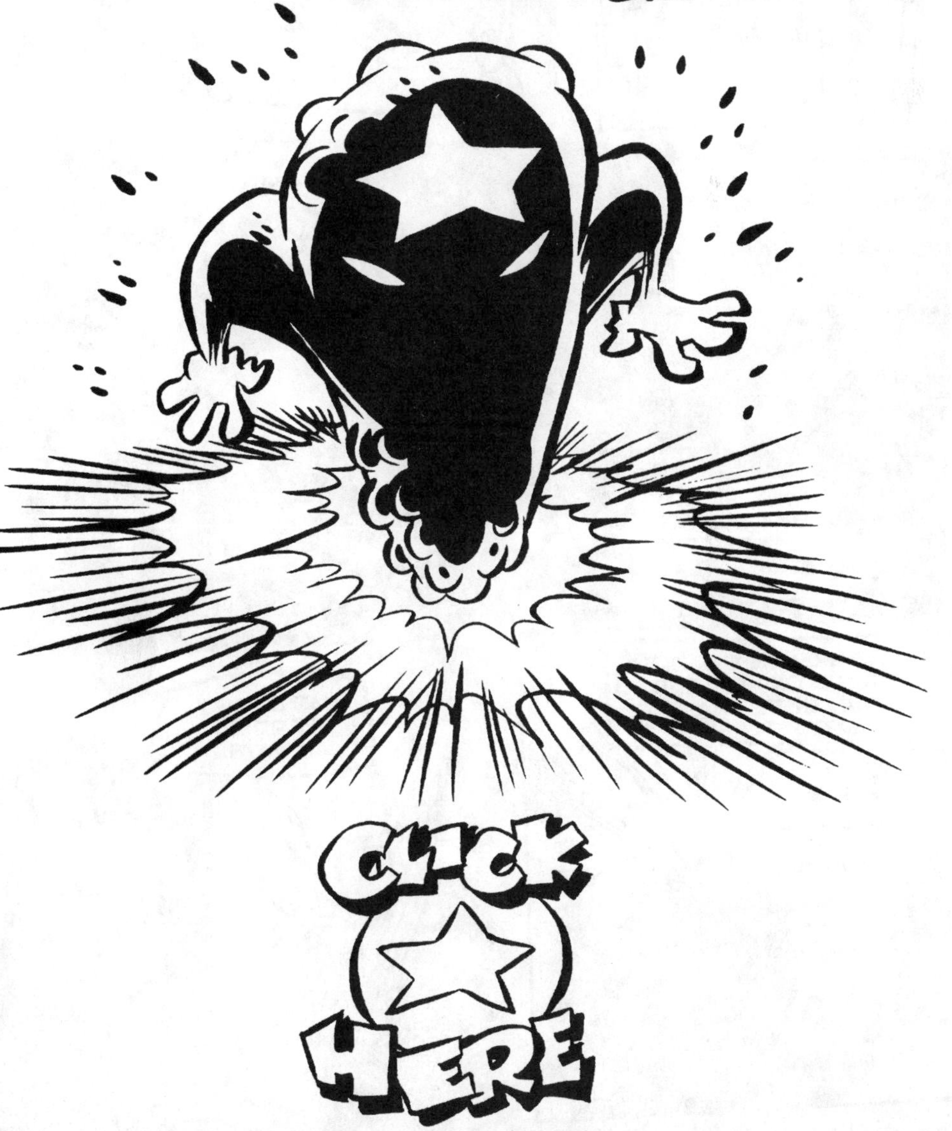

CLICK HERE

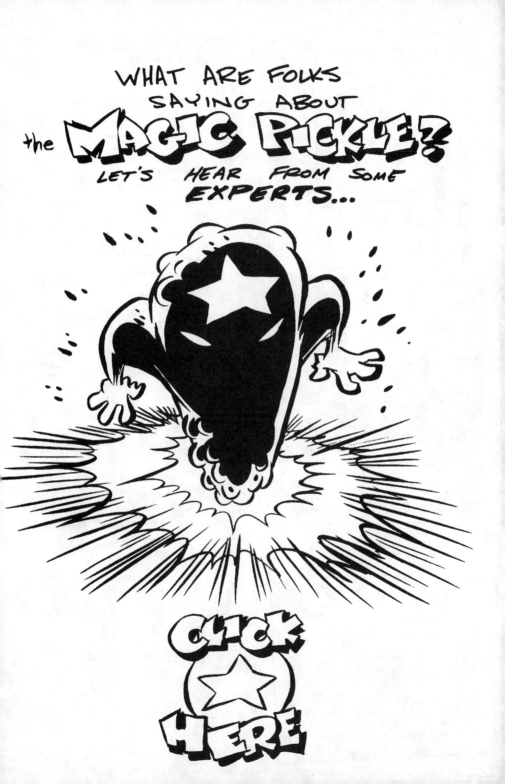

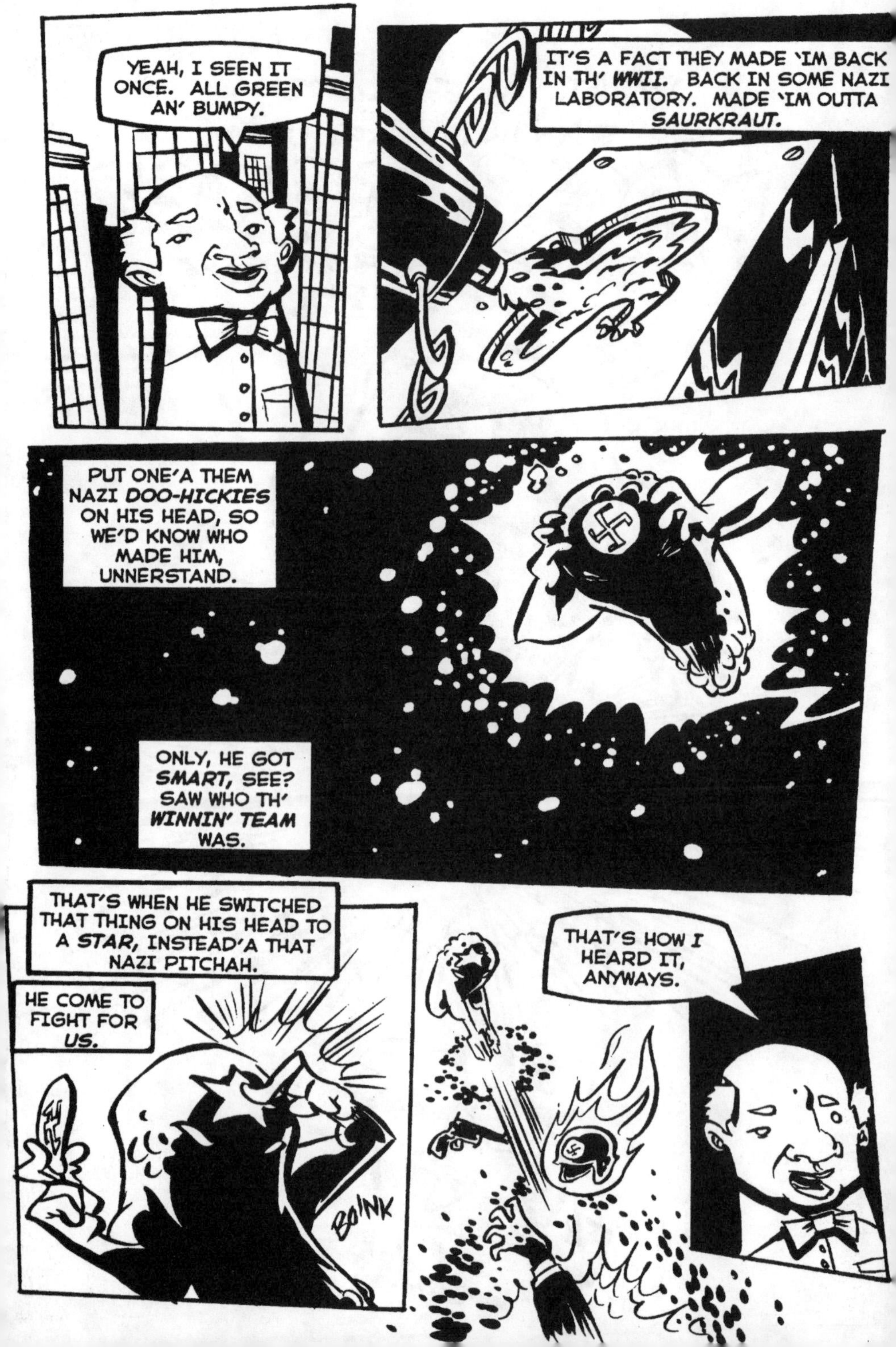
YEAH, I SEEN IT ONCE. ALL GREEN AN' BUMPY.
IT'S A FACT THEY MADE 'IM BACK IN TH' WWII. BACK IN SOME NAZI LABORATORY. MADE 'IM OUTTA SAURKRAUT.
PUT ONE'A THEM NAZI DOO-HICKIES ON HIS HEAD, SO WE'D KNOW WHO MADE HIM, UNNERSTAND.
ONLY, HE GOT SMART, SEE? SAW WHO TH' WINNIN' TEAM WAS.
THAT'S WHEN HE SWITCHED THAT THING ON HIS HEAD TO A STAR, INSTEAD'A THAT NAZI PITCHAH.
HE COME TO FIGHT FOR US.
BOINK
THAT'S HOW I HEARD IT, ANYWAYS.

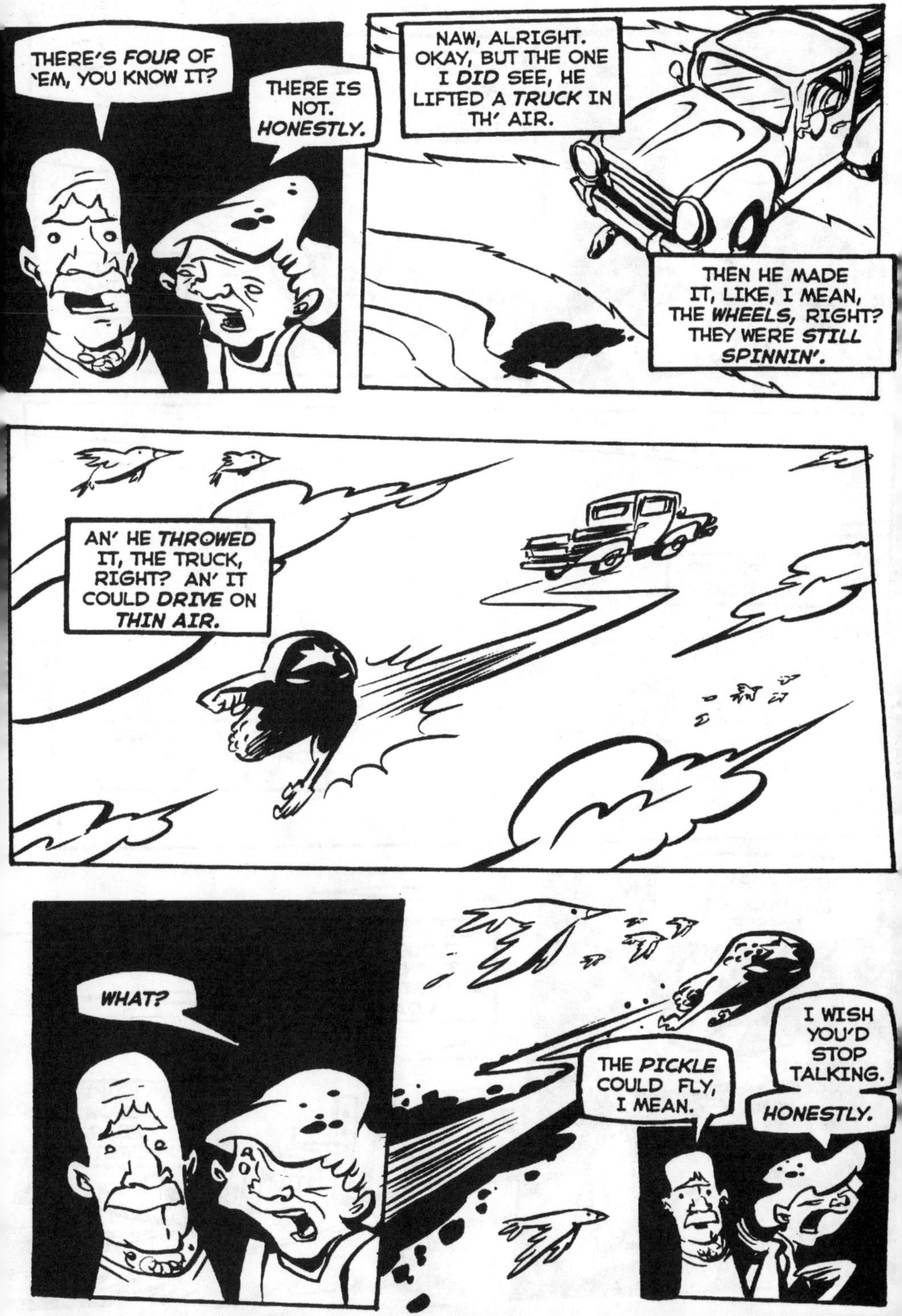
THERE'S *FOUR* OF 'EM, YOU KNOW IT?
THERE IS NOT. *HONESTLY.*
NAW, ALRIGHT. OKAY, BUT THE ONE I *DID* SEE, HE LIFTED A *TRUCK* IN TH' AIR.
THEN HE MADE IT, LIKE, I MEAN, THE *WHEELS*, RIGHT? THEY WERE *STILL SPINNIN'*.
AN' HE *THROWED* IT, THE TRUCK, RIGHT? AN' IT COULD *DRIVE* ON *THIN AIR.*
WHAT?
THE *PICKLE* COULD FLY, I MEAN.
I WISH YOU'D STOP TALKING.
HONESTLY.

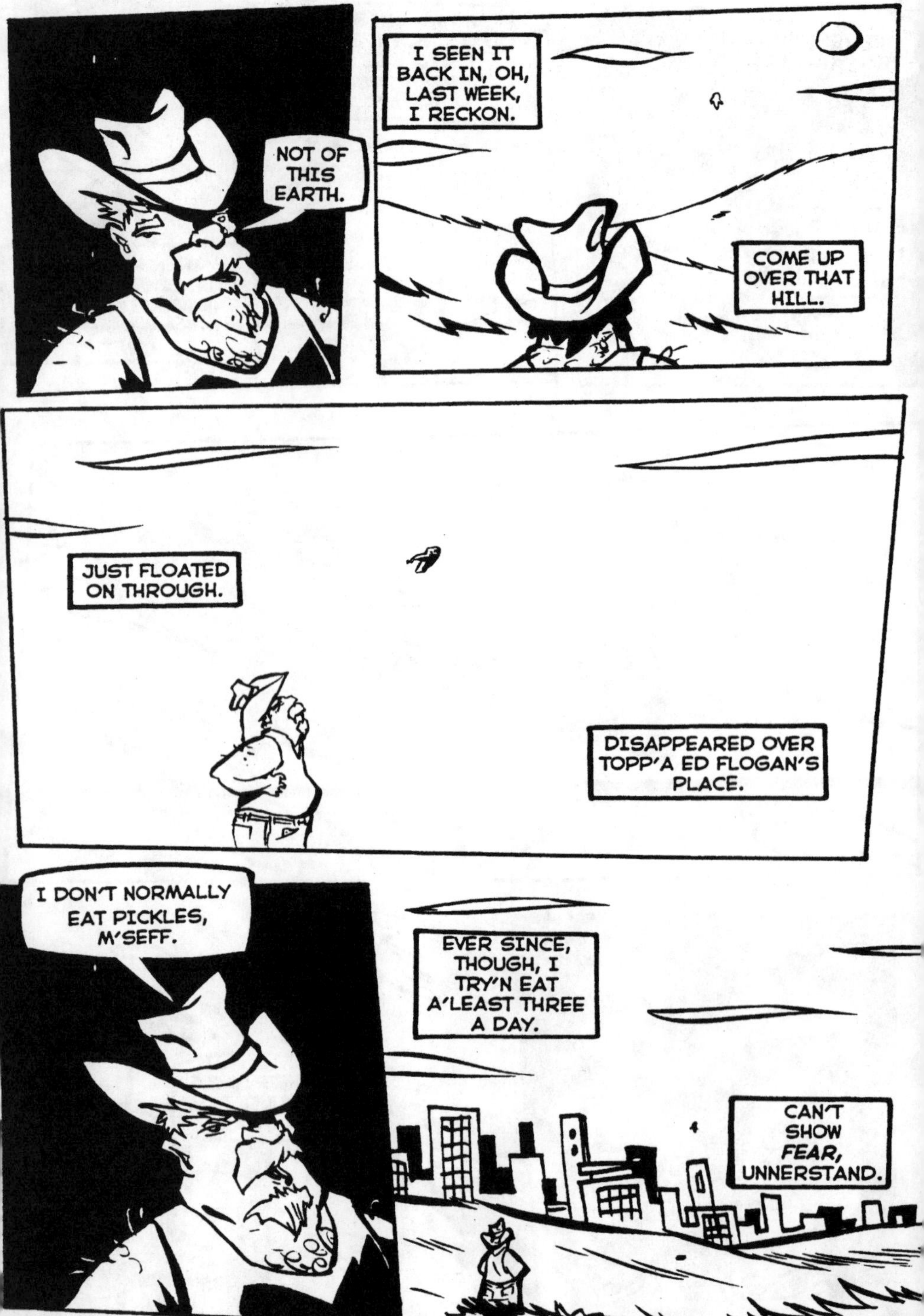
NOT OF THIS EARTH.
I SEEN IT BACK IN, OH, LAST WEEK, I RECKON.
COME UP OVER THAT HILL.
JUST FLOATED ON THROUGH.
DISAPPEARED OVER TOPP'A ED FLOGAN'S PLACE.
I DON'T NORMALLY EAT PICKLES, M'SEFF.
EVER SINCE, THOUGH, I TRY'N EAT A'LEAST THREE A DAY.
CAN'T SHOW *FEAR*, UNNERSTAND.

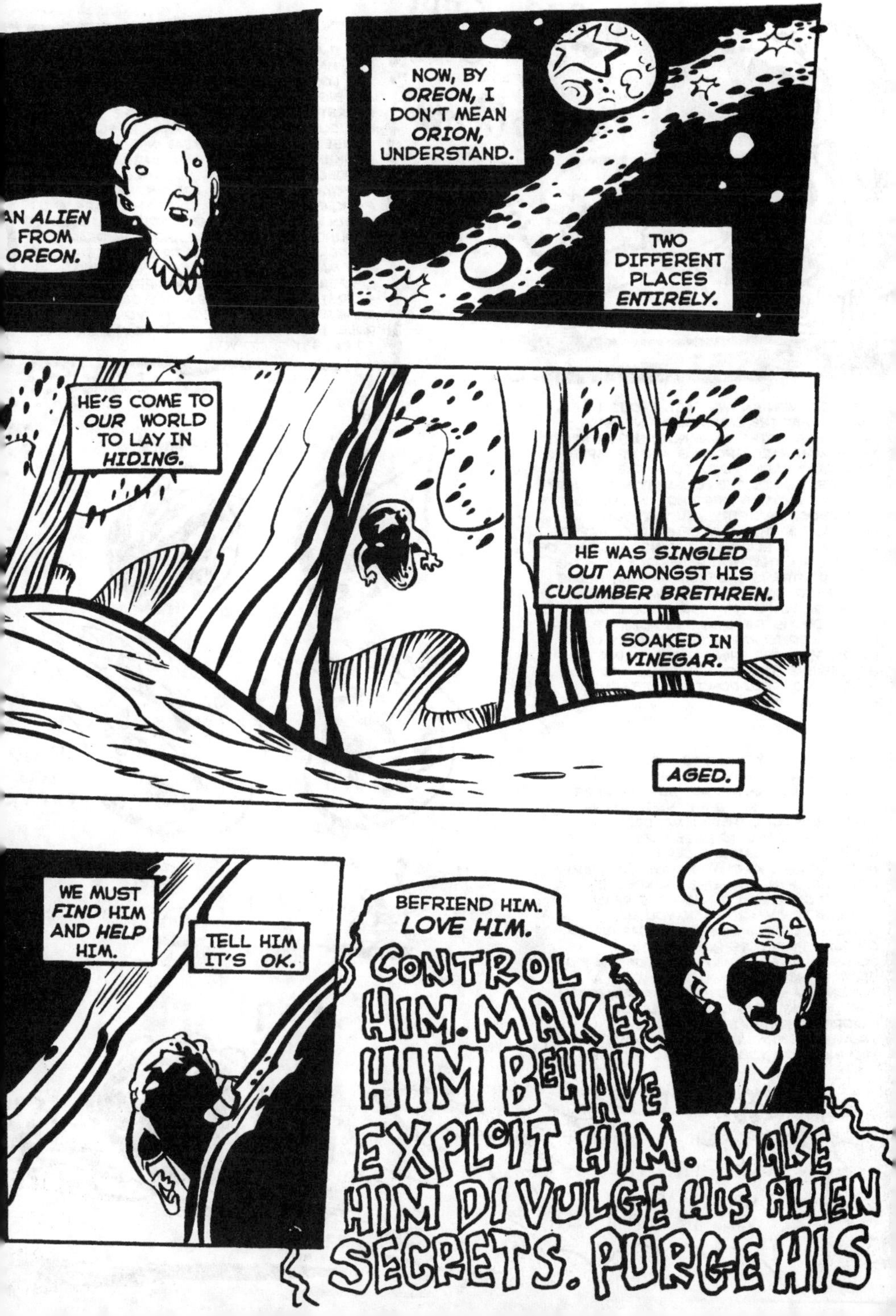
AN ALIEN FROM OREON.
NOW, BY OREON, I DON'T MEAN ORION, UNDERSTAND.
TWO DIFFERENT PLACES ENTIRELY.
HE'S COME TO OUR WORLD TO LAY IN HIDING.
HE WAS SINGLED OUT AMONGST HIS CUCUMBER BRETHREN.
SOAKED IN VINEGAR.
AGED.
WE MUST FIND HIM AND HELP HIM.
TELL HIM IT'S OK.
BEFRIEND HIM. LOVE HIM.
CONTROL HIM. MAKE HIM BEHAVE
EXPLOIT HIM. MAKE HIM DIVULGE HIS ALIEN SECRETS. PURGE HIS

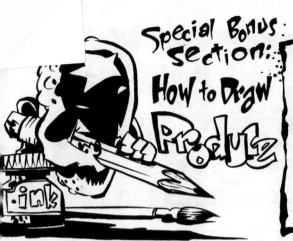

Special Bonus Section: How to Draw Produce

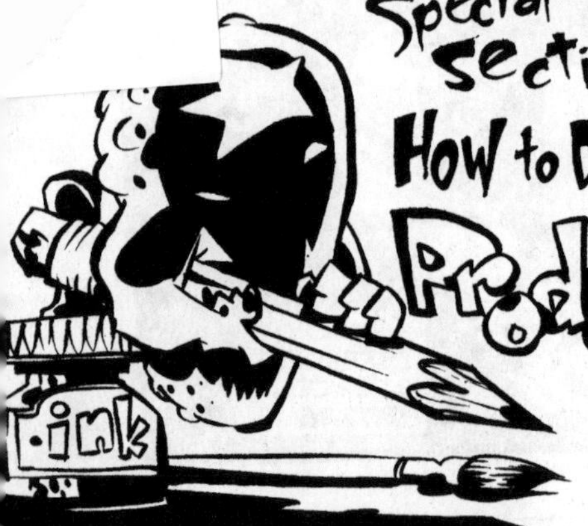
ink

IT'S TIME YOU WERE ALL TOLD THE TRUTH. THE LIES HAVE BEEN ALLOWED TO PROSPER FOR TOO LONG. THE COMIC BOOK INDUSTRY, LIKE ALL BIG BUSINESS ORGANIZATIONS, HAS SECRETS, AND I'M HERE TO LET THE BIGGEST ONE OUT OF THE BAG. MY NAME IS SCOTT MORSE. I'VE BEEN WORKING IN THE COMIC BOOK INDUSTRY FOR A FEW YEARS NOW, ON PROJECTS LIKE ***SOULWIND, VOLCANIC REVOLVER, ANCIENT JOE,*** AND ***MAGIC PICKLE.*** I'VE WATCHED, OVER THE YEARS AND LEARNED THAT THE COMICS INDUSTRY REVOLVES AROUND ONE BIG SECRET AND NOW, DEAR READERS, IT'S UP TO YOU TO TAKE THIS SECRET AND MAKE IT WORK FOR YOUR FLEDGLING CAREER ASPIRATIONS. JACK KIRBY KNEW THIS SECRET. JACK COLE KNEW THIS SECRET. WILL EISNER WILL NOT TELL YOU THIS ONE GOLDEN RULE. I'VE UNEARTHED IT AND NOW I'M GOING TO PASS IT ON TO YOU.

IT'S A COMMON KNOWN FACT, THOUGH WELL HIDDEN, THAT THE COMIC BOOK INDUSTRY SPRUNG FROM THE SAME NOTION THAT KEEPS THE HUMAN RACE GROWING AND PROSPERING ON A DAILY BASIS: FOOD. FOUR BASIC FOOD GROUPS. THEY'RE THE FOUNDATION OF EVERY GROWING ENTITY'S EXISTENCE, INCLUDING THE COMIC BOOK INDUSTRY. ALL THAT YOU PURCHASE IN THE FORM OF STAPLED PAPER, ALL THAT YOU SLIP SILENTLY INTO SLEEVES OF PLASTIC, ALL THAT YOU REINFORCE WITH THE NATURAL STRENGTH OF CARDBOARD, STEMS FROM FOOD. NO, NOT IN THE WAY YOU'RE THINKING...YOU CAN'T FEED A COMIC BOOK, SILLY. FOOD IS THE STARTING POINT OF EVERY LINE PLACED TO PAPER, THE GENESIS OF EVERY THICK AND THIN STROKE OF INK THAT GRACES THE FORM OF YOUR FAVORITE SUPERHERO. STILL DON'T GET IT? LEMME SHOW YOU.

IF YOU'LL KINDLY REFER TO *FIG. A*, YOU'LL NOTICE WHAT'S BEEN IN FRONT OF YOU SINCE THE BEGINNING. ALL SUPERHEROES ARE BASED ON FRUITS AND VEGETABLES. OVER THE YEARS, THERE HAVE BEEN IMITATORS, TRYING TO BASE SUPERHEROES ON, OH, SAY, BREAD AND CEREALS, OR MEATS (YEAH, LIKE THAT'S LOGICAL). EVERY NOW AND THEN, SOMEONE UNEXPECTED SHEDS SOME LIGHT ON HOW IT'S REALLY DONE...A FEW YEARS BACK, YOU MAY RECALL, A COUPLE OF CHARACTERS BASED ON DAIRY PRODUCTS ROSE TO THE OCCASION. IT WAS ONLY A HINT OF THE BIG SECRET, THOUGH. IF YOU TRULY TAKE A MOMENT TO BREAK DOWN AND ANALYZE THE BASIC STRUCTURES OF ALL YOUR OLD FAVORITES, YOU'LL BE BLESSED WITH KNOWLEDGE THAT THE BIG TWO HAVE BEEN KEEPING FROM YOU, THE LITTLE GUY.

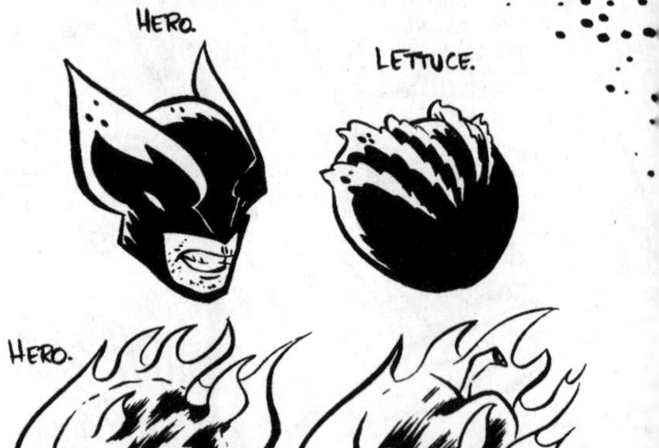
HERO.
LETTUCE.
HERO.
ROASTED BELL PEPPER
HERO.
PEA.

FIG. A

YOU'LL NEED:

- A PENCIL
- SOME PAPER
- SOME TIME TO KILL IN MATH CLASS

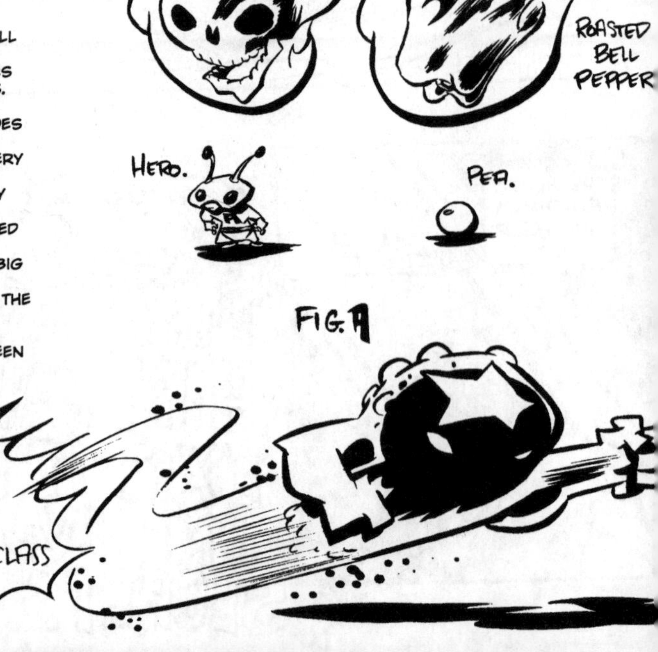

IG. B POINTS OUT YOUR FIRST REAL STEP IN RAWING YOUR OWN TRUE SUPERHERO. YOU UST FIRST THINK OF WHAT YOUR CHARACTER S ABOUT, WHAT HE'S TRYING TO ACHIEVE IN HE CONTEXT OF HIS STORY. THINK OF HOW HE VAS RAISED. THINK OF HIM AS A CHARACTER. ND THEN THINK OF WHAT FRUIT OR EGETABLE BEST REFLECTS THOSE SENSIBILITIES. IF YOU'RE GIVEN A CHARACTER THAT, SAY, IS A HOMEGROWN, ALL-AMERICAN HERO, BUT WHOSE TRUE POWER'S BEEN HARVESTED BY RADIATION, YOU MAY WANT TO CONSIDER CORN. THINK ABOUT IT, BREAK IT DOWN: ALL-AMERICAN, HOMEGROWN, HARVESTED. IT'S OBVIOUS STAN LEE AND JACK KIRBY WERE ON TO SOMETHING HUGE.

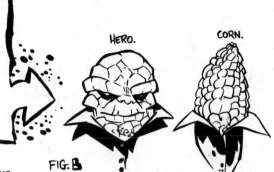

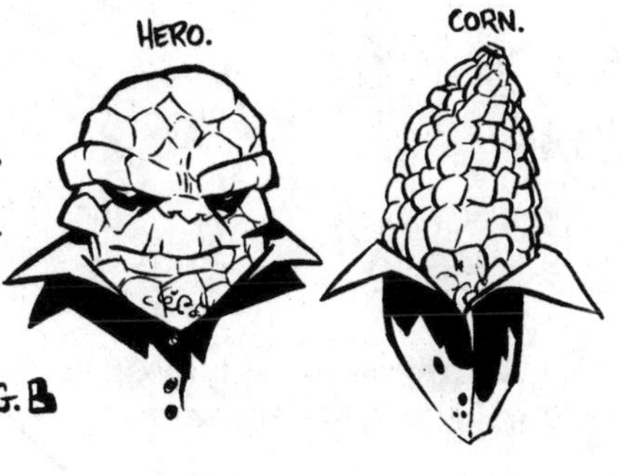
HERO.
CORN.

FIG. B

OUR MAIN FOCUS, SINCE WE'RE JUST LEARNING THE FAR-REACHING IMPLICATIONS OF SUCH A HUGE INDUSTRY SECRET, IS TO KEEP IT REAL. DECIDE WHICH FRUIT OR VEGETABLE BEST REFLECTS YOUR CHARACTER'S INHERENT ABILITIES, AND SELECT A MODEL. ALWAYS DRAW FROM LIFE. WITH PRATICE, YOU'LL LEARN THE BASICS ABOUT ANATOMY, STRUCTURE, FORESHORTENING, AND HOW YOUR MODEL BEHAVES, AND YOU CAN INCORPORATE THESE THINGS INTO YOUR HERO. MODELS ARE EASY TO FIND, THE BEST USUALLY HANGING AROUND THE FARMER'S MARKET OR THAT MISTY, COOL SECTION OF THE SUPERMARKET, OR ON THE SHELVES (BUT CHECK THOSE EXPIRATION DATES!). DON'T GO TO THE FROZEN FOODS ISLE--THAT'S FOR HACKS.

WE'LL ASSUME WE'VE BEEN GIVEN AN ASSIGNMENT TO DESIGN AND RENDER A HERO, A GOOD GUY, ENGINEERED BY THE GOVERNMENT, WHO'S SNAPPY, FRESH, AND PACKS A PUNCH. A PICKLE IS A PERFECT CHOICE FOR THIS: THEY'RE SWEET AND KOSHER, THEY'RE REALLY CUCUMBERS THAT HAVE BEEN ALTERED THROUGH SCIENTIFIC ENDEAVORS, THEY HAVE A SNAPPY SOUND WHEN BITTEN INTO, THEY'RE FRESH, AS LONG AS KEPT REFRIGERATED, AND THEY INDEED PACK A PUNCH TO THE TASTE BUDS.

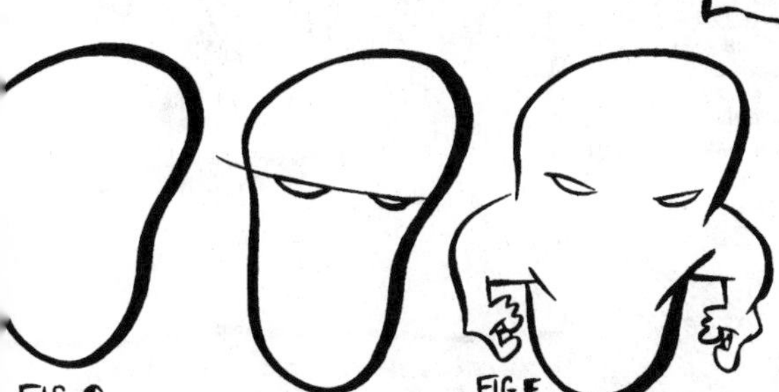

FIG. C FIG. D FIG. E

SO, WITH A PICKLE AS OUR MODEL, WE'LL BEGIN TO DESIGN OUR CHARACTER. AS IN *FIG. C*, WE'LL TAKE THE INHERENT OUTLINE OF THE VEGETABLE, A SORT OF SQUASHY (NO PUN INTENDED, FOLKS, THIS IS SERIOUS) OVAL, AND LAY THAT LINE DOWN ON PAPER. THIS INITIAL SHAPE IS THE BASIS FOR OUR HERO'S POWERS, AS WE CAN ASSUME HE'LL NEED TO FLY, AND A ROUNDED, OVAL SHAPE IS THE MOST AERODYNAMIC WE COULD HOPE FOR. DRAW IT WITH A QUICK, FLUID SWEEP OF THE PENCIL, KEEPING THE ENERGY OF OUR HERO INTACT. *FIG. D* SHOWS US THAT WE SHOULD NEXT DRAW LIFE INTO OUR HERO, SWEEPING A SIMPLE LINE THROUGH THE TOP THIRD OF THE CHARACTER, AND USING THIS AS AN INDICATOR OF WHERE HIS EYES SHOULD GO. *FIG. E*, OF COURSE, HELPS ROUND OUT OUR CHARACTER'S ATTRIBUTES, AND HELPS US BEGIN TO EXEMPLIFY THE EXTENTS TO WHICH THE GENETIC ENGINEERING OF OUR CHARACTER HAS AFFECTED HIS NEW LIFE. ARMS ARE IMPORTANT FOR MOST CRIME-FIGHTERS, PEOPLE, SO MARK THAT DOWN IN YOUR NOTES. THEY'RE COMPOSED OF TWO STRAIGHT LINES, AND ONE CURVED LINE ON THE OUTER EDGE, FULFILLING THE BASIC DESIGN AESTHETIC OF "STRAIGHT VERSES CURVED"...A DYNAMIC AND POWERFUL ELEMENT TO AN OTHERWISE SLICK AND SPEEDY CHARACTER DESIGN. *FIG. F* SHOWS YOU WHY THIS IS IMPORTANT, AS TOO MANY STRAIGHTS OR CURVES THROWS OFF THE CHARACTER'S OMINOUS PRESENCE. BALANCE IS NEEDED.

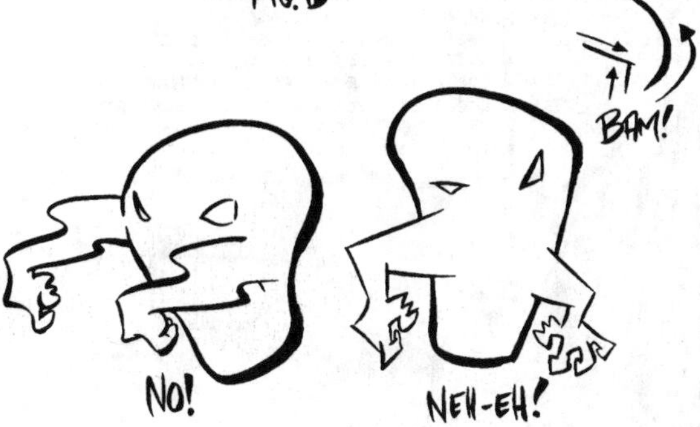
BAM!
NO!
NEH-EH!

FIG. F

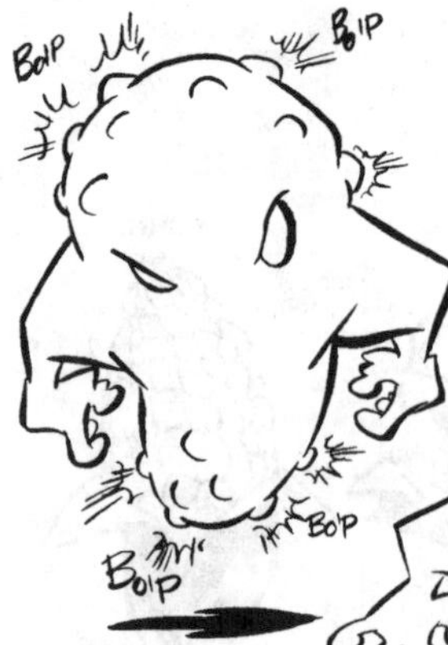
BOIP
BOIP
BOIP
BOIP

FIG. G

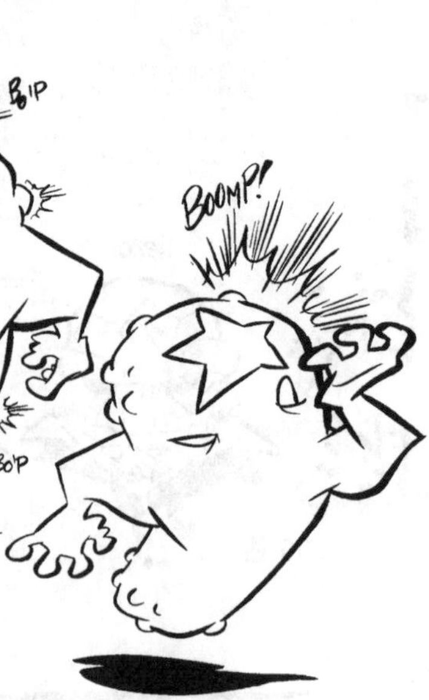
BOOMP!

FIG. H

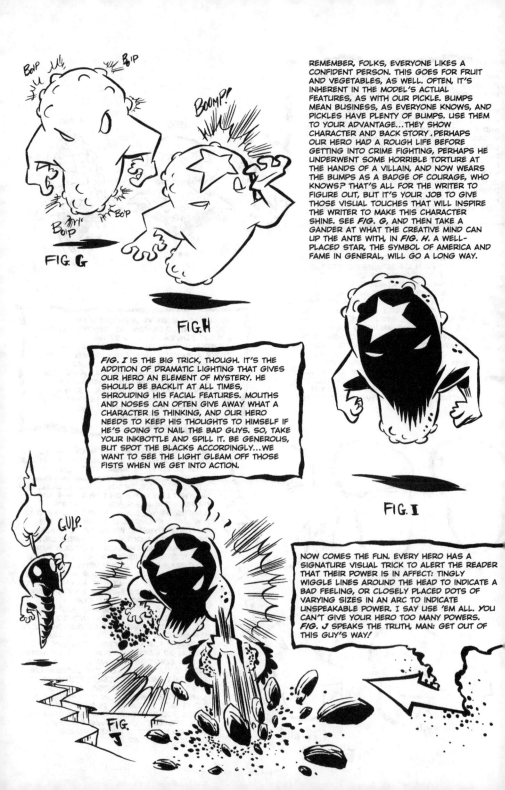

REMEMBER, FOLKS, EVERYONE LIKES A CONFIDENT PERSON. THIS GOES FOR FRUIT AND VEGETABLES, AS WELL. OFTEN, IT'S INHERENT IN THE MODEL'S ACTUAL FEATURES, AS WITH OUR PICKLE. BUMPS MEAN BUSINESS, AS EVERYONE KNOWS, AND PICKLES HAVE PLENTY OF BUMPS. USE THEM TO YOUR ADVANTAGE...THEY SHOW CHARACTER AND BACK STORY. PERHAPS OUR HERO HAD A ROUGH LIFE BEFORE GETTING INTO CRIME FIGHTING, PERHAPS HE UNDERWENT SOME HORRIBLE TORTURE AT THE HANDS OF A VILLAIN, AND NOW WEARS THE BUMPS AS A BADGE OF COURAGE, WHO KNOWS? THAT'S ALL FOR THE WRITER TO FIGURE OUT, BUT IT'S YOUR JOB TO GIVE THOSE VISUAL TOUCHES THAT WILL INSPIRE THE WRITER TO MAKE THIS CHARACTER SHINE. SEE ***FIG. G***, AND THEN TAKE A GANDER AT WHAT THE CREATIVE MIND CAN UP THE ANTE WITH, IN ***FIG. H***. A WELL-PLACED STAR, THE SYMBOL OF AMERICA AND FAME IN GENERAL, WILL GO A LONG WAY.

FIG. I IS THE BIG TRICK, THOUGH. IT'S THE ADDITION OF DRAMATIC LIGHTING THAT GIVES OUR HERO AN ELEMENT OF MYSTERY. HE SHOULD BE BACKLIT AT ALL TIMES, SHROUDING HIS FACIAL FEATURES. MOUTHS AND NOSES CAN OFTEN GIVE AWAY WHAT A CHARACTER IS THINKING, AND OUR HERO NEEDS TO KEEP HIS THOUGHTS TO HIMSELF IF HE'S GOING TO NAIL THE BAD GUYS. SO, TAKE YOUR INKBOTTLE AND SPILL IT. BE GENEROUS, BUT SPOT THE BLACKS ACCORDINGLY...WE WANT TO SEE THE LIGHT GLEAM OFF THOSE FISTS WHEN WE GET INTO ACTION.

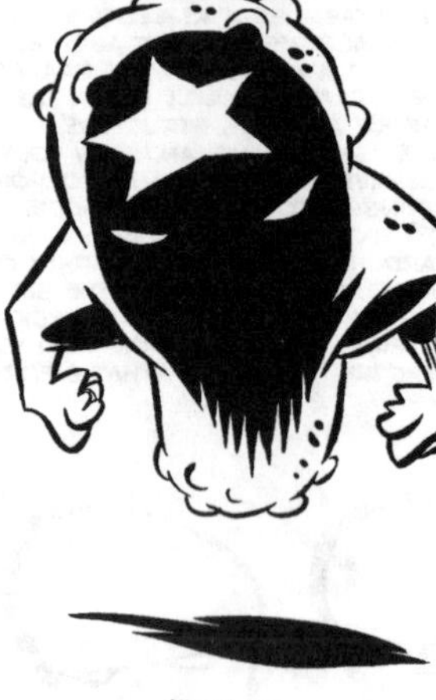

FIG. I

NOW COMES THE FUN. EVERY HERO HAS A SIGNATURE VISUAL TRICK TO ALERT THE READER THAT THEIR POWER IS IN AFFECT: TINGLY WIGGLE LINES AROUND THE HEAD TO INDICATE A BAD FEELING, OR CLOSELY PLACED DOTS OF VARYING SIZES IN AN ARC TO INDICATE UNSPEAKABLE POWER. I SAY USE 'EM ALL. *YOU* CAN'T GIVE YOUR HERO TOO MANY POWERS. ***FIG. J*** SPEAKS THE TRUTH, MAN: GET OUT OF THIS GUY'S WAY!

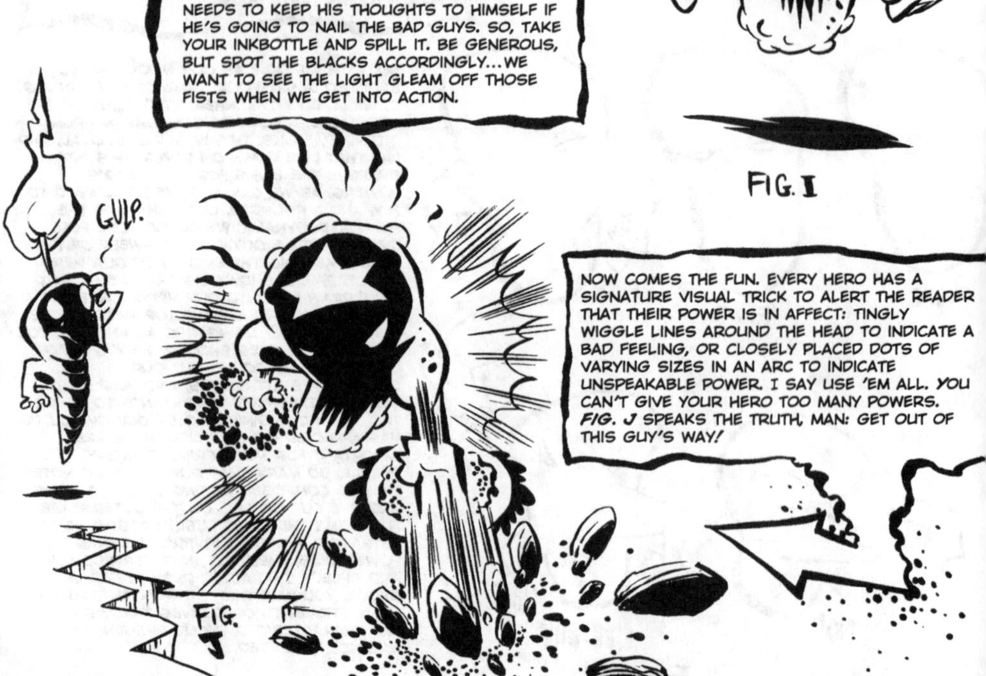
GULP.

FIG. J

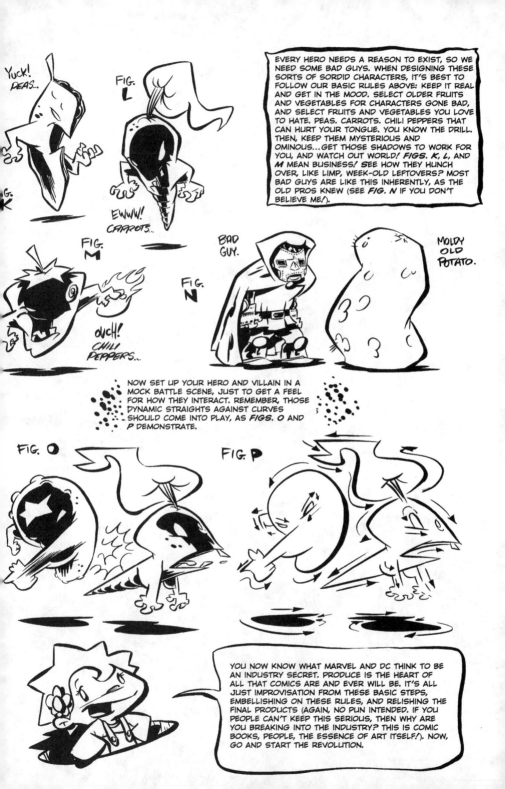

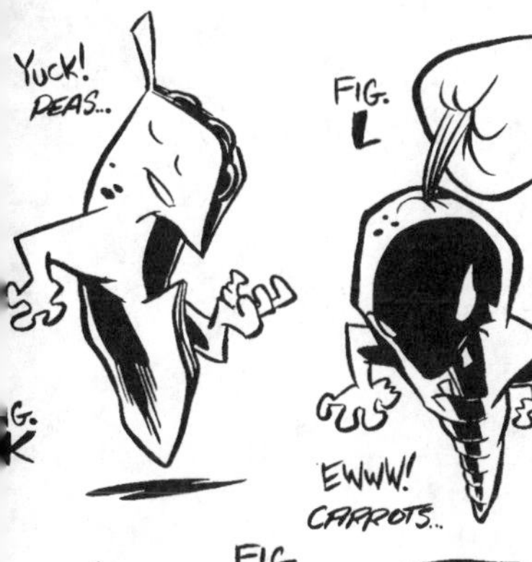
YUCK! PEAS...
FIG. K
FIG. L
EWWW! CARROTS...

EVERY HERO NEEDS A REASON TO EXIST, SO WE NEED SOME BAD GUYS. WHEN DESIGNING THESE SORTS OF SORDID CHARACTERS, IT'S BEST TO FOLLOW OUR BASIC RULES ABOVE: KEEP IT REAL AND GET IN THE MOOD. SELECT OLDER FRUITS AND VEGETABLES FOR CHARACTERS GONE BAD, AND SELECT FRUITS AND VEGETABLES YOU LOVE TO HATE. PEAS. CARROTS. CHILI PEPPERS THAT CAN HURT YOUR TONGUE. YOU KNOW THE DRILL. THEN, KEEP THEM MYSTERIOUS AND OMINOUS...GET THOSE SHADOWS TO WORK FOR YOU, AND WATCH OUT WORLD! ***FIGS. K, L,*** AND ***M*** MEAN BUSINESS! SEE HOW THEY HUNCH OVER, LIKE LIMP, WEEK-OLD LEFTOVERS? MOST BAD GUYS ARE LIKE THIS INHERENTLY, AS THE OLD PROS KNEW (SEE ***FIG. N*** IF YOU DON'T BELIEVE ME!).

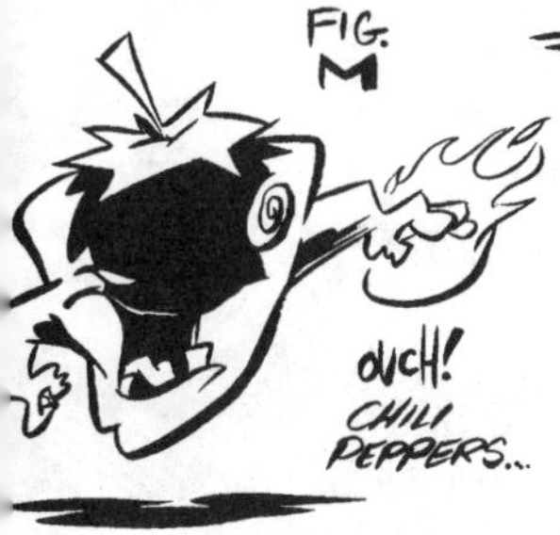
FIG. M
OUCH! CHILI PEPPERS...

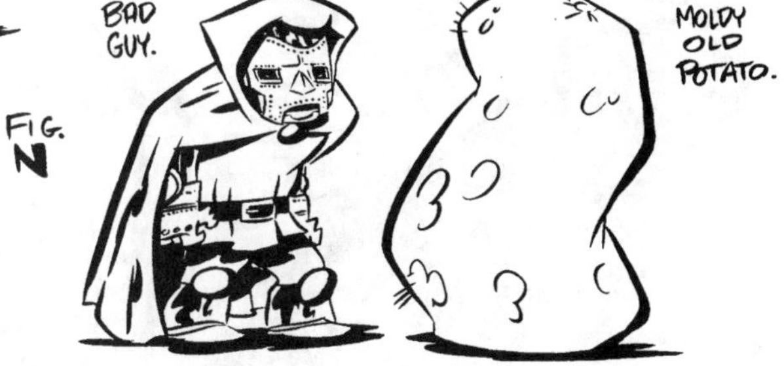
FIG. N
BAD GUY.
MOLDY OLD POTATO.

NOW SET UP YOUR HERO AND VILLAIN IN A MOCK BATTLE SCENE, JUST TO GET A FEEL FOR HOW THEY INTERACT. REMEMBER, THOSE DYNAMIC STRAIGHTS AGAINST CURVES SHOULD COME INTO PLAY, AS ***FIGS. O*** AND ***P*** DEMONSTRATE.

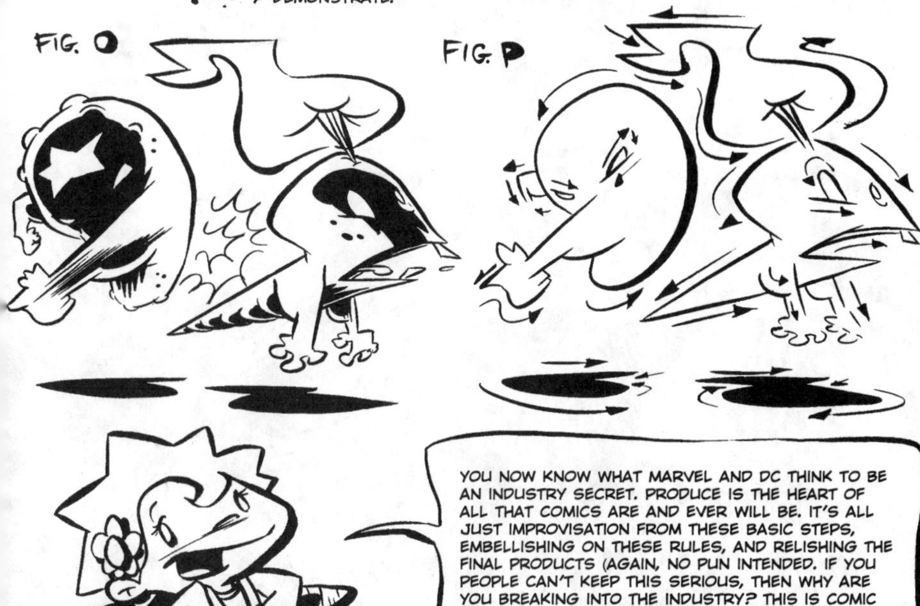
FIG. O
FIG. P

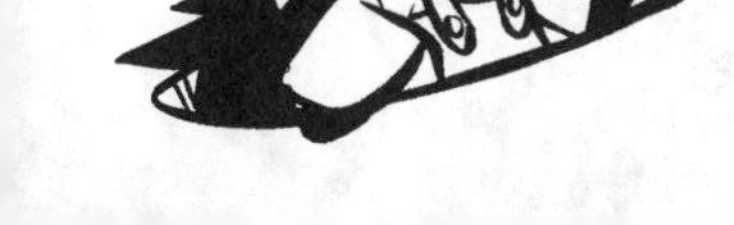

YOU NOW KNOW WHAT MARVEL AND DC THINK TO BE AN INDUSTRY SECRET. PRODUCE IS THE HEART OF ALL THAT COMICS ARE AND EVER WILL BE. IT'S ALL JUST IMPROVISATION FROM THESE BASIC STEPS, EMBELLISHING ON THESE RULES, AND RELISHING THE FINAL PRODUCTS (AGAIN, NO PUN INTENDED. IF YOU PEOPLE CAN'T KEEP THIS SERIOUS, THEN WHY ARE YOU BREAKING INTO THE INDUSTRY? THIS IS COMIC BOOKS, PEOPLE, THE ESSENCE OF ART ITSELF!). NOW, GO AND START THE REVOLUTION.

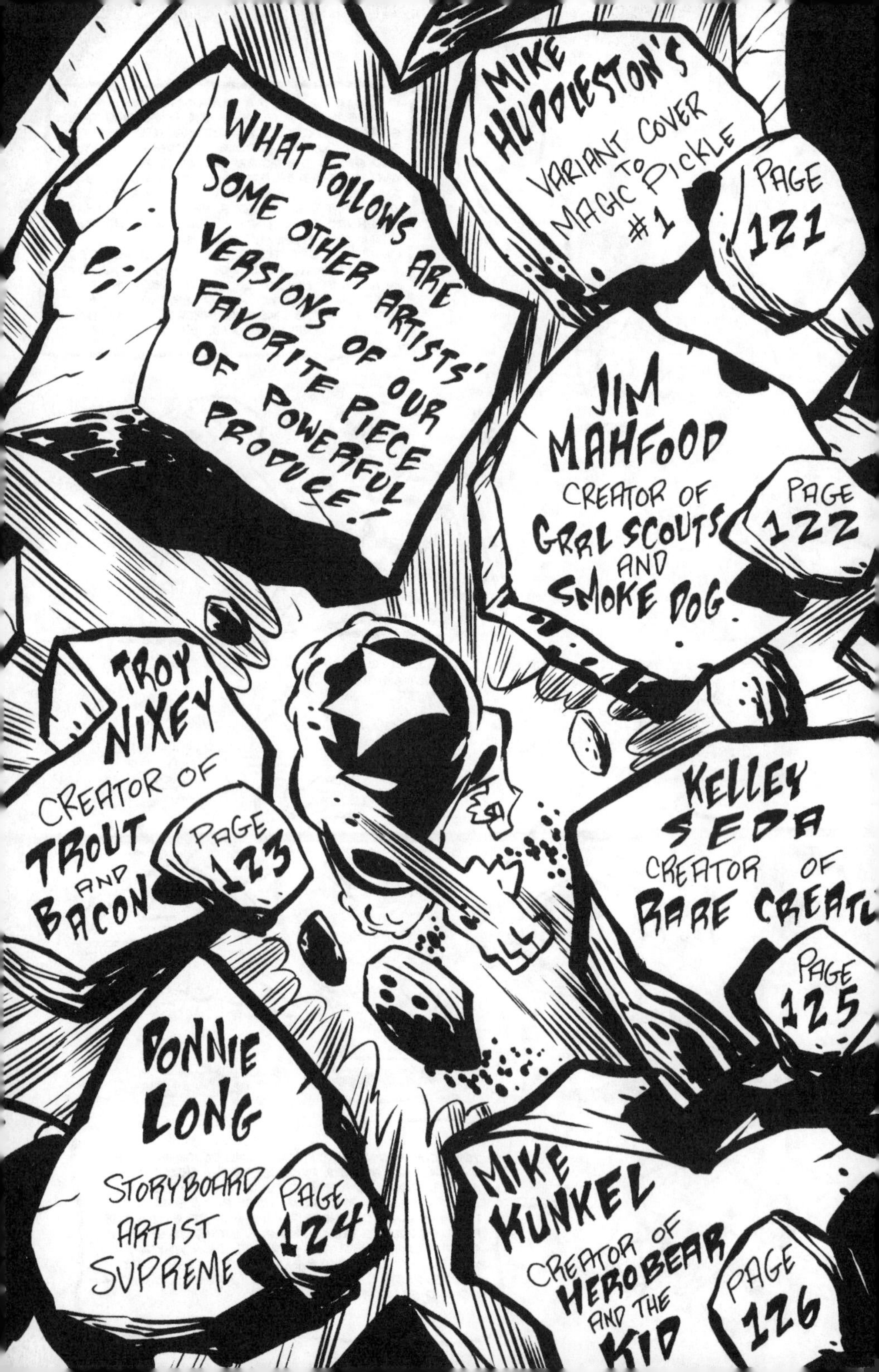
WHAT FOLLOWS ARE SOME OTHER ARTISTS' VERSIONS OF OUR FAVORITE PIECE OF POWERFUL PRODUCE!
MIKE HUDDLESTON'S
VARIANT COVER TO MAGIC PICKLE #1
PAGE 121
JIM MAHFOOD
CREATOR OF GRRL SCOUTS AND SMOKE DOG
PAGE 122
TROY NIXEY
CREATOR OF TROUT AND BACON
PAGE 123
KELLEY SEDA
CREATOR OF RARE CREATU
PAGE 125
DONNIE LONG
STORYBOARD ARTIST SUPREME
PAGE 124
MIKE KUNKEL
CREATOR OF HEROBEAR AND THE KID
PAGE 126

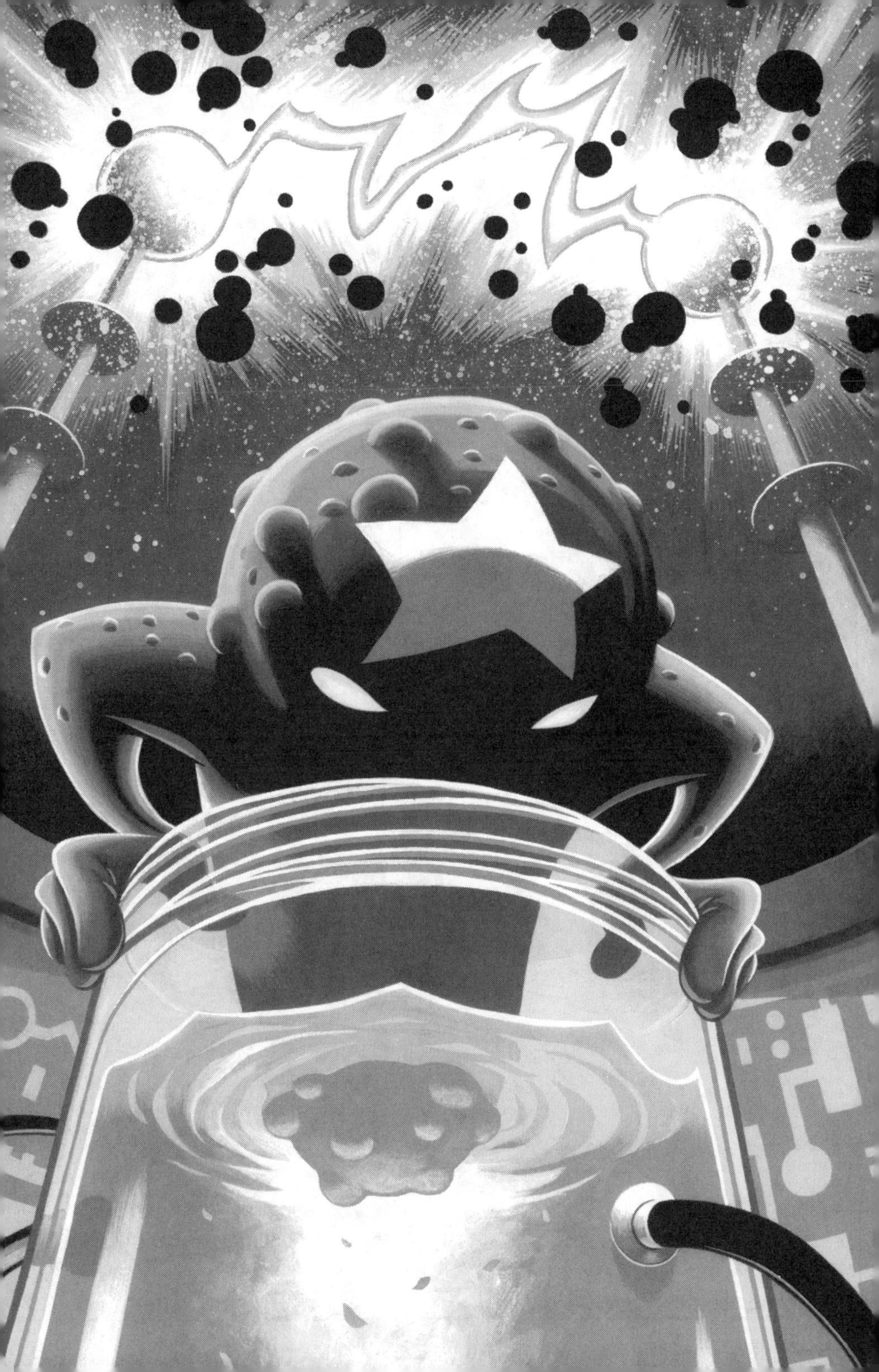

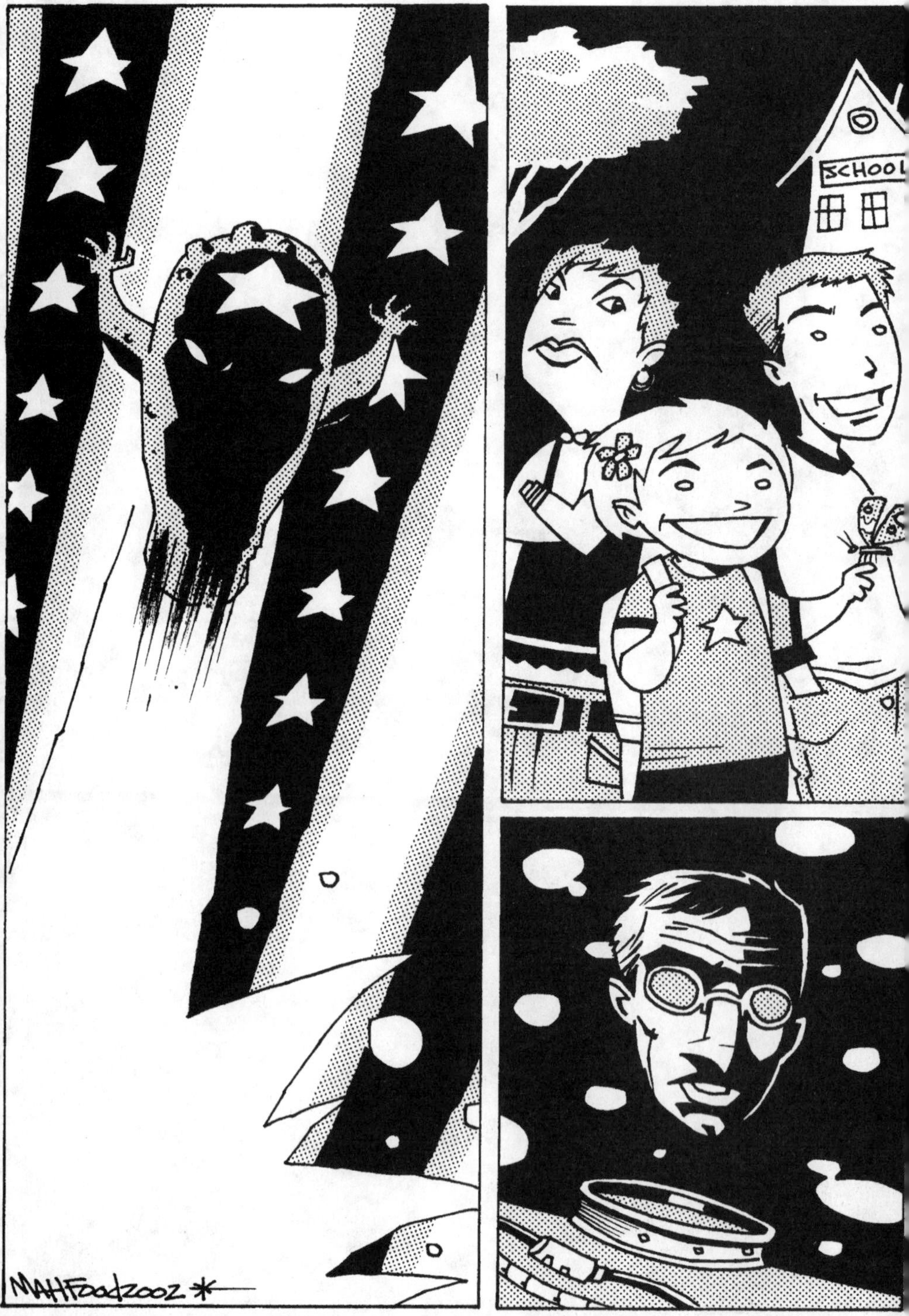
SCHOOL
MAHFOOD2002

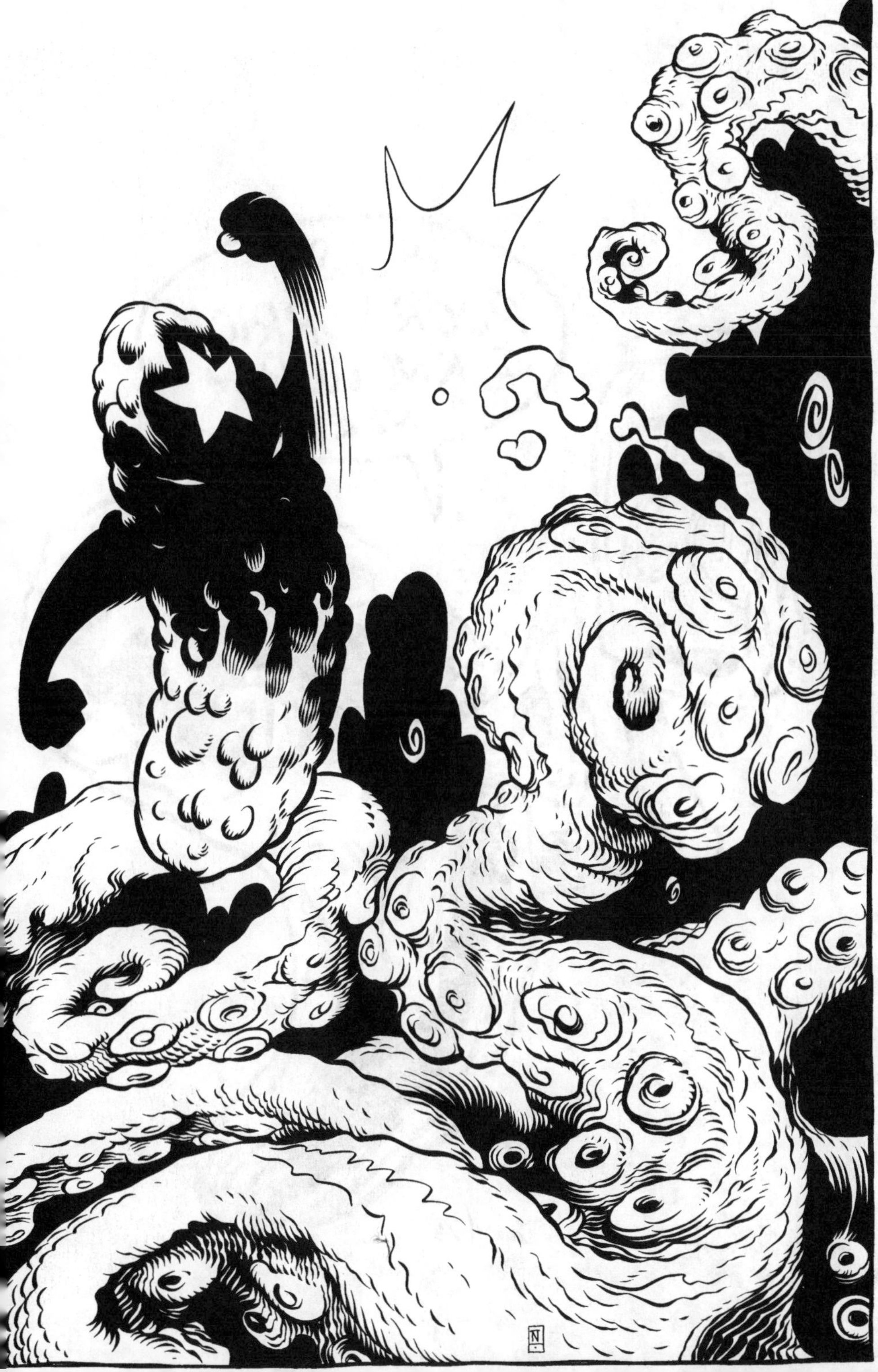

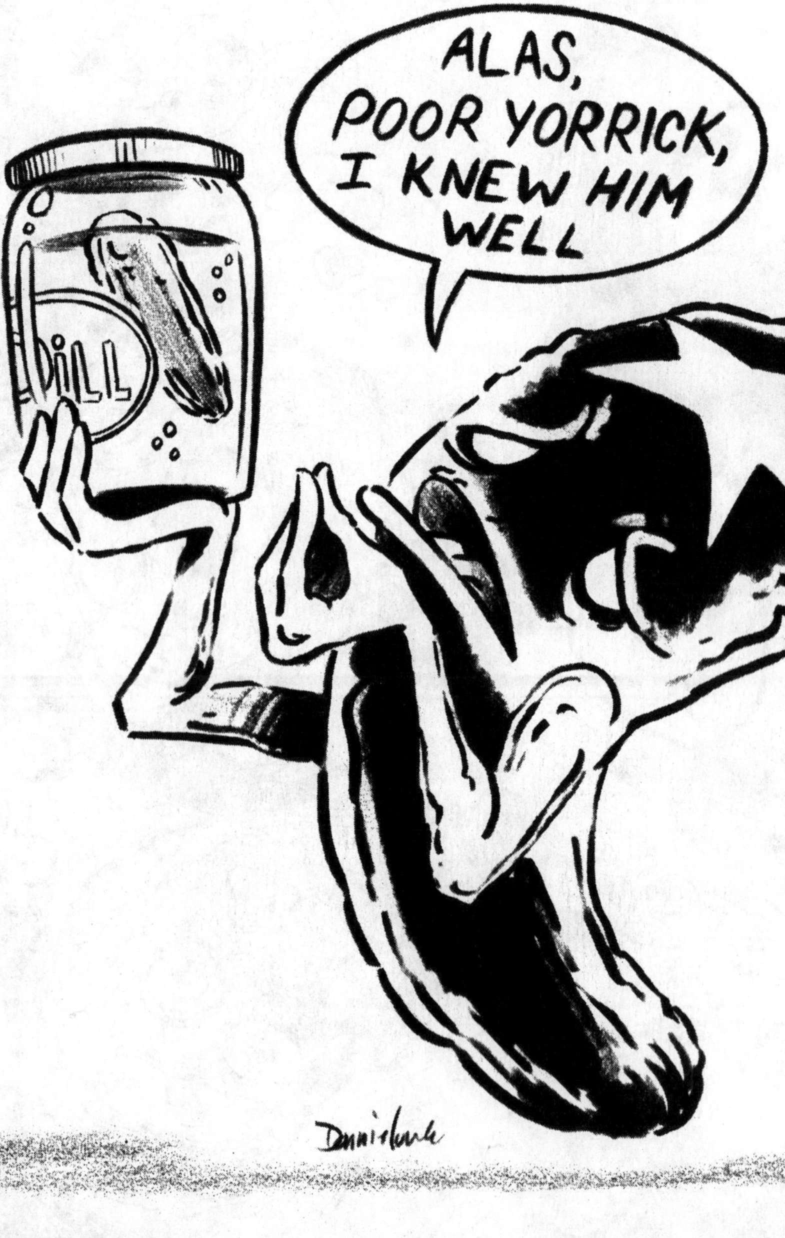
ALAS, POOR YORRICK, I KNEW HIM WELL
DILL

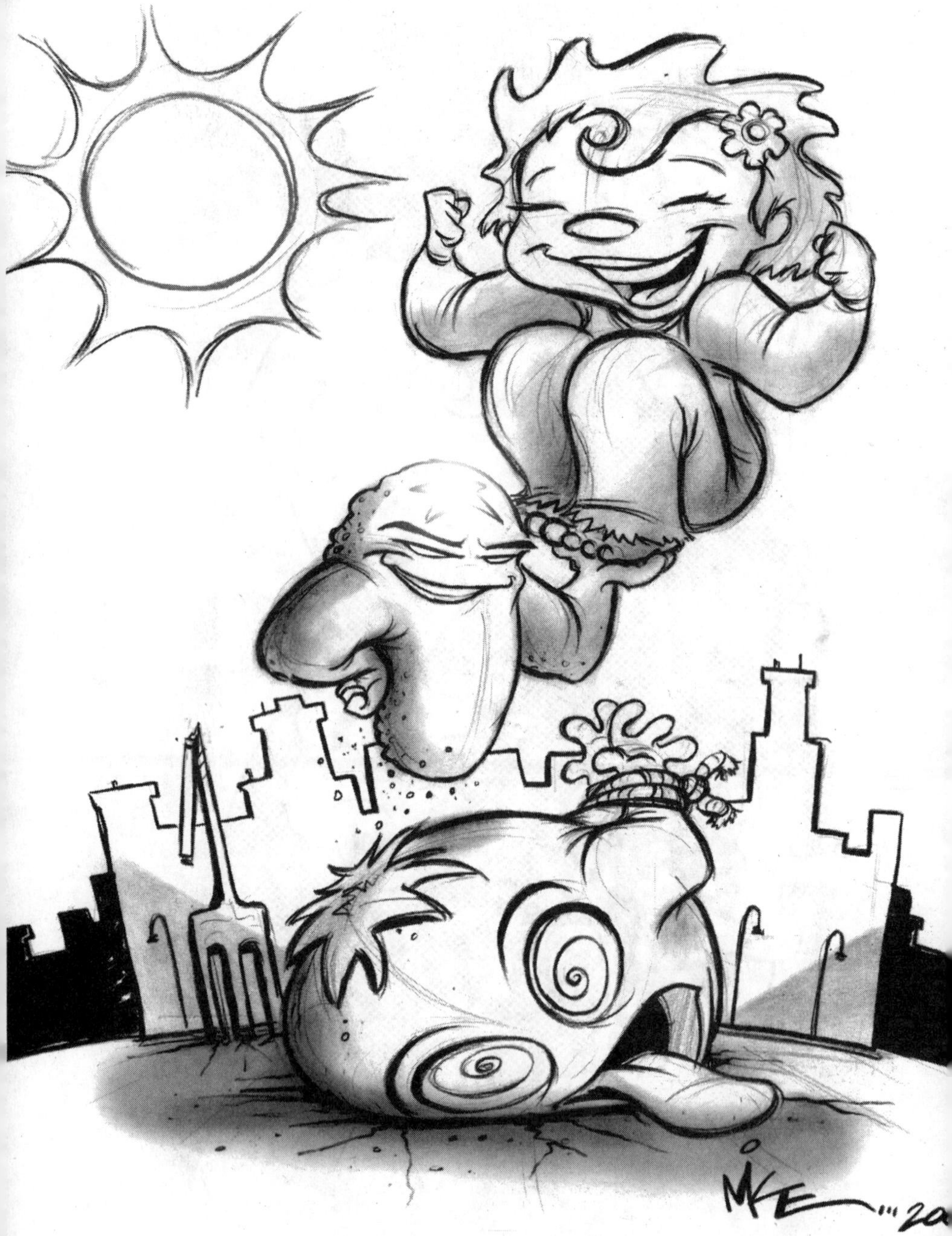

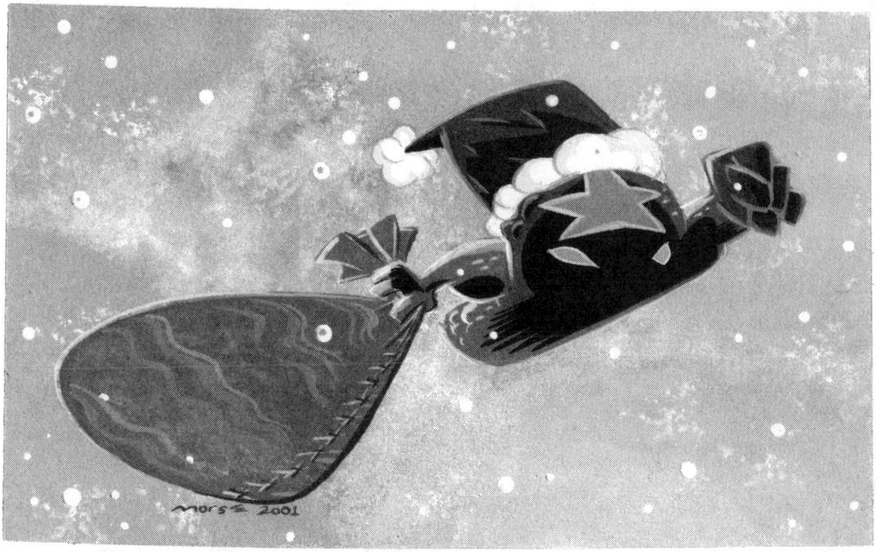
Morse 2001

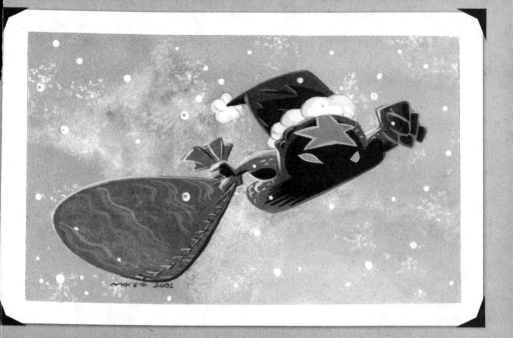

The star on his head
Lit the sky like a candle.
For Santa, this year,
Just had too much to handle.

Not chestnut, nor egg nog,
Nor bowl full of jelly...
This jolly green elf
Was a saint from the deli.

And all the wee tots
That were cruel, mean, or fickle
Got nary a gift
Save a smack from the pickle!

Happy Holidays

from Scott, Jim, Kelley, James
and the rest of the Oni crew!

OTHER BOOKS BY SCOTT MORSE...

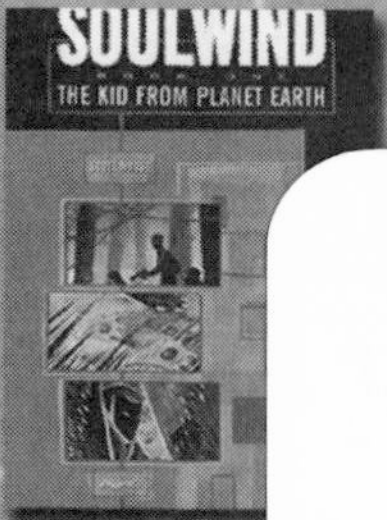
SOULWIND
THE KID FROM PLANET EARTH

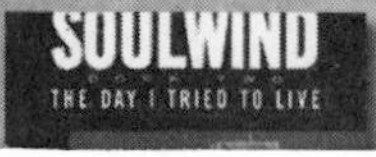
SOULWIND
THE DAY I TRIED TO LIVE

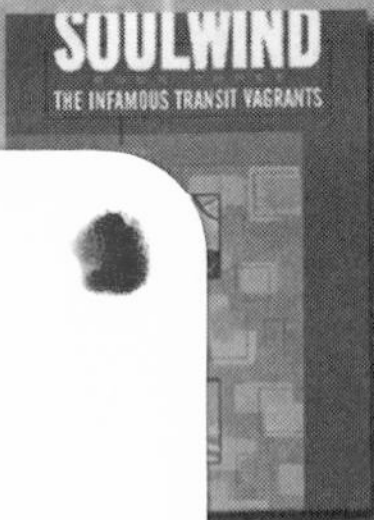
SOULWIND
THE INFAMOUS TRANSIT VAGRANTS

SOULWIND I:
THE KID FROM PL
128 pages, black-
$8.50 US, $12.50
ISBN 0-9667127-4

S TRANSIT VAGRANTS
ck-and-white interiors
2.50 CAN
127-7-3

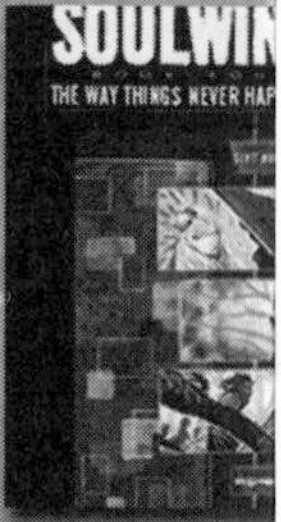
SOULWIN
THE WAY THINGS NEVER HAP

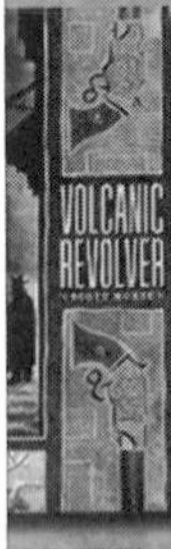
VOLCANIC
REVOLVER

SOULWIND IV:
THE WAY THINGS
96 pages, black-a
$8.50 US, $12.50
ISBN: 1-929998-0

VOLVER™
aders.
pia-and-white interiors
5.95 CAN
27-5-7

OTHER ... SS...

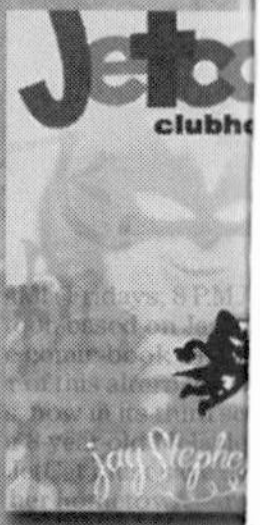
Jetca
clubho
Jay Stephe

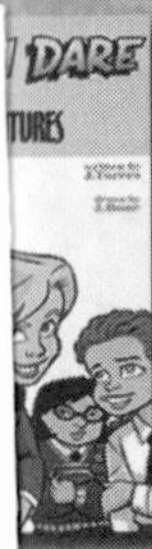
DARE
TURES

JETCAT CLUBHO
By Jay Stephens
80 pages, 24 co
$10.95 US, $16
ISBN 1-929998-

D ALISON DARE
Bone
-and-white interiors
95 CAN
20-1

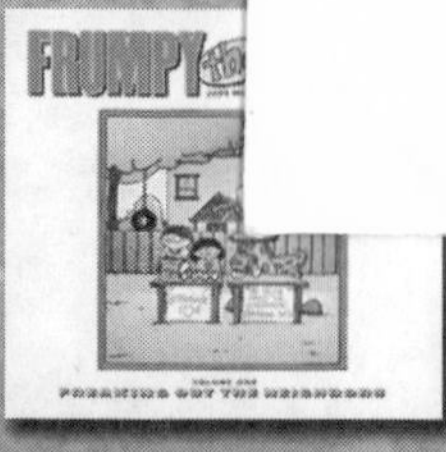
FRUMPY
FREAKING OUT THE NEIGHBORS

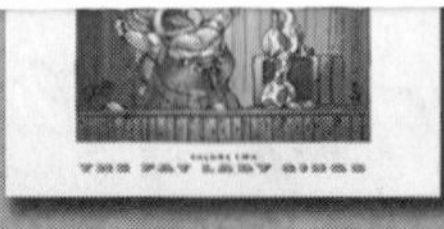
THE FAT LADY SINGS

Available at finer comics shop
everywhere. For a comics stor
near you, call 1-888-COMIC-BOO
or visit www.the-master-list.com
For more Oni Press titles and
information visit www.onipress.com

FRUMPY THE CLOWN,
VOLUME 1: FREAKING OUT THE NEIGHBORS
by Judd Winick
144 pages, black-and-white interiors
$15.95 US, $23.95 CAN.
ISBN 1-929998-11-2

FRUMPY THE CLOWN,
VOLUME 2: THE FAT LADY SINGS
by Judd Winick
136 pages, black-and-white interiors
$15.95 US, $23.95 CAN.
ISBN 1-929998-12-0

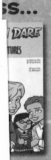